'David Hepworth's forensic sweep of this astonishing twelve months is thoroughly absorbing and appropriately rollicking, expertly guiding us through one miraculous year in all its breathless tumble of creation.' Danny Baker

'Soon every post-war year will have its own tombstone book, but this is already one of the best.' *GQ*, Editor's Hit List

'David Hepworth's argument is simple: 1971 was "the most febrile and creative time in the entire history of popular music". It's an enormous assertion but he makes his point with infectious enthusiasm . . . Whether you agree is beside the point. This is a compelling love letter to a year of timeless music.' *Q*

'An engaging and thought-provoking read. It's a dry-eyed but deeply felt love note to the date when rock was still busy inventing itself. Hepworth points out more than once that at the time he had no idea how lucky he was. He knows now – and so do we.' *Mail on Sunday*

'Engaging . . . Hepworth, who wears his nostalgia on his sleeve, concedes that the music of one's youth inevitably rings most potently. Yet he is surely right that '71 marked a step change in pop history . . . *Never a Dull Moment* lives up to its title.' *Observer*

'Action-packed . . . A good mix of entertainment, insight and odd facts. Hepworth's thesis is largely convincing.' *Mojo*

'So much music, so many players. Hepworth recreates 1971, convincingly, as an ensemble play in which characters are constantly bumping into one another and having life-changing encounters . . . [he] has a sharp appreciation for the rich detail.' *Washington Post*

'A slice of pop culture history from one of the best writers on the subject.' *Sunday Post*

'The book is like listening to Hepworth himself: highbrow detail and context is intersected with personal reminisces, and all threaded together with an infectious enthusiasm'. *Record Collector*

'Fond, funny, beautifully written and fizzing with sharp and sweeping theories that instantly feel like facts.' Mark Ellen

'Whether you agree will depend on your age. But this book shows 1971 was definitely a GREAT rock year.' *Sun*

'Laced with a wisdom gathered over many years as a journalist and industry insider and with an endless enthusiasm for the music . . . a highly readable assessment and a convincing argument for the importance of a year in which the culture of rock began to be aware that it was living out its good old days.' *New Statesman*

'A clever and entertaining book . . . Hepworth proves a refreshingly independent thinker. His style is pithy and his eye for anecdotal detail sharp . . . Hepworth's guide to 1971 proves a thoroughly provoking delight.' *Daily Telegraph*

'A mighty fine and convincing read.' *Classic Rock*

'Near the beginning, Hepworth argues that 1971 saw the pop era giving way to rock. Even so, his own approach is much more like the best pop: never taking itself too seriously, essentially out to entertain – but also an awful lot smarter than its absence of solemnity might lead you to think.' *Spectator*

'Entertaining and clever . . . [Hepworth's] writing might best be described as dapper, which is to say it's sharp, whip-smart, quick-witted, deeply knowledgeable beneath an occasionally knockabout veneer. Hepworth also knows how to work a room for laughs, of which there are plenty here, making *Never a Dull Moment* that welcome thing: a serious book about rock that doesn't take itself too seriously to be taken seriously.' *Uncut*

1971

NEVER A DULL MOMENT

David Hepworth

BLACK SWAN

TRANSWORLD PUBLISHERS
61–63 Uxbridge Road, London W5 5SA
www.penguin.co.uk

Transworld is part of the Penguin Random House group of companies
whose addresses can be found at global.penguinrandomhouse.com

Penguin
Random House
UK

First published in Great Britain in 2016 by Bantam Press
an imprint of Transworld Publishers
Black Swan edition published 2017

A CIP catalogue record for this book
is available from the British Library.

ISBN 9781784162061

Typeset in 11.25/15pt Minion by Thomson Digital Pvt Ltd, Noida, Delhi
Printed and bound in Great Britain by Clays Ltd, Elcograf S.p.A.

Penguin Random House is committed to a sustainable
future for our business, our readers and our planet. This book
is made from Forest Stewardship Council® certified paper.

MIX
Paper from
responsible sources
FSC
www.fsc.org   FSC® C018179

5 7 9 10 8 6 4

CONTENTS

THE LAST DAY OF THE SIXTIES

On New Year's Eve 1970 Paul McCartney instructed his lawyers to issue a writ at the High Court in London to wind up the Beatles.

The sixties ended that day, which was a year late, strictly speaking. You might say this was the last day of the pop era.

The following day, which was a Friday, was 1971. You might say this was the first day of the rock era.

1971 would also turn out to be the busiest, most creative, most innovative, most interesting and longest-resounding year of that era.

Nobody dreamed the rock era would last as long as it has done. In those days nobody expected any form of entertainment to last. Least of all rock music. In fact people joined rock bands to get away from things that lasted. But many of those who first achieved stardom in 1971 – David Bowie,

1

Rod Stewart, Pink Floyd, Led Zeppelin, Elton John and Joni Mitchell – have since gone on to enjoy careers longer than their contemporaries who became novelists, politicians, captains of industry and actors, let alone their old friends who remained at school when they hit the road with a guitar over their shoulder.

Similarly, nobody imagined 1971 would see the release of more influential albums than any year before or since. That influence hasn't merely been felt by later generations of musicians, most of whom weren't born in 1971, it's also been felt by the performers themselves. Many of them are still around and more popular than ever. They're still reaping massive rewards from that rock industry that began in 1971. They wish they could still write songs that are as good, make records that are as strong, and express themselves as unselfconsciously as they did in 1971.

For those of us who were listening, it never got any better than 1971. During those twelve months, in a surge of creativity, playfulness, ambition, technological breakthrough, ego and blissful ignorance, a huge proportion of the most memorable albums ever made were released.

How did it happen? This book explains. It's the story of 1971, rock's best year.

PROLOGUE

I was born in 1950. For a music fan that's the winning ticket in the lottery of life.

I grew up in the 1960s. At the time we didn't know these were going to become 'The Sixties' and follow us around for ever. Those years seemed no more unique than any other ten-year period.

I was thirteen on that Friday in November 1963 when JFK was shot. I felt a bat-squeak of patriotism a few months later when the Beatles conquered America. I was fifteen when Bobby Gregg's snare shot announced Bob Dylan's 'Like A Rolling Stone'. Bruce Springsteen, who was just six months older, heard it while he was in the car with his mother. He later described it as 'somebody kicking open the door to your mind'.

I came of age in 1971, the same year rock did. At the time I was at college and spending what little spare cash I had on records. Like many similarly inclined young men – and we were mainly men – all my consumer appetites were channelled through the record shop. Jerry Seinfeld says that for the first ten years of his life the only clear thought in his mind was 'get candy'. We were like that with records.

All the cash that came my way – the £40 I had each term for anything more than board, food and tuition, the pay I got for holiday jobs, birthday gifts from distant relatives, and record tokens, obviously – was instantly converted into albums. There was simply nothing else I wanted to spend money on. I spent every idle moment hanging around record shops, being in the presence of, learning the names of, combing the covers of and sometimes even listening to those things I wanted that I could not have. It was a life spent in pursuit of a gratification endlessly deferred.

At the time 1971 didn't feel like a particularly exceptional year. Nobody talked about 'The Year in Rock' back then. Nobody tried to take the temperature of the business. Nobody pontificated about where things were going or had been. The habit of looking back, which is now so much a part of the music media game, and of which this book is an example, hadn't been invented. It's only in retrospect – and only quite recently at that, since the great digital musical Niagara has made it possible to have all fifty years of recorded rock and roll at our fingertips, to shuffle it, sort it and subject it to endless listification – that I've come to realize just what an exceptional year my twenty-first year was.

At this point you may raise a sceptical eyebrow and say that for you too the music of the year in which you turned twenty-one, or eighteen or sixteen or whenever you felt most alive, still speaks to you in a way no other year does.

That's natural. That's just growing up. We all have precious memories of one soft infested summer when we were young. For us too the soundtrack thereof will always be rock's annus mirabilis.

There's an important difference in the case of me and 1971.

The difference is this: I'm right.

This book is a month-by-month journey through the past to discover what happened that year, in what order, why it did, how the changes on the surface were responding to huge seismic changes underground, how it shaped and was shaped by a few hundred people who were in their mid-twenties at the time, and why the music of 1971 still rings so clearly almost fifty years later. It's also to a certain extent about the world out of which that music emerged. It's a book about sex, drugs, hair, hot pants, tax, technology, class, race, gender and foolishness as well as Grammy awards, platinum albums and reviews in *Rolling Stone*.

On our journey we shall shatter the cliché that the early seventies were a mere lull before the punk rock storm, rather than the most febrile and creative time in the entire history of popular music; puncture the pious pretence that the words 'new' and 'exciting' are always interchangeable; wonder at the working practices which brought forth so many masterpieces; reconstruct the real-world background against which all this invention took place; and look at the lives of the artists who shaped that time and in turn were shaped by it. At the end of each chapter I've included a list of ten records associated with that month. Some were hits at the time, others were beginning their long march to classic status by being unveiled on stage that month, and a few are there because they deserve to be heard, particularly now that even the previously obscure gems of 1971 are just a click away.

There are moments in all creative stories when the right sort of talent meets the right amount of opportunity with just enough money and technology (but not too much) and then lays the result before an audience which is in the ideal state of readiness to ensure that things will happen in a way they have never happened before and will never happen again. 1971 was one of those moments.

JANUARY:
GET DOWN AND
GET WITH IT

The last days of pounds, shillings and pence. Average salary for a working man £2,000 per annum. A house in an up-and-coming area of north London worth £20,000. Bitter 11p a pint. Cigarettes 27p a packet. Long-playing records £2.15. Berni Inns' rump steak, button mushrooms, tomato, chips, roll and butter, apple pie and cream for 80p. Barclaycard the only credit card. Two-thirds of the population don't have a bank account. Every night a detachment of Coldstream Guards marches to the City of London to mount guard on the Bank of England.

Three TV channels. BBC1 Saturday night line-up with Cliff Richard, *Dixon of Dock Green* and Rolf Harris. Some shows in colour, others still in black and white. Henry Cooper advertising the great smell of Brut. Jimmy Savile promoting car seat belts. Clunk click, every trip. No commercial radio. *Daily Mirror* sells four and a half million copies every day. Major cities have a morning and evening newspaper. No celebrity magazines. Wartime titles *Reveille* and *Tit-Bits* still popular.

No mobiles. Seventy thousand red telephone boxes. Press button B to get your money back. The only ringtone is a ringing tone. Overseas calls via the operator. Police in touch with the station via police boxes. Urgent news delivered via telegram. Train tickets checked by eye, not machine. No magnetic strips. Most people have never seen a computer in their lives.

Smokers everywhere. On tube trains, in pubs, in offices, even in hospitals. No joggers, no health shops, no gyms, no leisurewear, no trainers, no mineral water, no Lycra, no fast food, no obesity. Wiry people. Biba's most popular dress sizes are six and eight. The only people with tattoos got them in the services.

Family department stores in most towns. Few supermarkets. People shop at their local butcher's, baker's, fishmonger's and greengrocer's and do so daily, not weekly. Petrol pump attendants, milkmen, paper boys, window cleaners, knife grinders, news vendors with shrill cries. Tramps.

No security industry. No gates on Downing Street, no full body scans, no surveillance cameras, no speed bumps. Football fans pay two bob at the turnstile and then shove. Only one black footballer. White faces everywhere. Psychiatric patients imprisoned behind walls of Victorian asylums. Plaster statues of 'spastics' collecting money outside

Woolworths. TV adverts starring chimpanzees dressed as humans. No political correctness.

In January 1971 Alfred Hitchcock arrives in London looking for locations for his new film *Frenzy*. The old Covent Garden market is about to move out to Nine Elms. Hitch, whose father was a market trader, complains the pubs have been made psychedelic and finds that the planners propose to flatten and 're-develop' Covent Garden to give it what they believe London needs most – a conference centre.

Later in the same year these plans are reversed in the face of unprecedented opposition from small traders, artists and architecture students, determined to preserve the unique character of the area. They succeed in preserving much of Covent Garden's fabric. Its character, however, will never be quite the same. What is a working market in Hitchcock's film will, by the turn of the century, become a major centre of the three industries that drive modern London: shopping, tourism and cool.

Nothing seems very cool in January 1971.

Much the same applies in New York. The United States is in recession. Unemployment in the inner cities is nearing 10 per cent. New York City subway tokens have just gone up to 30 cents. Transport, like much of the city, is in crisis. The streets are full of potholes. The wind that blows down the avenues blinds pedestrians with grit and makes uncollected garbage gather round their ankles. Gasoline is 36 cents a gallon. OPEC is imposing a 50 per cent tax on oil extraction. Ford is thinking about making smaller cars. A seventeen-year-old from Washington Heights who calls himself TAKI 183 is becoming famous for leaving his tag on subway cars.

People are leaving the city in the face of crime and filth. Property values are dropping. An apartment in one of Manhattan's smartest addresses is on the market for $225,000, half of what it cost in 1969. All the movies made in New York, such as the recent Jack Lemmon–Sandy Dennis hit *The Out of Towners*, depict it as a place only the foolhardy would choose to visit. The city's magazines carry sardonic survival guides. A picture of the half-finished World Trade Center illustrates an article in the *New York Times* promoting the unfashionable view that the city might yet be a desirable place to live. Someone in the convention business timidly suggests reviving a musicians' saying from the 1920s and christening the city 'the Big Apple'.

Some 85 per cent of New York's twenty-five thousand police patrolmen are on strike over a pay claim. A cop earns around $11,000 a year, just above the national average. According to a detective called Frank Serpico, giving evidence to an inquiry into corruption, many can earn an additional $600 a month in bribes from illegal gambling rackets. Serpico will eventually be played on screen by Al Pacino. Already in early 1971 the real-life corner-cutting detective Eddie Egan is the model for the fictional Popeye Doyle in the upcoming movie *The French Connection*.

Consumer prices are beginning to rise too fast to make it worth printing prices on menus. McSorley's Ale House, which has just been compelled to admit women for the first time, has adjusted its draught ale from 50 to 60 cents. However, a McDonald's is 20 cents and a Coke can be as little as 10. It's still possible to have dinner for four at a smart place like 21 for $130 including wine and tips. The new John

Lennon solo album is $3.49 at King Karol while George Harrison's *All Things Must Pass* is $6.98.

The *Johnny Carson Show* on New Year's Day 1971 is the last to carry a commercial for cigarettes. It's for Virginia Slims, a brand aimed at women with the slogan 'you've come a long way, baby'. Walter Cronkite presents the seven o'clock news. Ed Sullivan still fronts his variety show on Sunday nights. He is beginning to lose his memory. Sullivan won't be renewed, nor will *The Beverly Hillbillies* or *Petticoat Junction*. There are no celebrity magazines. The person currently monopolizing the headlines is President Nixon's daughter Tricia, who is engaged to be married. The big media organizations are terrified they are losing touch with the young audience. *National Lampoon* satirizes their attempts to stay in touch, such as *Cosmopolitan*'s search for a nude male model. A *Life* magazine survey finds America's most admired names are Robert Kennedy and Bill Cosby. Least admired are Fidel Castro and Black Panthers activist Eldridge Cleaver. Jimmy Carter, newly sworn in as Governor of Georgia, says the state may finally have accepted integration. In cities like Cleveland integration is resulting in the flight of second-generation European immigrants to the suburbs and the consequent hollowing out of the centres.

Hot pants are everywhere. 'They are the kind of fad that topples institutions,' one fashion observer tells *Life*. Barber shops are closing. Every businessman is growing sideburns. Jane Fonda, thirty-three, her curly blonde hair transformed into a harsh shag, has just completed her role as the call girl Bree Daniels in *Klute*. She has driven alone from California to New York to play the part. Once on set in a studio in Harlem she insists the director let her sleep the night in her character's apartment, the better to identify with her pain. The film glories in the squalor of the city. 'After you've been in New York a month you become tense and nervous and alienated,' says Fonda. Returning to California, determined to put her privileged life behind her, she sells her possessions and moves with her daughter into a house in a cul-de-sac in the shadow of a freeway.

Fonda puts her energies into supporting the increasing number of soldiers' organizations opposing the continuation of the Vietnam war. The nation is riven with mistrust over the conflict and its political poles seem incapable of dialogue. Speaking for the older generation, Bob Hope, profiled in *Life*, says 80 per cent of the hippies on Sunset Strip 'have a social disease'. The voting age is in the process of being lowered from twenty-one to eighteen. Employees report that the baby boomers now entering the workforce in unprecedented numbers want faster advancement and less formal dress codes, and in some cases even have to have the profit motive explained to them. From 12 January the gap between the older and the younger generation is dramatized in a new TV series called *All in the Family*, which pits Glenn Miller-loving working stiff Archie Bunker against his long-haired liberal son-in-law. Within months even Richard Nixon can be heard complaining about Bunker's son-in-law on the newly installed recording system in the Oval Office.

For most young people TV is an irrelevance, as are the movies. Music is where it's at.

In January 1971, up-and-coming New Jersey musician Bruce Springsteen was twenty-one and still unknown beyond the immediate area, which was leaving it perilously late. He had recently returned from a visit to his parents at their new home in California where he had time to reflect on the future of his two-year-old band Steel Mill. They had endured a rather traumatic night on 11 September 1970 – only three months after National Guardsmen had opened fire on demonstrating students at Kent State University, killing four of them – when local police had moved in with clubs swinging to enforce a curfew at an open-air show Steel Mill were playing in the deceptively idyllic-sounding surroundings of the Clearwater Swim Club. Although they met the invasion with a certain amount of bravado – reconnecting the power after the police had cut it off, band member Danny Federici pushing a stack of speakers in the direction of some officers who were trying to climb on to the stage and Springsteen using his emerging stagecraft to keep the crowd on side – the experience put him off any further rebellious rhetoric.

Like bands the world over in 1971 who weren't known for their own material, Steel Mill played anything and everything they could. Springsteen's band performed Iron Butterfly's 'In-A-Gadda-Da-Vida', knocked out an Allman Brothers tribute called 'Going Back To Georgia' and sometimes even played a thirty-minute rock opera called 'Garden State Parkway Blues'. When Steel Mill played shows in New Jersey, sometimes attracting as many as four thousand people despite never having been on the radio, hardly ever having been written about and certainly never having put out a record, their audience would overwhelmingly come from the proportion of the population born between 1946 and 1956. There wouldn't have been a single soul over the age of

13

thirty and there wouldn't have been many under the age of eighteen. Audiences were uniformly young and unjaded. Whatever they were hearing they felt as if they were hearing it for the first time, and consequently they tended to be receptive.

During Springsteen's holiday in the San Francisco area he had been listening to the local FM stations and his imagination had been captured by the breezy sound of Van Morrison's *His Band And The Street Choir*, with its attendant hit record 'Domino', and the soul revue force of Joe Cocker's *Mad Dogs & Englishmen*. Henceforth he decided Steel Mill would be no more. The band was going to boast horns, line up more like Morrison's and Cocker's, and the name on the marquee would be his.

There are few moves that require as much self-belief as taking a band which has previously been, at least notionally, a democracy and naming it after yourself. It can only occur if the leader has the nerve to lead and the musicians involved recognize the strength of his claim to do so. At the time Springsteen was living in a ground-floor apartment in Asbury Park which he shared with Steve Van Zandt, John Lyon and Albee Tellone. Once a week they invited more musician friends round and played Monopoly. (Sandy Denny and Trevor Lucas would invite friends round to their Fulham flat to do the same thing – a fair indication of how little was on the TV in 1971.) It was during those games, which involved rule-bending, secret treaties, bribery and other skulduggery, that the 21-year-old Springsteen took to referring to himself, his tongue barely an inch into his cheek, as 'the Boss'.

By the end of 1971 he would bestow similar honorifics on the rest of his growing crew – 'Miami' Steve Van Zandt, 'Southside' Johnny Lyon, Vinny 'Mad Dog' Lopez and Clarence 'Big Man' Clemons – as he played night after night at The Student Prince in Asbury Park and further afield, where the band's standard performance would consist of four forty-minute sets with breaks in between.

Recalling this time in later years Springsteen said 'sometimes you'd come home with five hundred dollars in your pocket and you could live on that for months. For a local band, that was a big success. And in that area, we were big local stars.'

In January 1971 Neville 'Noddy' Holder, born in 1946, raised in a council house with an outside lavatory, his only proper employment a short period buying and selling auto-parts, was the leader of a group called Slade. In his twenty-five years Noddy had already packed a lifetime of experience of playing live: in his native Black Country, in German dance halls where the waiters carried guns, up and down the United Kingdom, and on a two-month residency entertaining holidaymakers in the Bahamas.

On New Year's Day 1971 Slade played Wolverhampton Civic Hall, in the middle of their industrial heartland. This was the first of no fewer than 150 shows they were to play over the next twelve months. Through that year Noddy Holder, Jim Lea, Dave Hill and Don Powell toured the United Kingdom with an intensity that hasn't been equalled since.

One of the reasons it hasn't been equalled since is that the venues they played that year either no longer exist or no longer host amplified popular music. Slade still hadn't had a hit so they couldn't do the big dance halls where the hit acts played. They could only play what was known as the rock club circuit. Nevertheless, that circuit was extensive. Among the 150 places they played were such venues as the Queen Mary Ballroom at Dudley Zoo, the St Giles Youth Club in Willenhall, the curiously named Farx in Potters Bar and the misleadingly genteel-sounding Ballerina Ballroom in Nairn. Slade performed amid the art deco splendour of the Floral Hall in Southport and the provisional prefabrications of Blades in Bexley. They rolled up and rocked in venues whose names still reverberate down the years, like the Marquee in Soho's Wardour Street. They played no less energetically at scores of places whose names no longer reverberate down the years and still hint at a vision of a future which never entirely materialized in the way the namers might have wished, places such as Teenage Centre in Fareham, the Showboat in Mumbles and the Cosmos Youth Centre in Fife.

Like Springsteen's band, Slade didn't turn up their noses at any of this. They actively sought people to play to. Sometimes they seemed almost to be harrying them. At the end of July 1971 they played three consecutive nights for Scottish holidaymakers on the Isle of Arran. This was such a success that they returned to do a further show in late September.

Slade had no fear of distances. On 4 September they played the Kilmardinny Stadium in Glasgow; the following night they were at a Schizophrenia Benefit in London. In the days when the motorway system was not fully networked this was a journey that would have occupied an entire cheerless, tedious, smoke-wreathed, bone-rattling day.

Because Slade were not what anyone would call a marquee name they didn't only play in their own right. They also opened for others who were slightly better known. They supported Argent at the Lyceum in London, Yes at the Marquee, Atomic Rooster at the Kinetic Cinema in Birmingham and the Alan Bown in Exeter.

Slade's 1971 act comprised crowd pleasers all the way. They began with their version of Ten Years After's 'Hear Me Calling' (borrowed from the Woodstock sensations' recent album *Stonedhenge*), finished with Steppenwolf's 'Born To Be Wild', had room to 'slow things down a bit' with John Sebastian's 'Darling Be Home Soon' and the Moody Blues' 'Nights In White Satin' – which featured the group's most accomplished musician, Jim Lea, on violin – and climaxed with their speaker-shredding version of Little Richard's 'Get Down And Get With It'. Through it all they kept up a stream of patter and ribaldry. Nobody came away from a Slade show without understanding that they had been entertained, and entertained by a band who didn't look down on them. 'We wanted to have fun with our audience,' recalled Noddy many years later.

Scores of other groups would have followed a similar trail in 1971, rattling around in the backs of ill-maintained Ford Transits, sleeping with the wheel arch as their pillow, relieving themselves in milk bottles, doing the *NME* crossword with a blunt guesthouse pencil, dreaming of a cold Wimpy and chips, probing for each other's personal weak spots and exploiting them without mercy, often risking life and limb by putting themselves in the hands of a driver who had taken a few drinks and didn't wear a seat belt. (The British folk-rock group Fairport Convention had been involved in an accident in May 1969 when returning to London from a gig at Mothers in Birmingham. The driver had fallen asleep, the van had come off the road and two passengers, their nineteen-year-old drummer Martin Lamble and a friend, Jeannie Franklyn, were killed.)

In late October Slade went into Command Studios in Piccadilly, London and recorded this by-now road-hardened set for the record that became *Slade Alive!*. By then they had already had a hit with 'Get Down And Get With It', which was almost comically shrill but perfectly suited to the fine art of wardrobe mirror-miming, a sport in which Britain led and still leads the world.

The next step was to take the live energy into the studio and bake it into bite-sized biscuits. Like Brian Epstein bullying Lennon and McCartney into forming a partnership and Andrew Oldham locking Jagger and Richards in a room with instructions to compose, Chas Chandler insisted Holder and Lea write their own follow-up. Lea took him at his word and turned up, with his violin, at the Walsall council house where Noddy lived with his parents. Within half an hour they had written 'Coz I Luv You', the first of their deliberately misspelled money spinners. They thought it was a joke. Chas thought it was a number one. Chas was right.

The year that had begun on stage at the Wolverhampton Civic Hall ended with them at number one. They got the good news while playing the Melody Rooms in Norwich. The cover versions were gradually dropped from the set. They no longer had need of them because they soon had quite enough hits of their own, a string that would eventually make them

Britain's most popular band since the Beatles. Unlike the Beatles, the more records they sold the more shows they played. They began all over again on New Year's Day 1972 at the Cambridge Corn Exchange, and this time played more than 150 shows. Hit records were all very well but the heart of the music business – and, at the beginning of 1971, the money – was in playing live.

At the same time as Slade were starting out on their 150 dates the rising progressive group Yes were also trying to make their way via an apparently different route. They had recently finished recording their third album, *The Yes Album*. This record would be released in February, by which time they would have been playing the songs from it on stage for fully six months.

Yes were one of the first rock groups to build their career on the virtues of practice. Their growing live reputation was predicated on the fact that they didn't record anything that they couldn't play and, more impressively, sing on stage, without any help from technology. They were big favourites of BBC radio producers at the time because they could be relied on to turn up, set up and record three tunes in three hours, which is what a session with the corporation, the one route to wider exposure, demanded.

Although the record company Atlantic had not got involved in its making, *The Yes Album* was the record that had to pay back in order to ensure that their deal was renewed. Yes were one of a number of long-haired groups who had been picked up in a sweep conducted by Atlantic's Ahmet Ertegun when he recognized that the future was likely to be both album-shaped and white in colour. Ertegun had used his roots music calling card to sign Crosby, Stills & Nash, Iron Butterfly, Cream and many other groups he didn't really pretend to understand. He was a businessman who was smart enough to conceal the fact.

The repertoire of Yes, who had come together in London in 1968, had begun with what they would have called 'cover versions' of songs like 'Something's Coming' from *West Side Story* and the Beatles' 'Every Little Thing'. Then they had moved on to their own compositions, all of which involved a bewildering number of notes. Where Slade aspired to simplicity, Yes craved complexity. Their records were full of alarming stops and starts, unaccompanied choral pieces that would lurch without warning into breakneck instrumental gallops, sub-sections indicated by Latin numerals that begged to be compared to Tchaikovsky and lyrics that had to be celestial poetry because they clearly made no earthly sense.

The only way Yes's music could be quarried from their seething imaginations and brought into the open air was by rehearsing and recording it in short sections, often as brief as thirty seconds. These would then be edited together with the next section – a labour requiring almost monkish dedication given the rudimentary technology available at the time. When a track was finally razored and spliced into place the five musicians would take a deep breath and learn to play it from the finished record. This was a complete reversal of the way things had been done since the invention of recorded sound. Even the bleakest bebop and the most avant-garde classical music had not gone to the same trouble as the practitioners of this new progressive rock.

In January 1971 Yes joined a European package tour called The Age of Atlantic, which was an indication of how keen Ertegun was to brand his company as the home of the new rock. Bottom of the bill was a jazz-rock band called Dada (who would later become Vinegar Joe); top of the bill was the American heavy act Iron Butterfly. Yes came in between and stole the show with their epic unpacking of Paul Simon's 'America'. Iron Butterfly were on their last legs by then and decided to break up at the end of the tour. This meant they were looking for a buyer for their PA system, which had impressed the members of Yes because it involved such undreamt-of refinements as monitors, which enabled the band to actually hear for the first time what they were playing. Since they now had management via the film company Hemdale, they could afford to make the investment and their reputation for polished performance consequently grew.

Their new personal manager was Brian Lane, who was conversant with the dark arts of record plugging. When *The Yes Album* appeared in early February it sold respectably in most places and healthily in the head shops. Because there was a postal strike for the first two months of the year the record shops couldn't make their traditional returns so the Virgin Chart, which briefly had Yes at number one thanks to the unscientific preferences of shop staff and the promptings of Lane, got more profile than usual. To their chagrin it wasn't enough to get them on the 'album spot' that

21

the BBC's weekly chart show *Top of the Pops* was offering as a sop to the burgeoning market for long-players.

Even for nationally known names January 1971 was primarily about keeping a packed date book. Pink Floyd went into Abbey Road at the beginning of the month to begin recording *Meddle* but still ventured out at weekends to play universities. They would load up their equipment at Abbey Road and then head out to play the Student Union Bar at Farnborough, the Theatre at St Mary's College in Strawberry Hill, Lecture Block 6 & 7 at the University of Essex, wherever they could earn enough money to pay themselves and their crew.

In 1971, despite the massive publicity given to festivals at Woodstock and the Isle of Wight, live rock music was still a minority taste. Music business veteran Andy Murray lived in the northern town of Carlisle, which at the time had a population of seventy thousand, and remembers, 'If you went to see a rock band in that area in those days you would see the other fifty people who were also interested in seeing rock bands. You'd even nod to them after a while. If you went to see Greenslade one week and then Jethro Tull the next it would be the same fifty people. They were mainly blokes and they were mainly wearing army surplus greatcoats.'

They would also be readers of the weekly music press, about to enter its golden age. The leading UK title was the *Melody Maker*, which had traded its traditional support of jazz musicians for a similarly workmanlike focus on rock. Its lifeblood was its live news and listings pages, which were literally the only way a rock fan in Carlisle would have any idea that Rory Gallagher was likely to play in town. If you sat across a railway carriage from somebody else reading the music press you would know that you were both members of an alternative society with secrets the straight world simply couldn't hope to decipher.

Universities were an increasingly popular place to play, not least because they had halls big enough to be able to cater to the demand. The most prestigious of them, Leeds, had the advantage over the local Victorian town hall of being able to accommodate two thousand people in its refectory. Students wishing to see the Who, Led Zeppelin or the Rolling Stones, all of whom played that room in 1971, had to do their drinking in the bar downstairs before joining the audience upstairs. The pubs would be shut at 10.30, which was long before the show finished. Most of that audience sat cross-legged, often feeling the chill imprint of the parquet floor through the thin seat of their cheap mail-order loon pants, an item of clothing so snug it made no allowance whatsoever for the gender of its wearer. Outside the charmed circle of the bohemian enclaves of London and the alternative press, drugs were available only to those who had the budget to afford them and the contacts through which to secure them. Hence audiences were overwhelmingly sober.

Student audiences were also obedient. Despite the ferment that had been taking place at Berkeley, the Sorbonne and Hornsey College of Art, they were still inclined to accept authority, possibly in the knowledge that they would soon be wielding it themselves. They transferred their habit of deference to rock musicians, who were accorded unquestioning respect to the extent that the audience's interest in them seemed to start and finish when they walked on and off the stage. Stage invasions were entirely unknown and in most cases it wasn't considered necessary to post a guard to keep 'fans' (not the word they would have used) from getting backstage and pressing themselves on the performers, either for a photograph, which they would have had no means to take, or an autograph, for which they would have had no merchandise to be inscribed.

Smokey, odiferous, uncomfortable, usually cold, unleavened by mood enhancers and often ended by a walk home after the last bus, as an evening of entertainment live rock had little to recommend it beyond the music. It was, however, the place where the music happened. Material was developed and polished on the road in front of audiences. Pink Floyd had entered Abbey Road in January with no material. It was only when they got in front of student audiences that spring that they began to whip new tunes like 'Echoes' into shape.

At the same time Neil Young, who had peeled off from Crosby, Stills, Nash & Young after their tour of the previous year, was on a solo tour of the US and Canada, during which he played a set of songs which would become famous once he'd recorded them for *Harvest*. Elton John, who was being acclaimed as a big star in the United States, still played the last night of Mothers, a club above a furniture shop in Birmingham. The Who played a series of shows at the Young Vic, which were supposed to be filmed for *Lifehouse*, which was intended to be Pete Townshend's next grand project after *Tommy*. The road was how you paid the rent. Royalties weren't yet the main revenue stream of the music business.

This was something that even the former members of the Beatles were coming to realize in January 1971. Although

Paul McCartney had issued his writ to dissolve the group's partnership in London, the centre of activity for the members of the group was New York. John Lennon had made himself scarce by going to Tokyo, ostensibly because Yoko was trying to get access to her daughter Kyoko, but also because he knew it would be best to be out of the way before 21 January, when his interview with *Rolling Stone*'s Jann Wenner was published.

The main thrust of this interview, which was itself the culmination of primal scream therapy with Arthur Janov, was threefold: his new album, *Plastic Ono Band*, was the best thing he'd ever done, Yoko Ono was the only true artist, and everything else, and the Beatles in particular, was 'bullshit'.

Paul McCartney was in New York when the interview appeared, recording at Columbia Studios, ostensibly with his wife Linda although the hired session musicians were in no doubt that only one person was in charge. George Harrison was also in town, avoiding Lennon, who was making unkind remarks about *All Things Must Pass*, which was at the top of the US charts, where John wished to be.

What the former Beatles were discovering – and the court case which got under way in London that month would bring into sharper focus – was that none of them could simply walk away from the group. They were connected by a partnership agreement which they'd entered into just before Brian Epstein's death, and locked into a management agreement with Allen Klein, who derived his power from the fact that he represented them as an entity, and from the fact that all their individual album releases, which to some ears appeared to be intended as darts aimed at each other, came out on their label Apple, which they owned jointly. It was a pretty mess, and wholly without precedent.

Furthermore, they didn't have as much money as they'd expected to have. When their music publisher Dick James had sold his company in 1969 they were unable to afford to bid. The record business the Beatles had dominated during the sixties had been tiny compared to what it was about to become. Teenagers were growing into young adults and taking their teenage enthusiasms with them. Singles sales were turning into album sales. Cents were becoming dollars. The kind of deal Epstein had done nearly a decade earlier seemed like chicken feed next to what Peter Grant was negotiating on behalf of his clients Led Zeppelin. The plates were shifting.

Although Klein had built his reputation on his ability to get back royalties out of reluctant record companies, the big money was in advances, and that had to mean looking forward, not back. Which is why when McCartney met Harrison in New York in January and said, 'Look, George, I want to get off the Apple label,' Harrison came back with a line that perfectly encapsulates the sadness and venom that had brought the greatest group of all to an end: 'You'll stay on the fucking label. Hare Krishna.'

At the same time as the former Beatles were fighting over the spoils of the previous decade in New York, long-playing records were being completed elsewhere whose sales in the new decade would dwarf the ones the Beatles had managed, in the process creating a whole new industry with a whole new way of doing things. One of them was being made in California by a woman the Beatles had long admired, a woman who had hardly ever appeared in public and whose music seemed as far as it was possible to get from the tortured virtuosity of Yes, the deeply thought-out self-mythologizing of Bruce Springsteen, the holiday camp jollity of Slade and the volume of all of them.

That woman didn't particularly mean to, but she invented the album business.

JANUARY PLAYLIST

George Harrison, 'My Sweet Lord'
Slade, 'Get Down And Get With It'
Van Morrison, 'Domino'
Yes, 'America'
Elton John, 'Your Song'
John Lennon, 'Working Class Hero'
Dave Edmunds, 'I Hear You Knocking'
Status Quo, 'In My Chair'
Badfinger, 'No Matter What'
T. Rex, 'Ride A White Swan'

FEBRUARY:
I FEEL THE EARTH
MOVE

Jim McCrary was the house photographer for A&M Records in Hollywood, California in 1971. It was a sweet gig. It wouldn't make a man rich but no two days were the same. Any time A&M needed a picture of one of the company's artists Jim would be sent along. A&M, which had been started in the previous decade by musician Herb Alpert and his business partner Jerry Moss, was a happening label at the time. McCrary had taken the famous pictures of the Flying Burrito Brothers in their Nudie suits that appeared on the cover of their first album. He had photographed Richard and Karen Carpenter on a sailboat on Lake Tahoe. He had captured the muscle-flexing pose of Joe Cocker in the picture that became the brand of *Mad Dogs & Englishmen*.

On 27 January Jim drove to Appian Way, a residential street in Laurel Canyon in the hills above Sunset Boulevard. His assignment that day was to photograph the woman who lived with her two young daughters at number 8815. She was one of the many New Yorkers who had moved to the West Coast around the turn of the decade to get away from a city that seemed grimy, crime-ridden and in irreversible decline. Moving to California meant she and her daughters could enjoy some sunshine while working in a recording industry that was similarly stepping westward.

Carole King wasn't natural photographic material. Twenty-eight years old, snub-nosed, freckly and frizzy-haired, she had prepared herself for McCrary's lens by putting on a sensible pullover and jeans, much as she would have done had she been weeding the garden. Although she had been in the music business for thirteen years by 1971, this had mostly been in a capacity that didn't have much call for having her picture taken. She had little interest in or flair for glamour. She was fond of remarking, even then, that she was at heart a middle-aged Jewish lady from Brooklyn. When McCrary called she was in the middle of a tapestry.

They tried various shots around the house, then McCrary asked if he could move King's cat Telemachus into the frame. The cat was placed on a cushion on the window-seat in front of King who was holding her tapestry. It provided a nice domestic note.

McCrary went back to the office fairly satisfied with his work and unaware he had shot a cover that would prove more famous, more popular and more ubiquitous than everything else he had photographed put together. The presence of the cat helped the picture strike a note of calm, warmth and domesticity, a note that chimed perfectly with the music on the record inside that cover. It was an album destined to sell in quantities nobody had previously thought possible.

Tapestry, the album that recalibrated the record business, was made the old-fashioned way, in just five three-hour sessions in January 1971. It was recorded in a building on Hollywood Boulevard that had once been the home of Charlie Chaplin Productions. There were three studios at A&M on the corner of Sunset and La Brea. They were all busy that month: Joni Mitchell was in the small one, recording the songs that would make up *Blue*; Richard and Karen Carpenter were in the biggest one, recording the songs that would comprise their best-selling third album *Carpenters*; and in the middle one was this refugee from New York's Tin Pan Alley who had written plenty of hits for other people but had not had any major success on her own and not yet established herself as a performer. There was no particular reason to suspect that what was going on in Studio B would come to be seen as more significant than what was happening on either side.

Carole King's real name was Carol Klein. She had married her chemistry student boyfriend Gerry Goffin while still in her teens. That's what girls did in the early sixties upon finding themselves pregnant. She and her husband wrote hits together for a major song factory called Aldon Music. She'd subsequently divorced Goffin, who had taken acid with predictable consequences for his mental health, and relocated, with her two young daughters, to California.

King could afford a certain amount of independence because her credit was on songs such as 'Will You Love Me Tomorrow', 'Up On The Roof', 'The Locomotion', 'Pleasant Valley Sunday', '(You Make Me Feel Like A) Natural Woman', 'Going Back' and 'Wasn't Born To Follow'. Of all the songwriters who had laboured in the mills of Broadway's Brill Building, among whom were such fabled mechanics of the heart as Cynthia Weil and Barry Mann, Neil Sedaka, Neil Diamond, Howie Greenfield and Paul Simon, none was more admired than this undemonstrative young woman.

Like the Beatles, King was a triple threat: she could write, arrange and sing. Lou Adler knew how good she was. He was the producer at the board for those five days at A&M. Adler was a Chicago-born record business man who had worked with Sam Cooke and guided the career of the Mamas and Papas. He had sold his record company Dunhill to ABC and now he'd started another one called Ode, which he'd licensed to the larger independent A&M Records. Before growing his hair and promoting the Monterey Pop Festival in 1967, Adler had represented Aldon, the New York music publisher which employed Carole King. He noticed how the record companies to whom he'd sent out King's demos tended to hang on to them to listen to for their own enjoyment. There was clearly something about King's voice.

Adler wanted to make a record with that demo quality, a record that felt like a portrait of a woman at work. He wanted the listeners to visualize Carole King sitting at a piano singing just for them. James Taylor had sold a ton of copies of *Sweet Baby James* in 1970 and it wasn't merely because of the quality of the songs. There was also something about his steadfast, modest delivery that appealed to everyone, even soul singers like Marvin Gaye. Adler wanted *Tapestry* to have some of that feeling. The backing instruments were knocked back accordingly so that the finished impression had some of the integrity of a pencil outline. It was not a record that leapt out and collared you. It was a record, like Taylor's, that asked you to lean closer.

The engineer was Hank Cicalo, who had previously worked with Peggy Lee, Vic Damone and the Monkees. Cicalo understood the importance of getting a singer into the right frame of mind. Manipulation of mood was second nature to Hollywood people. When Sinatra had recorded at Capitol on Hollywood Boulevard in the sixties they'd placed him on a podium and invited all the secretaries down so that his sessions had the feeling of a club show in front of adoring fans. King, who had never performed live, needed something different. Cicalo turned down the lights, no matter what the time of day, and placed her in such a way that she could have eye contact with the band and conduct them with her head.

Cicalo had avoided the larger Studio A and installed her and drummer Russ Kunkel, guitarist Danny Kortchmar and bassist Charlie Larkey in B, which was more suitable for combos. The best piano was in the smaller Studio C, which had been locked out by Henry Lewy for Joni Mitchell, who was unwilling to give it up. King was so keen to use its distinctive sound that she and the band dashed in there one morning and recorded three tunes, the opener 'I Feel The Earth Move', her own version of '(You Make Me Feel Like A) Natural Woman' and a new one called 'You've Got A Friend'. It took them three hours, which was the standard length of a session as laid down by the musicians union.

The five days of recording were followed by some doubling-up of voices, using the 'sel-sync' technology that allowed artists to overdub without adding layers of tape hiss, the sparing addition of strings, and then mixing and sequencing, something that Adler considered particularly important. Here he was inspired by *Something Cool*, an album made by jazz singer June Christy in 1954. The whole thing was finished in less than three weeks. It cost $22,000.

Two weeks after McCrary had taken his picture the record was in the stores. It came out in the same week that the Los Angeles area was shaken by the Sylmar earthquake, which killed over sixty people; Britain, which was preparing to join the European Economic Community, said good-bye to pounds, shillings and pence and adopted decimal currency; and *The Yes Album*, Harry Nilsson's *The Point*, Janis Joplin's *Pearl*, Elton John's *Tumbleweed Connection* and the Faces' *Long Player* were all released.

On a break during the sessions young Charlie Larkey, the bass player who was also King's partner, had collared Adler in the corridor.

'What do you think of all this?' asked Larkey, a relative novice.

Adler, the old hand, looked at him and replied with the certainty that senior partners are permitted, 'I think it's going to be the *Love Story* of albums.'

Erich Segal's *Love Story* had been the best-selling book of 1970, and the movie starring Ali McGraw and Ryan O'Neal was the top box office film in January 1971 as *Tapestry* was being wrapped up. Larkey, like most longhairs of the time, shuddered at the parallel with a film that seemed to represent mainstream entertainment. He knew that, unlike *Love Story*, Carole King's album was in no way designed to be a blockbuster. The way it was made seemed to have little in common with a traditional Hollywood smash.

Lou Adler's prediction would turn out to be right. Released in February, *Tapestry* entered the *Billboard* album chart at number seventy-nine on 10 April, with the artist's name listed without the 'e'. Within two weeks it was at thirty-four, by which point they were spelling her name correctly. They would never spell Carole King's name wrong again. *Tapestry* kept on rising until in the week ending 19 June it was the best-selling album in the United States. The fact that they were overhauled by a record by somebody who wasn't a name and who had never even headlined a show (she was still playing piano in her friend James Taylor's band at the time) must have cast a shadow over the days of the artists who suddenly found themselves below her in that top ten, among them the Rolling Stones, Paul McCartney, the Carpenters, Crosby, Stills, Nash & Young, Aretha Franklin and the producers of the soundtrack of *Love Story*.

Tapestry had been carried to the top on the back of the popularity of its single 'It's Too Late', which went to number one, and of another of its songs, 'You've Got A Friend', which was also included on *Mud Slide Slim And The Blue Horizon*, the new album by King's friend, touring companion and celebrity patron James Taylor.

A small number of albums get to enter the charts, a tiny minority of those are best-sellers, and an infinitesimal handful of these go on selling long after the hit singles, the tours, the word of mouth and all the other promotional thermals are becalmed. In the previous decade the soundtrack of *The Sound of Music* was one such. Simon and Garfunkel's *Bridge Over Troubled Water*, released in 1970, was another. Carole King's *Tapestry* would eventually surpass both and in the process redefine success in the record business for the new decade. It remained America's number one album for fifteen weeks through the summer of 1971. By the end of the year it was still selling 150,000 copies a week in the United States alone. This was achieved without TV appearances, without headlining more than the occasional show and without stories in the press. At the close of 1971 this record which had been quietly released back in February had sold five million copies. It had burst the bounds of 'singer-songwriters A–K' and any of the other sub-divisions of the nascent rock retail industry and gone right into the same mainstream as *Love Story*, much as Lou Adler had predicted it would.

Although he had every faith in King's talent, Adler had hedged his bets by making sure that she included two songs that would already be familiar to record buyers. The first was 'Will You Love Me Tomorrow', which in this version sounded less like the plea for gentleness on the part of a trembling virgin and more like a mature woman requiring parity in a relationship. (The backing vocals on this put James Taylor in one channel and Joni Mitchell in the other. This was interesting casting since neither of them was a byword for fidelity, particularly in 1971. During the recording of the album Taylor had an affair with King's co-writer, the glamorous Hollywood scenester Toni Stern, and then moved on to begin an intense affair with Mitchell.) The other song was '(You Make Me Feel Like A) Natural Woman', which King and Gerry Goffin had written in response to Jerry Wexler's request for a song of that name for Aretha Franklin to sing.

Unlike most of the singer-songwriters who came in the wake of James Taylor, King had never really written on her own and the recruitment of the feisty Stern suggested the producers felt she could use some sass. However, the key song, 'You've Got A Friend', had none of that quality and was entirely King's own work. King said she had no idea where it came from, which is what songwriters generally say when they've come up with something exceptional. When these flashes of inspiration occur the best thing a songwriter can do is stay out of the way and, as it were, take dictation. When she played the song for fellow songwriter Carole Bayer Sager she was told it was too simple. When she played it for lyricist Cynthia Weil she was told it was too long. When she played it for James Taylor he recognized that the qualities of guilelessness and lack of edge were what made it perfect. He begged her to let him record it. Hence the song of the year became ubiquitous because two separate versions were recorded, using essentially the same musicians, in studios a few hundred yards from each other within a few days of each other, and went on to dominate the airwaves for the rest of the year and to attract cover versions by everyone from Barbra Streisand through Dusty Springfield to Aretha Franklin. But no matter how accomplished those versions might be, none would quite eclipse the modest conviction of King's original.

The 150,000 people who were picking up King's album every week in 1971 took it home and sang along to it as they finished their essays, did their housework or hovered nervously over their first chilli con carne. It was easy for them to believe that the sound that came out of their mouths was the same as the one they were hearing from the record player. That voice's concerns seemed to be the same as theirs, its temper no more extreme than theirs, its expectations of the world no greater than theirs. It seemed to be broadcasting on the same frequency.

Carole Bayer Sager described it as 'a voice every woman thinks she could have'. Certainly, nobody ever thought they could sing like Aretha Franklin or live like Joni Mitchell, but many of them felt Carole King was the sister they might have had.

As Lou Adler had noted, there had been very few best-selling albums fronted by women. Janis Joplin's *Pearl* had been the number one album for a while in February on the back of the publicity attending her death and her version of Kris Kristofferson's 'Me And Bobby McGee', but that was the exception. Bobbie Gentry had briefly been in the number one slot in 1967 but the top spot had largely been monopolized by male acts like Simon and Garfunkel, the Beatles and Led Zeppelin. That's because up to that point most of the people who bought albums had been men. *Tapestry* changed that and pointed to a future where in order to sell huge numbers of long-playing records you had to sell them to women too.

The first few reviews of *Tapestry* were lukewarm. The one that changed it was a lead review that appeared in *Rolling Stone* on 29 April in which Jon Landau said 'the simplicity of the singing, composition and ultimate feeling achieved the kind of eloquence and beauty that I had forgotten rock is capable of'. The core readership of *Rolling Stone* was male, hairy, leftish and inclined to believe that music worth their time was always loud and edgy. Landau's review was a reminder of the virtues of the pre-Woodstock era and the songwriting baby that might have been thrown out with the bathwater during the move away from the narrow back garden of the hit single to the rolling prairies of the album age.

In 1971 that market for albums was still quite small. The technology for playing records remained forbidding. Long-playing records came in inner bags with messages warning of the dire consequences that could flow from playing a stereo record on a record player which was only wired for mono. There was a widespread feeling that the old portable record players were no longer appropriate machines on which to play these new, self-important long-players in their fold-out covers. Stereo was acceptable only for hobbyists prepared to have their living space dominated by snaking leads.

This was beginning to change with the baby boomers, who were leaving college and setting up their own homes, often communally, in rented accommodation. In 1971 none of these people would have even considered having a TV. It was widely accepted that there was nothing on TV that a long-haired person with a college degree could have the remotest interest in watching (the most exciting event on US TV in the month *Tapestry* came out was the launch of *All in the Family*, the Archie Bunker vehicle based by Norman Lear on the British hit *Till Death Us Do Part*). Instead of a TV they bought a record player. Having bought it, they needed something to play on it. It was quite common in those days to go to a friend's flat and find a new, cheap, Japanese-made 'music centre' with a smoked plastic cover over the deck, dark-brown wood-effect boxes for the speakers, black mesh covering tiny woofers and tweeters. Propped up alongside it would be no more than half a dozen records. As likely as not there would be one by the Beatles, one by Simon and Garfunkel and one by Santana – and as the year went on, it was increasingly likely one would be *Tapestry*.

But those 150,000 people a week buying *Tapestry* in the United States were members of a new constituency. They didn't have *Easy Rider* posters on their walls or pictures of Marianne Faithfull in motorcycle leathers, they didn't hang around hip record stores puzzling over the smoking paraphernalia, they didn't carry around Richard Brautigan books and go to late-night showings of Peckinpah's *The Wild Bunch*. Most of those 150,000 were from a section of the population who ultimately decide whether a pop singer is a flash in the pan or here to stay. They were young women.

Chris Darrow, a respected Hollywood musician, went to see King play the Troubadour in the week of *Tapestry*'s release and was immediately struck by the emergence of this new constituency. 'It was crowded and almost all the people in the room were women, mostly high school and college age. Almost all of them were with their mothers.'

Something was happening which was so gradual and profound that nobody even thought of writing a song about it. In the month of *Tapestry*'s release *New York* magazine published a picture of ten women who worked for *Time* magazine. They were all white, casually dressed but well groomed, and they posed in the New York offices of their employer to mark the success of their efforts to force Time Inc, the massive publishing empire of *Time* magazine, *Life*, *Sports Illustrated*, *Fortune* and various other huge-selling journals, to recognize the fact that they were writers and not researchers. In this they were following in the footsteps of *Newsweek*'s women who had forced that magazine's owners, the Washington Post Company, to allow women to be recognized as writers. Up to then even star writers like Nora Ephron and Ellen Goodman had been forced to accept the lowly title of 'researcher' because the magazine's culture simply couldn't be seen to admit that women could write about mainstream subjects. All this despite the fact that *Newsweek*'s parent company was owned by Katherine Graham. In order to make the changes happen the women had to use legal instruments which had been introduced in the wake of the civil rights struggles of the sixties.

The fact that these women, at both *Time* and *Newsweek*, were the smartly dressed cream of the female graduates from some of America's finest universities gives some indication of the extent to which, in 1971, it was perfectly possible for women to be not so much overlooked as looked through. The fact that they had to threaten *Time* magazine, the citadel of sophisticated East Coast values, with this kind of action in order to get this most modest of changes underlines how far working life in 1971 was out of kilter with the blithe reassurances of the ad saying 'You've come a long way, baby.' Lynn Povich, who eventually became *Newsweek*'s first female editor, wrote a book about the events of 1970. She called it *The Good Girls Revolt* because it featured women who were well brought up, well dressed and well spoken and had been brought up to expect the world to function in a certain way. As she wrote, 'Until 1970 women represented 10 per cent of students in medical school, 4 per cent of law school students and only 3 per cent of business school students.' As Nora Ephron recalled, 'for every man there was an inferior woman, for every writer there was a checker. They were the artists and we were the drones.'

The Good Girls Revolt was a turning point. Nowhere in that *New York* magazine article will you find the word 'sexism'. Nor will you find it in Jill Tweedie's report in the *Guardian* on London's first Women's Lib demo, which took place at the beginning of March 1971. Nor did anyone at the time draw any line between these events and the fact that three of the big films of the year, *Get Carter*, *Straw Dogs* and *Play Misty for Me*, depicted women as sexually voracious and dangerously unhinged. Nobody made a connection between that and the women's movement and nobody ever suggested the music made by single mother Carole King could be thought of as in any way feminist.

A film made at Vassar in 1971 features female students who describe their ideal careers as if they don't quite believe they will actually happen. 'I want to be a music teacher,' says one, 'but I suppose I'll be married and have children.' One wants to be a paediatrician, another wants to be a recording engineer – which in 1971 would probably have made her the first one – but there was an acceptance that other things would get in the way.

While their male counterparts might be worrying about the draft, the key change in the world of young women in 1971 was the sudden availability of the pill. In Britain the Family Planning Association instructed its clinics to make the pill available to single as well as married women, a change which would have seemed seismic a couple of years earlier. This meant that the generation who went to college in the late sixties, who were not expected to settle down and get married quite as soon as the previous generation had done, suddenly had the major disincentive to sex taken out of the equation. This resulted in a short period of time when people living in close proximity to each other felt almost compelled to sleep together as if the act were merely a natural extension of familiarity. In the face of the fact that they couldn't get 'into trouble' any longer, girls who didn't choose to sleep with the first person to ask them were often asked, in all seriousness, 'Are you frigid?' King's record was made in the midst of a socio-cultural milieu which seemed intent on separating the physical act from its emotional consequences. By the autumn of 1971 she had achieved such eminence that Hollywood's senior cocksman Warren Beatty offered to sleep with her, on the grounds that he was curious to know what it was like to have sex with a pregnant woman.

The Good Girls who bought *Tapestry* identified not only with its tunefulness but also with its themes of shelter, stability and trust. Ever since her parents had broken up when she was a child, Carole King had been open about the fact that home was her dream. Nobody ever put King in the foreground of this movement. She was never held up as a symbol of fearsome independence and self-determination. She was a mild-mannered, quite shy person who had to be brought to the front when she played in James Taylor's band. She didn't go round doing interviews advertising her lifestyle. Nonetheless, as Cynthia Weil said, listening to *Tapestry* 'made you feel a friend was taking care of you'.

Tapestry was the first huge-selling record of the modern era. It was the first record to carry on selling once it had passed beyond its obvious commercial window. When you look back at lists of the biggest-selling albums of all time, *Tapestry* is the earliest one to be included. Even when King followed it with *Music*, which was written, recorded and released later in the same year, the public duly noted the new record but kept on buying the old one in a way that indicated that to them it would never be the old one. *Tapestry* was the first evergreen of the rock era. Its success would make the record business realize that it could extend the commercial life of certain albums for years by continuing to release the strongest tracks as singles. Fleetwood Mac's *Rumours*, Meat Loaf's *Bat Out Of Hell*, the Eagles' *Hotel California* and Blondie's *Parallel Lines* were all beneficiaries of this approach later in the decade. A select handful of albums, including *Led Zeppelin IV* and Pink Floyd's *Dark Side Of The Moon*, achieved evergreen status without apparent help from pop success, continuing to notch up sales on the basis that the few people who didn't have it felt they ought to have it.

Tapestry's success was such that none of the people involved with it have ever been able to follow it in the conventional sense. It's made a lot of reputations and bought quite a few homes. In 2013 King reunited with James Taylor to do a tour designed to recapture the spirit of 1971. Whenever she goes on stage nowadays she still plays the songs from *Tapestry*. She's had a film, *Grace of My Heart*, based on her story. *Beautiful*, a musical based on her songs, is running on Broadway and in the West End.

*

At the time of writing, *Tapestry* has sold twenty-five million copies worldwide. Carole King would never have achieved that without the changes that took place in American radio in 1971.

Lee Abrams was a radio nerd from Chicago. He had grown up in the sixties when the airwaves were the domain of fast-talking, self-promoting, sponsor-boosting names like Murray The K. Unlike most kids with a transistor under their pillow Abrams didn't just lose himself in the rhythm and chatter. He started to make a study of what he heard. He corresponded with the stations. He read trade papers. He turned up at industry conventions. He managed a covers band. Because he naturally wanted to know which songs the band should play, he did what nobody had done before in the entire history of the music business. He asked the audience.

Abrams would hand out questionnaires at gigs, personal appearances, record hops and radio station events, carefully compiling the results into typewritten reports listing the songs that people liked and the songs that they were about to like. He started calling the radio stations and offering to share this information with them. He took out ads in the trades which he called 'Better Ideas for Better Stations'.

What he and the radio stations needed to do was get ahead of the charts. If you were a programme director there was no use waiting until a record was number one before your station started playing it. You needed to be playing it when the affair between the public and the record was in the first flush of infatuation. That's the sweet spot radio needs to be in, where people's love of the record being played merges with their love of the radio station and spills over into a little bit of love for its sponsors and advertisers. It's therefore important information for any radio station. In the United States of the late sixties when a record could be red hot in Chicago and mean very little in Miami it was vital intelligence.

In 1971, radio in the United States was just emerging from its brief, heady experiment with free-form radio. Associated particularly with the whisky-voiced hipster Tom Donahue at KMPX and then KSAN in San Francisco from the Summer of Love onwards, free-form meant stations took barely any notice of what happened to be in the charts and instead took pride in serving up the most arcane and challenging music they could get their hands on. This was the time when you could turn on the radio and find somebody playing all twenty minutes of Canned Heat's 'Parthenogenesis' and then welcoming you back to the studio with the silence that indicated approval and eventually the word 'nice'. In Britain, audiences would sit listening to the endless ragas of Ravi Shankar on Radio One unaware that John Peel had put them on in order to go off and spend time with a girlfriend. The audience might not have always found the music to their taste but they approved of the very idea that it was long and proudly uncommercial.

But for every genius of free-form radio, for every jock who knew how to put together a show which could shift gears between the exotic and the familiar, there were twenty tin-eared snobs who were simply on the radio because they liked to be on the radio. Thus there were two kinds of radio: programming on the old AM model which seemed as if it belonged in the long-gone days of the Beach Boys and the Turtles, and free-form programming on the FM stations which had quickly become a self-indulgent bore and a turn-off for those people who didn't spend their days wondering what Grace Slick and Paul Kantner were up to. As one radio programmer put it, 'it was either too hip or too hype'.

By then Lee Abrams was getting his first job in radio. He believed the future was in FM radio. It offered a better signal, a warmer, less shrill sound and the stereo that people were increasingly used to hearing on their records at home. The problem was that the people who ran FM didn't programme the music that the mass audience wanted to hear. Abrams' idea, which he put into practice first at WRIF in Detroit and then at WPTF in Carolina, was to programme the hip music in unhip ways. His motto, which has dominated all radio since, was 'familiar music works'. The idea was that you didn't simply play the hot new record the DJ felt like playing or the one the programme director had been lunched to play. You polled the audience all the time, often by phone, and you asked them to name the acts they most liked. Then you programmed the most popular cuts by those artists. You might let a DJ choose in which order to play them – although over time even that latitude was denied him – but broadly you took the personality DJ out of the equation and replaced him with a strong format, a format which felt as if it was being put together by somebody as windswept and interesting as Clint Eastwood's character in *Play Misty for Me* but in reality was being read off a script provided by Abrams or one of his consulting partners. This was the format that moved the bulk of listening from AM to FM and laid the foundations of the massive sales achieved later in the decade by the Eagles, Fleetwood Mac and Linda Ronstadt. In 1971 it was just getting into its stride, and one of the first beneficiaries of its new way of doing things was the tuneful, female-friendly, easy-on-the-ear record made by Carole King, a woman who was as much a refugee from the AM dial as her listeners.

The artists who weren't on the playlist loathed it. The artists who were on the list thought it was just fine. By the mid-seventies more than three hundred stations across the United States were programmed according to Abrams' principles. Some called it AOR (Album or Adult Oriented Rock). It was certainly no longer underground. It was the new mainstream.

Television had only the haziest clue what was going on beyond its walls. On 15 February 1971 Johnny Carson, the king of late night, presented the *Tonight Show* as usual. As was the custom in the show's early days, it was broadcast from New York. Among Carson's guests that night, returning for her second appearance because he liked her so much, was a sassy twenty-six-year-old singer of Jewish extraction who had grown up in, of all places, Hawaii. Carson liked Bette Midler because not only could she sing, she could also hold her own in the wisecracking stakes and presented herself with a cheery brassiness which you didn't find in most pop singers of the era. Midler was what Carson and other members of the ring-a-ding-ding generation would have called a broad. She didn't have a record contract at the time, and in 1971 she was marking time by playing the Acid Queen on stage in the first production of Pete Townshend's *Tommy* at the Seattle Opera or entertaining closely packed houses of gay men clad only in towels in the Continental Baths in New

York City. This was not directly referred to in her TV appearances. In 1971 you still couldn't use the word 'gay' on the TV, certainly not in a light entertainment context. Midler, saucy tongue sheathed in rouged cheek, would simply say it was full of 'happy people'. Her act at the Baths, which earned her the name 'Bathhouse Betty', was made up of sixties pop favourites, chin-up tunes from wartime and tearful torch songs that she cooked up and arranged with her accompanist, the equally unknown Barry Manilow, who sometimes entered into the spirit of things by playing wearing only a towel.

A particular favourite in the latter category was confusingly known as 'Groupie (Superstar)'. Neither the original name nor its parenthetical name featured in the lyrics. It had been the idea of Rita Coolidge, a member of the teeming cast of Joe Cocker's *Mad Dogs & Englishmen*, and had been inspired by her observation of the way certain impressionable girls seemed to queue up to be misused by the famous men on stage. The ballad had been written by the tour's musical director Leon Russell with Bonnie Bramlett, and Coolidge had sung it every night on the *Mad Dogs* tour. It had subsequently been covered by Cher and Vicki Carr. Midler found that its theme of being used and abused by a man also resounded with her moist clientele at the Continental Baths.

Watching the Carson show that night in the new five-bedroom house he and his sister Karen had recently moved into in the Los Angeles suburb of Downey was Richard Carpenter. The Carpenters, who were originally from Connecticut, had put out their first album in late 1969 but already he was under pressure to come up with their third. They had spent the day in A&M's studio on La Brea recording tracks for this third album, and he knew he needed follow-ups to huge hits of the previous year like 'For All We Know' and 'We've Only Just Begun'.

The success of the Carpenters, which was already considerable, had been achieved at the expense of some of Richard's pride. As the older sibling and an accomplished pianist and arranger, Richard might have expected to be in charge. Things hadn't worked like that. Although he wrote his own songs, the Carpenters' hits tended to come from composers like Paul Williams and Burt Bacharach. Although Richard did some singing his vocals were nothing like as distinctive as those of his gawky kid sister Karen. Richard had steeled himself for stardom only to find that its mantle had fallen instead on his sister, who seemed manifestly unready for it. Their parents, the original driving force behind their children's efforts, still saw Richard as the talent. The rest of the world didn't agree.

Karen Carpenter had been included as a package with her older brother ever since they were teenagers. Their gimmick was that she played the drums. The session musicians who played on the Carpenters' records, who came from that loose federation of brilliant pop instrumentalists known as the Wrecking Crew, knew that while average drummers were ten a penny, voices like Karen's happened along only rarely. Joe Osborn, the bass player in whose garage they first learned to record, said 'she got no credit for anything. Richard was the star as far as the family was concerned.' Drummer Hal Blaine, who played along with her on some of the studio recordings, says 'that voice was just incredible. She was born with that. She didn't learn that.'

Karen Carpenter's problem was that while the requirements of show business demanded that she come out front
and be the band's lead singer, her self-consciousness about
her appearance meant she preferred to stay behind the kit.
'She was kind of a tomboy,' said Sherwin Bash, who managed
them, 'and the drums were traditionally a male instrument.
She wasn't sure she was slim enough, svelte enough, pretty
enough, any of those things.'

Richard and Karen Carpenter prospered greatly in 1971
but they were scorned by those who considered themselves
hip. They popped up on the old-fashioned TV shows fronted
by stars terrified that they were losing their way in a country
which appeared to have gone youth crazy. In any show fronted
by a comedian in a tux you could guarantee they would be
the musical guest. There wasn't the ghost of anything edgy
about them. In a world where people were expected to flaunt
their attitude they didn't appear to have any. They sounded
like creamed rice.

The fact that the Carpenters made it big speaks volumes
for the willingness of a few record companies to invest in
unconventional talent. A&M was a company that had made
a lot of its money with the easy listening sounds of Herb
Alpert's Tijuana Brass and the Sandpipers so it knew as well
as anyone how to promote an act like the Carpenters. They
were one of the first acts to sell big on eight-track and cassette. Their buyers were the great bulk of the American and
overseas public who just liked good tunes and also found
something in Karen Carpenter's profound contralto that
spoke to them about their lives every bit as much as Leonard
Cohen, Carole King or Neil Young did to their listeners.

So 'Groupie (Superstar)' was an odd choice for a Carpenters song. Then again, 'We've Only Just Begun' was originally a jingle for a bank. Richard had never heard the song Midler sang before, which is an indication of the direction in which his personal radio was tuned, but he guessed his sister could sing the song, as she could sing pretty much any ballad.

He was right. Karen was less convinced but she did what she was told. They made one change to the lyrics, 'to sleep with you again' becoming 'to be with you again'. She did a guide vocal for the musicians to play along with. Even with only half her mind on the job she delivered a perfect performance. The guide vocal never needed to be replaced. That was the special quality of Karen Carpenter, a quality which became even more poignant following her anorexia-related death in 1983. When Bette Midler performed, half the impact was in the twinkle in her eye, her coquettish body language, the way she carried herself. With Karen Carpenter it was in her voice and her voice alone.

Russ Solomon started selling records in his father's drug store in Sacramento just after the war. He named his business after the building in which it was housed, the Tower Theatre. He opened the first big store in Watt Avenue in Sacramento. In 1968 he opened another at Columbus and Bay in San Francisco. In 1970 he bought a plot on Sunset Boulevard in Hollywood, within walking distance of the Whisky a Go Go. It had its own parking lot. At busy times it even had its own parking attendant directing traffic in that lot.

Tower advertised itself as 'the largest record-tape store in the known world', a claim also made by The HMV Shop in London's Oxford Street. Claims of that kind are impossible to measure but the key feature of Tower was that all the stock was out on the floor rather than in the storeroom so it certainly felt like that. New releases would be literally piled on the floor near the door and advertised at discount prices, making it impossible to resist buying them. At the same time they would carry a depth of catalogue which would be unknown in your local record store. They could do this because they were sited in busy cities with growing populations of young people who would buy records.

Tower took some of the ambience of the hippy record shacks like Rather Ripped in Berkeley or Virgin in London – Solomon promoted the fact that he wouldn't allow his staff to wear ties – while behind the scenes his staff were playing hardball with distributors and using their growing muscle to negotiate discounts the hippy shacks could never match. They organized in-store gigs and personal appearances (War drove a tank into the car park to promote their album), they became outlets for the growing market for local listings magazines, and turned into de facto social centres, encouraging people to spend all day in the shops secure in the knowledge that it would be difficult to come out of there with just one record. They had hand-written price labels above the racks, they did all the things that the little hippy stores thought they were too cool to do and the old-fashioned mom and pop stores would never have thought to do, and they achieved the objective of the record companies by making new releases seem like the most important thing in the world.

By early 1971 Tower on Sunset already seemed like the capital of the worldwide record business. It was within walking distance of the studios where *Tapestry* and *Mud Slide Slim* had been made, and the Troubadour where all the happening acts played and where on Tuesday nights a line of hopefuls – including, that spring, young Thomas Waits from Pomona – would turn up for their chance at the big time. It was near enough to the new West Coast headquarters being set up by all the record companies as they fled New York in search of a more congenial lifestyle for newly wealthy executives and in pursuit of a feeling that this was now the centre of a different kind of world. For those people who weren't that excited about what was going on in the cinema, didn't own more than one set of clothes and couldn't afford anything more than a beaten-up twenty-year-old car, Tower on Sunset was the most exciting place in the world, a temple into which all consumer desire was channelled. The pulse quickened on entering it in the sure and certain knowledge that you would experience some shock of the new in the shape of a new record by either an old favourite or a new name you had only just heard about, had never heard sing and had certainly never seen. The record shops were medium and message combined. Most of the people who bought Carole King's *Tapestry* would not have had an earthly clue what she looked like until they picked up her album and turned it over in their hands. The new generation of record shops had a magic which replaced the radio. They were the place where you came into contact with the product. You didn't merely shop at a place like this. You parsed every last detail of your surroundings at the same time. You stood among the racks studying every recent release, memorizing paragraphs of the sleeve notes, piecing together your knowledge square by square. It was the love of rock turned into its purest expression – shopping.

The recorded music business was beginning to diversify into new product ranges. In their 1971 ranges American motor manufacturers were starting to offer cassette or eight-track decks as extras on their luxury cars, and Philips were advertising the previously undreamt-of sensation of 'stereo in your car' with their own in-car players. In 1971 Henry Kloss introduced the Advent 201 which incorporated Dolby noise reduction and chromium dioxide tape, which improved the sound, meaning that a technology that had once been considered only good enough for dictation was suddenly a perfectly acceptable way to listen to music. That meant that the record companies for the first time had the possibility of selling something in more than one format, which suggested you could conceivably sell it more than once. For those people coming into the market for music who were not hooked on the romance of the 12-inch album and preferred convenience above all things, the cassette was an exciting new way to join the fun. By the end of the decade it would be the leading music carrier.

Those lucky people who were able to sweep out of the parking lot of Tower on Sunset while inserting a cassette of a freshly purchased new album by the hottest, least-tried new artist into their new auto-reverse in-car player with the promise that it would bloom into stereo using the cabin of the vehicle as a huge sounding-box felt they were having a hit of human pleasure, a pinch of ease, a brief transport of delight that nothing else in their daily life would ever be able to match. They weren't entirely wrong.

In 1971 even the most comfortable people didn't get to indulge their fantasies; to live, even temporarily, the luxury life. In that year the United States and Europe were still a long way apart. Transatlantic travel was the exclusive preserve of the wealthy, the business traveller or people making once-in-a-lifetime trips to visit relatives who might have emigrated in the years after the war. Mass transit hadn't yet arrived. The first jumbo jet full of ticket-buying passengers hadn't landed at Heathrow until 1970. There were very few airlines and few of them were offering budget fares. In 1971 Southwest Airlines opened its commuter routes between Dallas, Houston and San Antonio, selling tickets which at $20 were marketed as being roughly comparable to the price of gasoline needed for the trip. The other key feature stressed in the advertising of Southwest Airlines was that their flight attendants wore bright orange hot pants and go-go boots.

The routes across the Atlantic were dominated by the old carriers who didn't discount. The USA was not a holiday destination for many Europeans. In London, people who had actually visited the States were interrogated by friends hungry for the smallest detail of this far-off land of dreams. In 1971 the average twenty-four-year-old Londoner would entertain small hope of ever making the trip themselves. That might be a source of mild sadness for many of them. For somebody so obsessed with America and its popular culture that he had changed his name in honour of an American frontiersman it was more painful than that.

On 24 January 1971, David Bowie took his first flight to the United States. It was the most important journey of his life. Bowie's career had stalled since 'Space Oddity' was a number one single in 1969 but he had a deal with Mercury Records, who were putting out his record *The Man Who Sold The World* in the USA. He also had a new manager, a solicitor's clerk called Tony Defries, who had managed to persuade Mercury to fly him out to do some promotion. In 1971 artists had to have an official exchange agreement with the American Musicians Union in order to be able to perform on such a visit. Since he had no such permit Bowie couldn't play any dates. However, he had a few enthusiastic supporters in the US media and on the staff of Mercury Records. One of these, the East Coast publicity boss Ron Oberman, met Bowie when he arrived at Washington's Dulles Airport. There was barely any budget for the visit and therefore it was agreed that he would stay with Oberman, who at the time was living in his parents' home in Silver Springs, Maryland. For the Obermans it was an adventure to go to the airport so Ron took his parents with him. Like most of the people in the terminal they were taken aback by Bowie's appearance when he came through customs. He had been detained for forty-five minutes by officials unaccustomed to seeing young men in electric blue fur coats with velvet trousers tucked into black motorcycle boots and hair swept into a style reminiscent of forties screen actress Veronica Lake. If they had looked in the traveller's bags they would have seen that he had packed one of the men's dresses by the London designer Michael Fish that he and his wife Angie had picked out.

Angie didn't travel with him because the budget didn't stretch that far, and also because she was six months' pregnant. She remained at their home, a rambling mansion in Beckenham, Kent called Haddon Hall. The people she was sharing with had pretensions to be a commune but in fact were largely dedicated to trying to launch the career of David Bowie.

The three weeks Bowie spent in the United States in January and February 1971, which took him to New York, Detroit, Minneapolis, Texas and California, were the most formative of his professional life. Like any young man in the early seventies coming from England, a country which had just one pop music radio station and a total of three TV channels, he was stupefied by America's plenty and intoxicated with the relative ease of life. Far from the responsibilities and well-trodden pavements of home, Bowie was free to make himself up, to say things he wouldn't have said back in the UK, describing his last LP as 'reminiscences about my experiences as a shaven-headed transvestite' to a San Francisco DJ and delighting in his ability to stop the conversation in any restaurant by the simple act of walking in.

Those three weeks changed his view of music. He was played the Velvet Underground's *Loaded*, which included 'Sweet Jane' and 'Rock N Roll', a record that would not be released in the UK until March. He was sufficiently enthused to see them at the Electric Circus in New York and was so overcome that he talked his way backstage to shake the hand of the man he thought was Lou Reed. It was only later that he learned that Reed had left the band and he'd been enthusing over the hastily elevated Doug Yule – further evidence of how shrouded in mystery it was possible for a cult band to remain in 1971. In Manhattan he met the avant-garde street musician Moondog. In San Jose he heard the Stooges for the first time. Having failed to make a commercial breakthrough and seeking consolation in heroin, the band was on the point of breaking up. Bowie and Iggy Pop would meet for the first time later in the year. By the time he arrived in Los Angeles on 13 February Bowie had told his new friend, the radio plugger, scene maker and provider of female companions Rodney Bingenheimer, that he had an idea for a whole album based on a character called Ziggy Stardust.

In Hollywood he stayed with RCA executive Tom Ayres who lived just off Sunset Boulevard in a home previously owned by the silent movie star Lillian Gish. Bowie and Bingenheimer borrowed Ayres's convertible Cadillac to drive to radio interviews. This would have been a kick even for someone from suburban California. For a boy from Beckenham it was unimaginably exciting. There was recording equipment in Ayres's house, which Gene Vincent was using at the time. Bowie took advantage of this to record a demo of a new song called 'Hang On To Yourself', which he offered to Ayres for Vincent.

The week in Los Angeles passed like a dream. Wearing his Fish gown, Bowie performed a few songs at a lawyer's party in the Hollywood Hills, perched on a waterbed – the item of furniture all rich hippies favoured at the time – and playing his acoustic guitar. He went to a party for Ultra Violet, one of Andy Warhol's superstars, and socialized with the handsome young film actor Don Johnson. Like all first-time visitors from Britain he didn't quite get to grips with the lack of public transport. On Valentine's Day he walked two miles down Sunset Boulevard to attend a rehearsal with Christopher Milk, the band led by *Rolling Stone* writer John Mendelsohn. This took place in the same studios where Carole King had just completed *Tapestry*. Together they played the Velvet

Underground's 'Waiting For The Man', which would soon become a part of Bowie's act.

Like any musician on the make he focused on Ayres as somebody who might be able to help him. His contract with Mercury expired after *The Man Who Sold The World* and he was looking for a new home. Ayres said he should consider his employers RCA because the only thing they had was Elvis and that wasn't going to last for ever. It was thanks to the contact that he had made with Ayres that the Ziggy Stardust album, when it arrived, would be on RCA alongside those of the King, the singer with whom he shared a birthday. Ayres introduced him to Grelun Landon, the company's august head of publicity. Landon, who had worked closely with Elvis Presley, said 'he's very bizarre but I think he's going to be the Bob Dylan of the seventies'.

When Bowie flew back to London on 18 February it was clear that he was infatuated with the USA, babbling excitedly to friends and audiences about the freeways, the subways and even the violence, in a way that seemed to be boasting as much as anything else. Rubbing shoulders with American music business people and listening to American radio made him think outside the box of his suburban Arts Lab world. The collision between English sensibilities and the actual experience of visiting America had seven years earlier led the Beatles and the Rolling Stones to create their defining music. Now it was David Bowie's turn. By the end of the month he had organized a session at Radio Luxembourg's studio in Mayfair to record 'Hang On To Yourself' and 'Moonage Daydream', another song which would eventually find its way on to his breakthrough album.

He wasn't planning to sing it himself. He was going to be the puppet master for a cute young gay guy called Fred Burrett. He and Angie had taken to spending time at a London club called The Sombrero. There they had met the tiny handful of people in London happy to describe themselves as gay. His plan was to transform young Fred into Freddie Burretti and make him a star. David would be the one pulling the strings Simon Cowell-style. It didn't work out quite the way he planned. It would be another year before Ziggy Stardust was properly set before the public, and then Bowie would find himself playing both puppet and puppet master. However, the seeds of his breakthrough idea had been sown during his intoxicating trip to the New World and, although they probably wouldn't have believed it, Lou Reed and Iggy Pop were rescued from the obscurity that seemed to be beckoning before their English fan made that fateful trip.

FEBRUARY PLAYLIST

Carole King, 'It's Too Late'
James Taylor, 'You've Got A Friend'
Joni Mitchell, 'Little Green'
Janis Joplin, 'Mercedes Benz'
Todd Rundgren, 'We Gotta Get You A Woman'
Roy Budd, 'Get Carter'
David Bowie, 'The Man Who Sold The World'
The Velvet Underground, 'Sweet Jane'
Jesus Christ Superstar soundtrack
The Temptations, 'Just My Imagination'

MARCH: ROCK AND ROLL

I n the early years of the present century I took a holiday in the Highlands of Scotland. I stopped in a lay-by at the side of Loch Ness, one of the most desolate, beautiful parts of the country. Here it's possible to escape the crowds and feel pleasantly cut off from your fellow man. I took a few moments to contemplate the chilly depths of the loch and brood on the stillness of the surrounding mountains.

There was only one other vehicle in that car park. It was a small van, dispensing drinks to passing tourists. On this occasion it was staffed by one young woman. She might have been a postgraduate university student, working her way through the summer, or just a member of that vast army of polite young people with surprising flecks of colour in their hair and runic tattoos on their ankles who nowadays can pop up anywhere in modern Europe, passing their time in a job far below their education and capabilities as they wait for life to provide them with a road map.

To while away the time between customers she had a book and, oddly enough, a cassette player. From this old-fashioned machine arose a piece of music which reached back even further, all the way to the spring of 1971, its melancholy merging perfectly with the view of the loch. It also provided the ideal soundtrack for the dispensing of a cup of tea in a polystyrene cup, marrying sound and image in a way that made me unsure whether I was watching a commercial or actually in one. The music was 'At The Chime Of A City Clock' by Nick Drake from his 1971 album *Bryter Layter*.

The patina overlaying Drake's music has been steadily built up over the years with so many layers of hindsight that it's impossible to know whether that twenty-something alongside Loch Ness was responding to the actual music as put on tape by engineer John Wood in Chelsea in November 1970 or to the identification of a certain quality of bruised soulfulness in Drake's music, an identification which has grown over recent years thanks to the music's frequent use on soundtracks. We have probably experienced it in movies like *The Royal Tenenbaums*, TV series like *Parenthood*, or the VW commercial in which a bunch of educated young people born in the era of mobile phones and satnav choose to spend the evening driving around listening to Drake's music and looking at the moon rather than mixing with the beery oafs at their local bar. Drake's music lives in the mainstream as a signifier for 'alternative'.

Of all the records put out in 1971, none was more heedlessly passed over at the time than Drake's *Bryter Layter* and none has been more warmly adopted by subsequent generations, most of whom weren't even born at the time he died. Some music from 1971 sounds more pertinent now than it did when it originally came out. This is certainly the case with Drake's work. Linda Thompson, a fellow musical striver and girlfriend of Drake's back in the early seventies, heard his music in the twenty-first century over a supermarket tannoy in Los Angeles and, as she remarked, 'couldn't believe how right it sounded. How did he know?' Drake's career, if we can call it that since he was absent by reason of death throughout it, has been the slowest burn in rock.

At the time *Bryter Layter* came out, in March 1971, Joe Boyd, the talent scout who had first signed Drake to his Witchseason Productions, produced him, found him live shows, established him in a flat and did all the other things Drake showed no sign of doing for himself, was already on his way to a new job in his native United States. Hence Drake was without the patron, advocate and twenty-four-hour irritant every artist needs if they are to elbow their way into prominence. However, Island, the larger independent to whom he was in fact signed, continued to pay him a £20-a-week retainer, comparable to the earnings of somebody who actually worked for a living. Later in 1971 he dropped in on John Wood, the engineer who had been at the board on his previous albums, and in two nights recorded the unadorned *Pink Moon*, which came out in 1972. That was the end of Drake's recording career. He died in 1974 at his parents' home in Tanworth-in-Arden, apparently after an overdose of antidepressants. He was twenty-six.

In the years that followed Island kept his records in the catalogue out of respect but there was no groundswell of interest. It wasn't until 1992, when the country rock artist Lucinda Williams released a version of Drake's 'Which Will', that his music began to exert a powerful fascination on the many artists who think of themselves as refugees from the established categories. His songs were done by everyone from the rock band the Flaming Lips to the jazz artist Brad Mehldau. Robyn Hitchcock and Mogwai are just two of the acts to write songs named after him. Prominent people were eager to tell us how much they liked him. It seemed to advertise their sensitivity. Brad Pitt waived his fee to narrate a BBC radio documentary about Drake's life. The film actor Heath Ledger claimed to be obsessed with him and was eventually found dead in circumstances that echoed Drake's death. These days Drake's reputation is greater than those of many of the people whose success he most envied in 1971. Nobody talks about Lindisfarne or Brewer and Shipley with the same reverence. Drake is a latter-day James Dean, revered as much for what he's seen to represent as for what he did.

The Pulitzer Prize-winning writer Louis Menand has written about what he called 'the iron law of stardom'. This law decrees that in show business you've only got three years. Three years is about as long as you can remain interesting and as long as an audience can maintain its interest in you. There are exceptions but it's surprising how many rock careers are effectively about three stylistically linked albums made over a period of three years. Drake's brief career, which started with *Five Leaves Left* in 1970 and ended with *Pink Moon* in 1972, is a classic case. His death meant he never got the chance to let anyone down. He is the epitome of the artist who, in the words of Elvis Costello, didn't stick around to witness his own decline. Now that his life is safely bounded by just three albums he remains not only an artist who made some appealing music but also a perfect emblem of misunderstood genius.

In the year 2013, Universal Music, the huge multinational entertainment company that swallowed up A&M, Motown, Island and many of the most charismatic independent record labels of the seventies, announced yet another reissue of Nick Drake's album *Bryter Layter*, forty-two years after its original release. This time his second album would be presented in a box set containing a record pressed on '180 gram virgin vinyl for the audiophile' and packaged inside a fold-out cover which had been painstakingly and expensively aged to replicate the original textured cover of the 1971 LP. It would also be accompanied by a replica shop poster. Especially for the collectors who were expected to file their copy away unplayed to make sure it retained its value, it came, too, with a code enabling the buyer to download the music on a choice of formats including High Definition 24 Bit and a version Dubbed From Disc.

With its curious combination of antique trade fakery and digital sheen the 2013 *Bryter Layter* project was the most elaborate example yet of the heritage rock industry's attempt to conjure the allegedly magical moment in early 1971 when that record was released. In truth there was no such moment, magical or otherwise, no feeling that something precious was happening, or even that an opportunity had been missed. The concept of rock posterity hadn't yet been invented.

Drake died unknown in 1974. Those few music fans who read the down-page news item at the time knew Drake as the guy who made the quiet watercolour music they might have heard on Island sampler albums like *Nice Enough To Eat*. Here, his 'Time Has Told Me' was sequenced immediately before King Crimson's bludgeoning 'Twenty-First Century Schizoid Man', which seemed destined to obliterate all traces of anything that had come before.

In 1971 Nick Drake had no noticeable following. At the time you had either made it or you were about to. Nobody had yet settled into that position of middling cultdom in which most of today's rock bands live, breathe and have their being. The cult of the noble underrated hadn't been invented. Drake's name didn't resound. Fashionable people didn't drop his name. He didn't stand for anything. Nobody had his picture on their wall. He was just another singer-songwriter making music, nothing like as celebrated as Al Stewart, let alone Leonard Cohen; more like Harvey Andrews or Amory Kane, a provider of the kind of music which was vaguely and approvingly described in the nasal argot of the day as 'nice', but bought by absolutely nobody you knew.'

The early weeks of March 1971 should have been the fullest of Nick Drake's life. He was twenty-two, comfortably off, devastatingly attractive to women, a guitarist that other players tried to copy but couldn't, and one of the handful of performers who had a sound and a style of their own. He'd just had his second record released on Island, which was Britain's hippest record company, and yet his day slipped by unseized. He almost didn't have a day at all.

Bryter Layter's release was held up by the British postal strike, which interrupted deliveries to shops. This action, in pursuit of a 15 per cent pay rise (fairly standard at the time), began in January 1971 and lasted for seven weeks. It made the nation's switch to decimal currency in February even more complex, and meant that the Post Office was forced for the first time to license private firms to carry the mail. The strike ended on 4 March, and *Bryter Layter* was released in the UK a week later. There was no single and barely any radio play. There was a half-page advert in the *Melody Maker* and a short interview in *Sounds* in which he talked to Jerry Gilbert about his dislike of live performance. It was the only interview Drake did in his life.

Other things were going on. Bigger things. *Bryter Layter* came out in the same week that Muhammad Ali fought Joe Frazier at Madison Square Garden for the heavyweight championship of the world. Ali had been stripped of his title because of his refusal to fight in Vietnam. This was his way back. It was billed as the Fight of the Century and it lived up to that billing. It went to fifteen rounds. Frazier had Ali on his backside at one point and eventually won on points. The only way Frank Sinatra could get a ringside seat was by serving as the accredited photographer of *Life* magazine.

Bryter Layter came out in the same week that three off-duty Scottish soldiers, one of them only seventeen, were lured away from a pub in Belfast city centre to a field on the outskirts of the city and shot in the back of the head by a Provisional IRA death squad. It was said that girls had done the luring, which made everyone shudder. The papers started to use the word 'honeytrap' with a new familiarity. The soldiers' deaths indicated that the British army's presence in Northern Ireland, which had begun as a police operation to protect besieged Catholics, could turn out to be more difficult to end than it had been to begin.

Bryter Layter came out in the same week that Michael Caine's film *Get Carter* opened. Caine played a London gangster travelling to Newcastle to find out who killed his brother and mete out brutal treatment to anyone who got in his way, whether male or female.

Things were grim whichever way you looked, and in such a climate a record as pallid and lyrical as *Bryter Layter* was blown away in a gust of grit.

This was not helped by Drake's reticence. Among sons and daughters of the upper class such as Drake, shyness often masquerades as arrogance. A further problem was that Drake just wouldn't take any of the simple steps that are generally associated with achieving popularity. The curious contradiction of the singer-songwriter's trade is that while the music has to hint at a soul which does not easily yield its secrets, it needs to be accompanied by an iron-clad confidence which enables the artist to get up in a crowded room and demand attention. It's a quality that peers such as Bob Dylan, Richard Thompson, John Martyn and Joni Mitchell had. Drake, for all his privileged upbringing, didn't.

His few efforts to play live resulted in performances that didn't project much further than the lip of the stage. During one show he left halfway through a song. This was either the understandable retreat of a soul too sensitive to live or the gross dereliction of duty of a person who has set himself up as an entertainer. As Joe Boyd said years later, dismissing the idea that all the Hollywood interest in Nick Drake might result in a biographical film about him, 'Nick didn't have a very interesting life. He spent most of his time alone in his room, smoking a joint.'

Drake was an upper-class hippy. The members of Led Zeppelin may have had similarly long, apparently unkempt hair, which at the time was the mark of the hippies, and they may have had a lot of the same interests in arcane music, mysticism and travel to the Third World, but their approach to their music and the selling thereof could not have been more different. Whereas Drake believed that success was his due, the members of Led Zeppelin knew that it had to be fought for. Thanks to their manager they were one of the first groups put together in order to achieve massive success and to make a great deal of money. Precisely how massive the success and how much money that would mean, they had very little idea.

If Nick Drake wouldn't stir from his room there were in 1971 many people who would. P. G. Wodehouse's advice to aspiring writers is 'first apply the seat of the trousers to the surface of the chair'. In 1971 a new generation of rock musicians were beginning to realize that if they wished to make their name and their fortune they had to adopt the same kind of work ethic. There was a feeling that this could be a perfect time to do so. While the former members of the Beatles were arguing in court or plotting their own solo records, the Rolling Stones trying to get themselves organized for relaunch and Bob Dylan moving back to New York and thinking about what to do next, their established positions in the hierarchy were being usurped by a band that was appealing to a generation who had been too young to be wholly under the spell of those sixties acts and reaching these people by going out and playing for them.

On 5 March, on the same night that the Rolling Stones played two shows at the Free Trade Hall in Manchester and Aretha Franklin recorded in front of the love crowd at San Francisco's Fillmore, Led Zeppelin began their 1971 tour at the citadel of unionism, the Ulster Hall in Belfast. They were still putting the finishing touches to their new album, which wouldn't come out until the winter. The problems of Northern Ireland hadn't yet hardened into 'the Troubles' and it was still just about possible for visiting bands to appear there. This wouldn't be the case for the next forty years.

This March tour entered the burgeoning lore of the band known familiarly to its young, hairy fan base as 'Zep' as the 'back to the clubs tour'. Announcing the plan to the *Record Mirror*, guitarist and group leader Jimmy Page explained, 'the audiences were becoming bigger and bigger but moving further and further away'. He said this tour was an attempt to say thank you to the clubs that had helped the band in its early days and enabled them to play in cities that didn't have large venues; tickets and fees would be pegged at the level they would have been in the past. Thus the tour took Led Zeppelin, who were at the time the biggest-grossing, most popular band in the world, to such venues as the Nottingham Boat Club, Newcastle's Mayfair Ballroom and the Belfry in Sutton Coldfield.

Although it resulted in small venues being swamped by the demand and made no financial sense for the band, the back to the clubs tour was interesting because it seemed to be trying to make amends for injuries the British audience had yet to sustain. Only the band knew the explosion in demand which was coming down the road. Led Zeppelin had glimpsed the scale of this demand for their live shows in the USA the previous year and they knew that when they went there later in 1971 they would be playing for crowds five times the size of the biggest crowd in Britain. The back to the clubs tour was doubly curious because the club days they were planning to get back to had been a mere three years earlier, in 1968. Since then they had released three albums which had sold massively (although the third one had not done as well as the previous two), but even so the largest venue they had played in Britain, apart from the odd festival, was the Albert Hall. This was considered the biggest place any band could reasonably expect a British audience to tolerate. It seated just four thousand people. When Page was talking about the audience appearing to be just specks on the horizon he was clearly thinking about some of the venues in the USA, where Led Zeppelin were starting to play arenas.

Meanwhile back in the Ulster Hall, which had a capacity of less than two thousand, the *Melody Maker*'s Chris Welch reported that the MC who was working on behalf of the hall still addressed the audience as 'boys and girls' and was asking them to leave when the band came back for an encore. This wasn't unusual. Nobody had yet worked out how they were supposed to behave at a big rock concert. Tickets were 16 shillings, less than a pound. Welch, who had flown out to cover this big moment, spoke to one young fan who had previously thought Led Zeppelin were American and had only laid eyes on them once before in one picture she had on her wall. He also noted that among the new songs the band played that night was one called 'Stairway To Heaven'. Because this was the *Melody Maker* he felt duty-bound to tell his readers that for this tune Jimmy played his twin-necked guitar, giving him a six- and a twelve-string sound on the same instrument. 'An excellent ballad, it displayed Robert Plant's developing lyricism,' he added, approvingly.

Recalling that night many years later, bassist John Paul Jones said that during 'Stairway To Heaven' the audience were bored to tears waiting for something they knew. It certainly took a while for the song to be greeted with any apparent enthusiasm. At first it was received with polite puzzlement, its early passages seeming to belong on their previous record *Led Zeppelin III*. Nobody at the time suggested it owed anything to the rock instrumental 'Taurus' by the American band Spirit. After a while it started to get more reaction, and Peter Grant, doing what great managers always do, which is watch the audience during the show, realized that it was hitting home and therefore made one of the very few artistic suggestions he ever made to the band. When it finishes and the last chords have died away, he suggested, don't immediately start tuning up for the next one. Don't go out of character. Hold the moment. Milk the drama. Maintain the mood. Grant had spent some time as a wrestler. He knew about hokum, which at the time very few rock bands did.

In 1971 Peter Grant was thirty-six, more than ten years older than the youngest members of Led Zeppelin. Like many of the managers and fixers who were beginning to come to the fore in this new music business, he was a member of an older generation. Born in the 1930s, he'd known hardships that his band hadn't, which made him more inclined to value whatever success they were having. Grant was always happy to have people know that he was a former professional wrestler, appreciating that if you have a reputation for violence it often saves you the trouble of resorting to it. In later years the band's preposterous success and his immersion in cocaine led him to behave in a way he had previously only threatened to; in the early days he was as important a member of the band as any of the people who carried instruments. Like the besotted parent of a gifted child, he was dedicated to implementing the vision of his favourite, Jimmy Page. The mere fact that Led Zeppelin had a vision marked them out from all the bands who had come before them and meant that their legacy was, if anything, greater. The biggest bands usually have an influence which is anything but benign. The Beatles made bands think they had to write their own songs. The Stones made bands think they had to be rebellious. Led Zeppelin made bands think they had to be loud.

Grant's original business partner was Mickie Most, who managed and produced the Jeff Beck Group, the band that established the template for the four-piece group with lead singer – in many people's eyes the perfect division of rock labour and since emulated by U2, REM, the Killers and hundreds more. But whereas Beck simply didn't have the patience for the long march, walking out on his own group in the middle of a US tour, Page had a little bit of money saved up and in Grant he had the man prepared to go to the big record companies and demand an advance. Page and Jones banked their £3,000 share of it (that was almost two years' salary for the average British worker at the time). Like many good-looking singers Robert Plant had to think about sheltering the girlfriend he'd hurriedly married when she became pregnant, and he used his money to make a deposit on a house. Drummer John Bonham went out and bought a sports car, which was a clear indication of how he planned to deal with success.

When Led Zeppelin played the University of Kent in Canterbury on 12 March tickets were 60p (12 shillings for those who hadn't yet adjusted to decimal) and they were sold out immediately to the people who queued up outside Eliot College on the appointed day. A few of them, reported the student paper, had actually been there since the night before. Although they had inherited the mantle of the Yardbirds, Led Zeppelin's success was built on a new generation of fans who had been born just slightly too late to experience the mid-sixties as teenagers and had come through their adolescence to the sounds of Jimi Hendrix and Cream. This meant they were wired in a slightly different way and were inclined to regard rock as something that needed to be measured rather than enjoyed. Unlike Led Zeppelin's fan base in the United States, who were already inclined to whoop, the disciples in their home country thought that the best tribute you could pay to a group was to appreciate them and believed that this was something best done in silence – and, given the restrictions of sight lines, from a cross-legged position.

The report in the student paper of that Canterbury show, which the band performed against the very red brick which had given the new universities of the sixties their name and from on top of the kind of platform better suited to a cookery demonstration, suggests a certain awkwardness in both band and audience. During 'Moby Dick', Plant had to actually chide the audience into standing up. This was on the eve of the release of their fourth album, the one that was to put them in a commercial category that neither the Beatles nor the Stones ever reached, and yet still their shows had more in common with classical recitals than pagan rites. At the end of the back to the clubs tour they played at the Paris Theatre in Lower Regent Street for a John Peel recording. The Paris was a two-hundred-capacity seated venue where the BBC recorded many of its comedy programmes. Peel, who would in due course come to deny Led Zeppelin thrice, introduced them nervously and the crowd received them as though they were a mayoral party come to open a fete. Even young, long-haired people tended to be restrained in public places in 1971, and easily intimidated by the sheer majesty of the BBC. When they played 'Rock And Roll', a song which was invented in the studio when Bonham started playing Earl Palmer's intro from Little Richard's 1957 hit 'Keep A Knockin'', they were clearly summoning up the primal throb of the jungle music which had shocked fifties America; the performance was received as if they were tackling Beethoven's late quartets.

What impressed Led Zeppelin's audience, who were now at university and therefore even further advanced in their wrong-headedness than before, was that this music appeared difficult to do. That's why they were more inclined to appreciate the passages during which Page bowed his guitar on 'Dazed And Confused', the periods of relief from the groove rather than the groove itself. Nobody at the time suspected that it was the groove that made Led Zeppelin remarkable.

That certainly accounts for how sampled they are more than forty years later. It's the groove that escaped most of the hundreds of bands who set out to follow in their footsteps, in the mistaken belief that volume was the end rather than the means. Then there was the breadth of their musical hinterland. Led Zeppelin created their music from a diet of Bert Jansch, Memphis Minnie, John Fahey, Billy Fury, Phil Spector, Richard 'Rabbit' Brown, Moby Grape, Manitas De Plata and Om Kalsoum. Those who came afterwards were content with a diet of Led Zeppelin, which is not the same thing at all.

Most sixties groups didn't tour as we would understand it today. Instead they played regularly, recording during the week and going out at weekends to play gigs that were within driving distance to make money. Led Zeppelin would change all that. Ever since forming in 1968 around session guitarist Jimmy Page, Led Zeppelin had toured with a steely determination. In fact they didn't appear to tour so much as campaign, a recognition of the fact that like politicians running for office they appeared to have an objective in view. They were perfectly equipped for this because they were built around Page and John Paul Jones, two musicians who had been around the music business long enough to realize that the people who made the money were the ones with the songwriting credits, and they were formed at the behest of Peter Grant, a manager from an earlier generation who had learned that there was far more money to be made than promoters and agents would readily admit, because much of it would have to be gained at the direct expense of those promoters and agents.

This is where Grant, together with the band's American agent Frank Barsalona, was reinventing the concert business in 1971. They started with the finances. The old promoters had paid a fee for a band's services and made their money out of the difference between that fee and the amount they could make out of tickets. People like Bill Graham, who was famous for running the prestige hippy showcase the Fillmore in San Francisco and New York, became rich because he had a brand and even the biggest bands, including Led Zeppelin, would play his venue for a flat fee. Barsalona put a stop to all that, which is one of the reasons why Graham closed both Fillmores in 1971. He was tired of dealing with the agent's demands for more money and the musicians' demands for special treatment.

In 1971 Barsalona was in his early thirties and he dressed like an old-fashioned show business agent. He ran an agency called Premier Talent which also represented the Who, another loud band with a strong live reputation. Premier Talent was the first agency to specialize in representing rock acts rather than renting them out alongside jugglers and light comedians. From this position of strength Barsalona was able to flip the model, as Silicon Valley would subsequently say. Instead of letting the promoter dictate to the band how much of the ticket money they could have, he told the promoter how much of the band's money they would be permitted. He knew Led Zeppelin didn't need any actual promoting, that they would sell out on the growing strength of their name, and therefore the promoters should consider themselves fortunate to be invited to have the honour of hiring a hall for them and providing them with fresh towels. What Barsalona and Grant realized was that live performance was no longer the music business's disreputable rodeo clown, as it had been in the days of package tours. It was now a massive business on its own. For acts like the Who and Led Zeppelin, the concert business was even more important than the record business.

Barsalona was starting to develop acts that could sell their presence even if they couldn't move product. In 1970 he signed two acts, one from London and another from Boston, Massachusetts, who would prove his point. The first was Humble Pie, a band fronted by Steve Marriott and Peter Frampton, two refugees from teen pop groups whose whiskery prettiness seemed to suit the 1971 taste for fallen angels; the second was the J. Geils Band, an act from Boston that purveyed Chicago blues with the expeditious razzle-dazzle of a soul revue. With the best will in the world, neither of these groups had an original musical idea to their name and they couldn't write songs to save their lives, but wherever they played they could be relied upon to tear it up.

Premier Talent was also the agent for Grand Funk Railroad, a young three-piece from Flint, Michigan who openly advertised themselves as 'heavy rock'. Grand Funk were put together by an older hustler called Terry Knight who could see that there was a market for music that was above all loud, particularly if it was purveyed by a bare-chested high-school adonis such as Mark Farner. In July 1971 Grand Funk sold out Shea Stadium and got a lot of coverage on the basis that this was the first time since the Beatles a musical act had managed to do that. In the same week they played a free show in Hyde Park in London. At both they were supported by Humble Pie. Whereas Led Zeppelin's chosen path had been to let their deeds speak for them, Knight was a believer in the fact that the media would take a band at its own estimation so he talked Grand Funk Railroad up relentlessly; this got under the skin of a number of people, from *Rolling Stone* magazine to bands like Led Zeppelin who feared that people couldn't discriminate between their rich textures and Grand Funk's callow riffing. When Jimmy Page talked in interviews about the 'other bands' that Led Zeppelin were not like it was Grand Funk he was talking about. It's not surprising that he felt this way. Grand Funk were almost entirely without merit musically but were far advanced in showmanship. One of the highlights of their act was when the drummer Don Brewer played his kit with his head. This seemed an eloquent testimonial to the group's approach to life.

Both Humble Pie and the J. Geils Band were managed by Dee Anthony, a pugnacious character built along the lines of Benny the Ball from *Top Cat*, often to be glimpsed at the side of the stage at their shows. Like Peter Grant, Anthony was a carpetbagger when it came to rock. He was born in the 1920s and had worked with nightclub singers Jerry Vale and Tony Bennett. There was nothing peace and love about Dee Anthony. He had three mottos: get the money, don't forget to always get the money, and remember not to forget to always get the money.

Anthony also brought with him something that too many rock bands, then and now, prefer to think is optional: an emphasis on showmanship. It was Anthony who told the J. Geils Band that they should never go on stage without being introduced first. It was Anthony who instructed Humble Pie on how to move in front of an audience and ensured that their set was put together on the basis of its ability to please a crowd rather than the need to play a string of songs from the new album. It was Anthony who told the J. Geils Band's Peter Wolf to go out to the lip of the stage because, he argued, it worked for Al Jolson. This was basic professional practice in most areas of show business, but many rock and roll bands hadn't yet come to terms with the fact that they were in show business. Old soldiers like Dee Anthony never for a moment doubted it, and he knew that the bigger the venue the greater the need to project, the grander the gestures had to be and the more the showmanship would matter.

Both Anthony's bands started out trying to make it on their original compositions. Both eventually gave in to Anthony's argument that they had to record live in order to bottle what it was that people liked about them. In April 1971 Humble Pie went into the Fillmore in New York and recorded a set which became almost as famous for its overplayed cockney introductions ('We go 'ome on Monday, but it's been a gas this time') as for their crunching assaults on warhorses like 'I Don't Need No Doctor'. The album *Performance: Rockin' The Fillmore* was the making of them. It sustained their career for the next few years, providing them with a template as unchanging as the Harlem Globetrotters' or the Glenn Miller Orchestra's. It didn't matter if individual members moved on. The brand was fixed.

By the time the live record was mastered Peter Frampton had left the band to go solo, but he didn't leave Anthony. Dee oversaw Frampton's solo career, eventually persuading him to record all his most-liked numbers in front of an audience and put it out as *Frampton Comes Alive!* in 1976. It eventually sold eleven million copies. The live album, which had started life as the souvenir of the live concert, became the item which made you want to go to the concert in the first place in order to taste in person the experience it had so artfully synthesized.

There never was a great deal about the rock concert experience that was actually spontaneous. It was always learned behaviour. Most of the learning was done by listening to live recordings, which poured forth in unprecedented profusion in 1971, and watching films like *Woodstock*. *Woodstock* the film was a greater watershed than Woodstock the event. For all the people who actually endured three days in the mud and chaos of that field in Bethel in 1969 the festival was the standard mixed experience. The people whose heads were really turned were the millions who had the experience mediated through the dazzling split screens and Martin Scorsese edits of the film and drank it all in in the dry warmth of their local cinema. For this younger generation *Woodstock* was a gateway to a new entertainment experience, one in which they were keen to play their part.

In the previous decade there had been two kinds of audience: teenage girls who came to scream and serious young men who came to nod their heads approvingly and applaud respectfully. In 1971 the audience was growing dramatically and bursting those old categories. As the crowds got bigger they had to behave differently. Eventually they had to behave like the sports crowds who normally occupied the places the bands were beginning to play. They were no longer just there to watch. They were there to become part of the spectacle.

In the Who's *Live At Leeds*, which had been recorded a year earlier, the crowd are just a distant presence, as distant as the traffic outside, because nobody has bothered to point a microphone at them. Things hadn't changed much by March 1971, when the Rolling Stones played Leeds. The recording is a faithful account of what the band played and nothing more. In subsequent live recordings by the band the audience becomes a character in the drama and the venue becomes a space which vibrates with accumulated associations.

One English band starting to get a reputation for being able to tear up the dance halls was Free. Their *Free Live!* was recorded in Sunderland and Croydon in 1970 and 1971. The producer, Andy Johns, could rescue only two songs from the Sunderland shows but he used the crowd noise from the traditionally more demonstrative North-East audience throughout the album. What producers like Johns were starting to realize was that the sound of the crowd was a key element in rendering an impression of the live music experience. It was a matter of communicating the excitement of the live show, and if necessary exaggerating it. Emerson, Lake & Palmer's first album had come out at the end of 1970 but it was with the release at mid-price of the 26 March recording of their *Pictures At An Exhibition* at Newcastle City Hall, also in the North East, that they broke through. Here the audience noise has been promoted in the mix, to ensure that everybody gets the message that gigs are above all about excitement and the joy of abandon. Similarly, Crosby, Stills, Nash & Young's 1971 live album *Four Way Street* was designed as a sound experience, from the way it begins with a number just coming to its end, to Graham Nash's introduction of Neil Young, to the pregnant silence that accompanies his intro to 'Cowgirl In The Sand' and the explosion that greets the first line.

Four Way Street is short on music but long on drama. It's a band's rather inflated view of itself, made even grander by the audience's willingness to participate in the illusion. That March, Richard Williams wrote about a Neil Young concert at London's Festival Hall. It was a favourable review but he couldn't help taking issue with the way the audience still demanded encores long after Young had clearly given his all. 'They seemed more concerned with applauding themselves than acclaiming the musicians,' he wrote. At the time few would have known what he was talking about. We do now.

The new generation of managers, agents, promoters and fixers were bulkier, balder and brusquer than the softly spoken PR men who had managed big acts in the sixties. They came from earlier generations and could remember World War Two. There wasn't a hippy among them. The promoter Bill Graham's mother died in Auschwitz, Dee Anthony had been in submarines, Peter Grant had been a wartime evacuee from London. Tom Dowd, who played a crucial role in the defining live album of 1971, was a cut above: he had worked on the project that perfected the first atomic bomb.

Dowd was the best recording engineer in the world. He'd been doing it for a long time. He had started off working on Eileen Barton's 1950 hit 'If I'd Known You Were Coming I'd Have Baked A Cake'. He was the man who conjured the magic of Atlantic Records' sixties sides from studios improvised in offices or in radio stations. Born in 1925, Dowd was the epitome of old school. Nonetheless he had great admiration for the musicianship of lots of the hairy rock players Atlantic increasingly paired him with. He had produced Eric

Clapton's 'Layla', which was beginning to climb the charts in an edited single version in 1971. He had recorded one album with the Allman Brothers Band, the southern group who were fast gaining a reputation as one of America's premier live bands.

On 10 March, Dowd arrived at Kennedy Airport on a flight from Paris. A couple of days earlier he had been in Accra, Ghana, recording the live performances of Wilson Pickett and the Staples Singers, who had flown there as part of the 'Soul to Soul' concert project, the first attempt to take contemporary African-American music back to Africa. He had intended to have a few days relaxing in Europe but was disturbed by the fact that it was snowing so he decided to go home. On the 11th he called the Atlantic office who told him that the Allman Brothers were due to begin a three-night stint at the New York Fillmore in a few hours' time.

Dowd immediately took a cab down to the venue in time to catch the first shows from the recording truck. He was horrified to discover that the Allmans had decided to bring along an under-rehearsed horn section for this, one of the most important performances of their career. After the Thursday shows he went backstage, got the band together and gave them the kind of dressing-down they would only have accepted from this grey-bearded father figure. 'I was pissed,' he remembered, 'and I gave them hell.' Specifically he instructed them to 'get those horns out of my life. They are out of tune and they don't know the songs.'

Amazingly, the Allmans did as Dowd told them. They respected his genius for listening and his ability to get on with musicians. The group's Dicky Betts recalls that when Dowd started working with them in 1970 he would address them as if they were a 1940s big band. He called them 'cats'. He applauded their ability to solo and to play in mathematically demanding time signatures; he also admired the way they could sweetly return to the main theme. Their performances had ample room for improvisation but it was always within the context of an arrangement, and that arrangement always served the tune. In that sense they were very much like a big band. Dowd recognized what neither the band, their fans nor the legions of imitators they subsequently inspired recognized: the Allman Brothers Band swung.

The nights between Thursday 11 March and Saturday the 13th (although this last show didn't actually start until early Sunday morning) were billed as 'an evening featuring Johnny Winter And [this was how the name of the Texan guitarist's hard rock quartet went out at the time] the Elvin Bishop Group' with the Allman Brothers Band as a 'Special Added Attraction'. In 1971 people were relaxed about questions of billing, particularly at a Bill Graham show, which you were generally invited to play by the promoter rather than being booked in there by the agent. The Allman Brothers were on last, starting their final Saturday show at 2.30 in the morning and leaving the venue in time to mingle with early Sunday morning churchgoers.

The other brusque older man watching over the Allmans that night was Bill Graham, who was forty at the time. He was a German-born refugee from Nazism who had come up through the theatre scene. Graham wasn't a rock and roll person. One of the things he tried to do was expand the horizons of the people who came into his theatres, presenting the jazz instrumentalist Roland Kirk to the fans of Santana and putting Woody Herman on before Delaney and Bonnie and Led Zeppelin. Graham was a controversial figure. His standard card was to present himself as the hapless victim of selfish fans, arrogant musicians and greedy managers and agents. He was an impresario, an egomaniac and a snob but he was all for trying things, and this seemed the ideal time to do just that. As he told me in the 1980s, 'what you have to remember about that time is we were out there with no compass'. Graham came on stage himself to introduce the Allman Brothers' last performance. He said that they were one of the greatest bands the Fillmore had ever hosted, and that what the people were going to hear was 'the finest in contemporary music' – a form of words that was no doubt picked up on by some of the San Francisco bands Graham had come up promoting, the bands who fancied themselves as being the last word in looseness and improvisation. It seemed to him that the Allmans were on a different level. He was right.

The music the Allman Brothers Band played that weekend, the music which thanks to Tom Dowd is preserved on *The Allman Brothers Live At The Fillmore East*, redefined what was possible on a rock stage. It was perfectly suited for the size of the venue. Like so many of the best halls for rock and roll the Fillmore was anything but purpose-built. It had started life as a Yiddish Theatre and seated two and a half thousand people, which would in today's terms make it ideal for an atmospheric showcase. What came out of that weekend turned the band into one of the biggest concert draws in the USA. It was musically extraordinary. From the insouciant loosener 'Statesboro Blues' through the jazz-flecked instrumental 'In Memory Of

Elizabeth Reed' to the impassioned 'Whipping Post', the twin guitars and two drummers of the Allmans played like a large truck which had found a way to handle like a Ferrari, in the process rendering all comparable attempts to record the rock jam as ragged and clumsy. The album was such a touchstone that even the strangled shout for 'Whipping Post' which rose from the audience during a gap between songs was widely copied by wiseacres in the audiences at other bands' concerts. It happened so often through the rest of the decade that Frank Zappa eventually learned a version of 'Whipping Post' and made it a part of his show.

At the beginning of that weekend in March 1971 the idea of rock improvisation was still somewhat unproven. By Monday the following week it was arguably all over. Within six months lead guitarist Duane Allman was dead in a motorcycle accident. He'd already played with the world's finest musicians, put his name on some of the signature records of the age, been widely acclaimed for the soul and uncanny maturity of his playing, and on that March weekend had taken his band to the mountain top and recorded there. He was twenty-four.

The same weekend that the Allmans played the Fillmore the Rolling Stones were appearing at the Roundhouse in London for the last night of their pre-tax exile tour; Led Zeppelin had moved on to play Bath Pavilion; the more adventurous British record shops were taking delivery of their copies of the Velvet Underground's *Loaded*, David Crosby's *If I Could Only Remember My Name* and John Lennon's 'Power To The People'; James Taylor and Carole King were playing Madison Square Garden; the *Doctor Who* episode on the BBC was 'The

Claws of Axos' (starring Jon Pertwee); Elaine May's comic masterpiece *A New Leaf* was on release in US cinemas; a venue called the Museum on Broadway was advertising 'a punk mass at midnight' featuring the avant-garde duo Suicide; and war was brewing in East Pakistan, a region which the world, particularly the long-haired, music-loving bit of it, was soon to know by a different name: Bangladesh.

MARCH PLAYLIST

Nick Drake, 'Poor Boy'
Led Zeppelin, 'Black Dog'
J. Geils Band, 'Whammer Jammer'
Humble Pie, 'I Don't Need No Doctor'
Allman Brothers Band, 'Statesboro Blues'
Jethro Tull, 'Aqualung'
Nancy Sinatra, 'Hook And Ladder'
Judy Collins, 'Amazing Grace'
Johnny Winter, 'Rock And Roll Hoochie Koo'
Freddie King, 'Going Down'

APRIL:
INNER CITY BLUES

I n 1971 Berry Gordy Jr, the boss of Motown, was forty-two. He was the third man to bear that name and had already passed on the same one to his son. Berry was big on family and ran his record company like a traditional family enterprise. It was founded in 1960 with a loan from his father. Two of his sisters were involved in the company in senior positions. He liked to think of the artists on his Motown label owing him the same fealty as he expected from family members. Wherever possible he sought to secure those professional ties through marriage. His artist development specialist Harvey Fuqua married his sister Gwen Gordy. Marvin Gaye, the handsomest and most eligible artist on his label, married his sister Anna.

The latter was not the most obvious match. Anna was seventeen years older than her husband when they got married in 1963. Three years later, finding herself unable to conceive, she faked a pregnancy, at the culmination of which she produced Marvin III. Although nobody knew this at the time, the child had actually been born to Denise Gordy, a fifteen-year-old niece of Berry's. In later years Marvin confessed this to his biographer David Ritz, but it wasn't until Steve Turner's posthumous biography *Trouble Man* that the further assertion was made that he was actually the father. Whatever the truth, life in the Gaye–Gordy clan required Jacobean levels of duplicity. Berry Gordy, the dapper, compact former amateur boxing champion, liked to feel he controlled everyone around him. When the success of his label meant he could move to Detroit's millionaires row he bequeathed his old house to Anna and Marvin. This was a reminder for the singer of where he stood in the value chain of Motown, a company which prided itself on being as much about process as those other great businesses that gave the Motor City its nickname.

All families have a secret. The secret is they're not like other families. This was even more the case in a family firm like Motown. In April 1971 Gordy's personal favourite performer and Motown's biggest star, Diana Ross, was expecting her first child. The press naturally assumed the father must be Robert Silberstein, a presentable young white man she had first met when she went into a men's fashion shop in Los Angeles to buy a gift for Berry. Ross and Silberstein had married in January 1971. 'What you see is what she got!' announced one magazine aimed at black readers, the inference being that any black woman marrying a white man was clearly moving up in the world. The wedding in Las Vegas came as a surprise to everybody at Motown because as far as they knew the couple had never been associated before. Furthermore, some people in the company's inner circle also knew that Diana and Berry had been sleeping together.

The marriage to Silberstein was accomplished so swiftly it even came as a surprise to the groom. Neither Berry Gordy nor the bride's mother knew about the wedding until the day after. Just two weeks later Diana, by then fully occupied in rehearsals for the ABC TV special which seemed the inevitable next step in her elevation into the pantheon of light entertainment, announced she was pregnant. Berry did his calculations and concluded the baby had to be his. He dealt with the shock by decamping on a short holiday in the sun with Chris Clark, the six-foot-tall Californian blonde he would repeatedly and unsuccessfully try to launch as America's Dusty Springfield. There was nothing Berry did that didn't have at least some element of social climbing about it.

Although it had only been seven years since the high noon of Motown's fame, in 1971 the stars of the company increasingly lived the kind of lives which previously existed only in the feverish imaginings of airport novelists. But then, as Cyndi Lauper was to observe many years later, money changes everything. Some even said that mob money had always been behind Motown and Gordy was being slowly eased out. Certainly a greater proportion of the company's senior executives were now white than had been five years earlier. What's also certain is that now that he had made his fortune Berry preferred to spend his time in climes warmer and more congenial than Detroit, a city where the signs of urban blight were apparent even to the people who remained on the wealthier side of town.

When Berry Gordy had been born in 1929 Detroit was the fastest-growing city on earth. There were only thirty-two million cars in the world at the time and 90 per cent of them had been made in the USA, most of those in Detroit. Although he was later to claim that he had modelled his label on the production-line methods of the big three automobile manufacturers, Gordy was far too polished an individual to personally submit to life in the plant. Many of the people, black as well as white, who migrated from the southern states to work in those plants in the period between the wars were attracted by the fact that it was one of the few places where a lack of formal education wouldn't be a handicap. The work certainly paid far more than a man could make on the land. Tens of thousands came north and duly prospered, notably during the war years when the plants were turned over to making the machines with which the Allies would liberate Europe.

The first hit record put out by Berry Gordy in 1959 was 'Money (That's What I Want)' by Barrett Strong. This was the most sincere and succinct mission statement ever made by a record label boss, before or since. Motown was social mobility set to music. In the sixties Gordy's label put out some of the most aspirational pop music ever made. In sound and deed, through the cut of their cloth and the swish of their arm movements, the likes of the Four Tops, the Supremes, the Temptations and Smokey Robinson and the Miracles may have been making 'the sound of Young America' for the kids but in Gordy's mind they were also looking to move uptown, to sashay their way into the supper club circuit, to overcome the de facto apartheid of American TV and to stand toe to patent leather toe with the Sinatras and Streisands of the world.

This relentless ascent often meant Berry was badly out of step. His misfortune was to make it to the far side of the red rope in the year 1971, just as the glitterati decided the action was on the other side and began to dress in work wear. At the end of the sixties, when everyone else was growing their hair and carrying themselves in a counter-cultural way, Gordy was still showcasing his big acts via live albums recorded at Squaresville spots like the Copacabana in New York or the Talk of the Town in London, pressing them into musical shotgun marriages so that he could bill their new records as jazz-style summit meetings and obliging them to do tiresome Christmas albums. With all this in mind, and his growing passion for golf, Gordy was slowly moving his company to Los Angeles, which everyone but the artists and executives regarded as a betrayal.

Back in Detroit, the growing prosperity of the sixties had not proved to be the solvent of old racial divisions. In July 1967, at the climax of the Summer of Love, a raid by white police on an unlicensed Detroit bar patronized by black people turned into a riot. This escalated so quickly the Governor called in the National Guard and the President ordered in the army. Forty-three people, most of them black, were killed. It was the worst civil disturbance in the USA for a century. Few felt the same about Detroit after that. The population of the city, which had been 60 per cent white, started to change as 'white flight' to the suburbs took place, followed by a hollowing out of the inner city and a resulting growth in violence and crime.

By then many of the Motown family had fallen by the wayside. Liver problems forced Paul Williams to retire from the Temptations. Florence Ballard of the Supremes sued Motown over royalties and lost. Tammi Terrell, Marvin Gaye's duetting partner, was taken by a brain tumour. Among the living there were jealousies. Anyone whose career didn't flourish would inevitably blame their plight on not enjoying the favour of Gordy, who was lavishing all his time and money on Diana Ross. Even the Jackson Five, who were Motown's cash cow in 1971, had been presented to the public as Diana's discovery, when in truth she had nothing to do with them. On 29 April young Michael appeared on the cover of *Rolling Stone* with the line 'Why does this eleven-year-old stay up past his bedtime?' Found in Gary, Indiana, the Jacksons had not been discovered by Gordy and did their recording in Los Angeles rather than with the motor city's Funk Brothers. They weren't touched at all by the old machine, and even that old machine had a new master in the shape of Norman Whitfield, the producer who was behind such extended grooves as the Temptations' 'Cloud Nine' and the Undisputed Truth's 'Smiling Faces Sometimes', which were pointing out the route dance music would take in the 1970s.

The acts who had made it at Motown were dealing with the financial consequences of success. The more artists earned on the back of their hit singles the more they stored up tax problems, and here they found the company's legendary paternalism didn't extend to helping out. Tax demands for the fat years inevitably arrived in the lean ones. For some of them at least there were also problems with drink and drugs.

The thirty-two-year-old Marvin Gaye's career was certainly becalmed. The massive success of 'I Heard It Through The Grapevine' in 1968 should have made him secure but he couldn't claim to have authored it and resented the fact that he didn't have the kudos of a self-sustaining creative unit like Stevie Wonder or Smokey Robinson. He didn't like performing live and didn't care for the way he was positioned in Berry Gordy's firmament. He couldn't imagine himself in Vegas. Marvin Gaye was Berry's male sex symbol and that's how Berry preferred him to remain. Consequently he stayed at home, fought with Anna, who was known occasionally to set about him with the sharp end of a shoe, and got high. This last may explain why he also at this time entertained a delusion that he could make it as a professional athlete. Marvin was in reasonable condition – for an entertainer. Since this is far from the fitness required of a professional athlete, the Detroit Lions, his NFL team of choice, didn't even bother to give him a trial. Marvin made this decision easier for them by hardly having played a game of football in his life. Throughout his life, much like Ronald Reagan, Marvin was apt to think that if he was photographed doing something he could actually do it. Lover, golfer, thinker, athlete, sophisticate; if he could look the part that was as good as actually fulfilling the role.

The album that Marvin Gaye released in 1971, *What's Going On*, has come to be seen as occupying a pivotal position in the story of pop music, to a certain extent because of the direction music has taken in recent years. In some lists of all-time great albums, many of which are compiled by white rock critics with inevitable guilt complexes, it has been known to come top. Albums that figure in these lists generally have a back story. The narrative behind *What's Going On* runs something like this: artist grows tired of obeying the suits at his record company, gets in touch with his inner feelings and then, moved by the plight of his brothers and sisters in the inner city, delivers a searing personal statement, then fights the powers-that-be to get it released.

It wasn't quite as mythic as that. It rarely is. The song 'What's Going On' began, like most things at Motown, with a wisp of melody rather than a big idea. That wisp occurred to Obie Benson, the bass singer in the Four Tops, who developed it with Motown songwriter Al Cleveland. Obie saw it as a gentle exhortation to worldwide brotherhood, much like the Coke commercial 'I'd Like To Teach The World To Sing', which came out in the same year, and claimed that he tried to plug it to Joan Baez during an appearance on *Top of the Pops*. Benson and Cleveland developed the idea over a few weeks and thought it might suit Marvin, the Motown artist who had a talent for the soft jazzy style the song seemed to demand. They sang it to him. He wasn't impressed. They pressed him for over a month without apparent success. Reluctant, as most artists are, to be caught following someone else's lead, Marvin eventually made some tweaks of his own and was apparently thinking of giving it to the Originals, a group he had been producing. Marvin was never brilliant at making up his mind and perhaps suspected, with some justification, that Berry would not want to see his label's great lover waving a placard.

Eventually he went into the studio in July 1970 to produce himself singing it. Here his lack of experience as a producer paid dividends. He brought a few football buddies in to make the party noises at the beginning. He was indebted to the saxophone player Eli Fontaine for improvising the opening solo while warming up over the track. Having thus invented one of the most distinctive intros of the era, Fontaine was sent home. The story goes that Gaye got bassist James Jamerson, by then so advanced in the drinking that eventually killed him that he would carry a bottle of Metaxa at all times, out of a bar and let him play the bass line while reportedly lying on the floor. The story, which has attached itself to the myth of 'What's Going On', is denied by people who were there. Certainly the double-tracked vocal came about by accident when Gaye happened to hear both during a playback and decided he liked the effect. Like Paul McCartney and other artists suddenly enjoying the luxury of not having anyone to argue with in the studio, he preferred to turn yesterday's mistakes – the false starts and sounds stumbled upon, the smudges at the edge of the canvas – into today's marks of unique authorship.

There was still no certainty that the record would ever come out. At Motown singles were supposed to pass a Quality Control Panel before they were deemed worthy of release. 'What's Going On' eventually emerged in January 1971 and was a hit before the West Coast-based Berry Gordy could object. When asked, he loudly proclaimed it a disaster for Gaye and the label. He thought its jazzy feeling, 'that Dizzy Gillespie shit' as he called it, was dangerously retrograde and he was quoted as saying it was 'the worst piece of crap

I ever heard'. He also worried that the record's sentiments would prevent it getting on the radio. Conversations with his brother Frankie about experiences in Vietnam were as near as Marvin had got to the nightmare being undergone by thousands of his contemporaries. Marvin's complaints about how much the government was spending on arms were indirectly connected to his reluctance to pay the back taxes he owed. However, radio took to 'What's Going On' immediately and within a week it sold a hundred thousand copies. As soon as the single was number one on the soul and number two on the pop charts the mogul in Berry Gordy took over. He forgot his previous objections and immediately demanded to know why they had no album to follow it with.

The accompanying album was recorded hurriedly in March and released in May. It was mixed once in Detroit in early April and then re-mixed by Marvin in Los Angeles. Considering that mixing had previously been a job thought too important to be left to the artists, this was a very bold thing to do. Gaye's Los Angeles mix, which is the one that came out in May, was like an inkwash version of the Detroit mix. It reduced the crisp separation of the Motown sound and replaced it with the shimmer that became its winning characteristic. On this he worked with the engineer Larry Miles, who is quoted in Ben Edmonds' book *Marvin Gaye: What's Going On* as saying that 'Marvin wanted to keep the rhythm going throughout like the heartbeat of a late night party'. In that sense it belonged in the tradition of Marvin Gaye, an artist more at home in the boudoir than the barricades.

In the UK, where EMI packaged it as shoddily as they did most albums by black artists, and fans were looking for the kind of singles that filled dance floors and not much else, it passed without any great fanfare. In America it changed people's expectations of a Motown album, which at the time rarely amounted to much more than a couple of recent hit singles, something by the Beatles and a standard for the Vegas crowd. Even though Berry Gordy hadn't noticed, things had moved on. People were starting to expect long-playing records to amount to more than the sum of their parts. Critics were desperate to see them as statements, record companies were eager to position them as luxury items, artists started to see each one as their bid for some sort of immortality.

The critical establishment was so keen to hail a long-form record by a black pop artist that they either went overboard with their hosannas for *What's Going On* or were so busy acclaiming it for having its heart in the right place that they missed the qualities which made it popular. Some critics in the broadsheets compared him to Duke Ellington. If so it was the rather stiff, sanctimonious Ellington who was always trying to get into the concert hall rather than Ellington the genius of the dance hall.

No white artist would have dared serve up anything quite as stagey as a track like 'Save The Children'. Had they done so they would have been ripped apart for their pains, probably by the same critics who hailed it, as Gaye's official biographer and collaborator David Ritz later did, as 'a socio-religious work of astounding originality'. Vince Aletti, the man *Rolling Stone* used to call when they wanted to cover soul, broadly approved but even he said the lyrics were 'hardly brilliant' and pointed out that its continuity of mood, which was itself quite unusual, was in danger of being boring.

The myths around *What's Going On* cloud the truth, which is more interesting. The idea that it was an expression of what Marvin felt about the drift of American society masks the contributions of many people around him who were closer to that society. These people ranged from Obie Benson to James Nyx, the elderly lift operator in one of Motown's office buildings who contributed the title 'Inner City Blues'. Because 1971 is seen as the moment when Gaye emerged from the factory years into a period of heroic individuality it's forgotten how much he owed to the professionals like David Van De Pitte, who turned his stabbed piano notes into arrangements, and players like Eli Fontaine, whose delicate touches are what keep the record alive nearly half a century on. *What's Going On* might not be a product of the Motown factory system but it owed a huge amount to the people who laboured there, often in complete anonymity. There is nothing on it Gaye could have done alone. Equally there is nothing here that would have been even half as special without him.

Ultimately, *What's Going On* is a beneficiary of the halo effect provided by a great opener and, in 'Inner City Blues', an even stronger closer. What nobody can refute is its influence. It made Marvin Gaye a force with those white rock fans who had tended to dismiss those they patronized as 'singles artists' and it set him up for a golden period which he was too fragile to take full advantage of. It was like a jazz record not merely because it had jazz manners and was slathered in strings and employed congas and triangle as its most prominent form of percussion (Gaye, a drummer by trade, was determined that the record would not have Motown drums, which was a major departure). It's also jazz in the sense that nobody would put it on to listen to just one track. It plays like one long single. Although, like the overwhelming majority of records made at that time, it was done without benefit of automated percussion, it anticipated a lot of contemporary music where the sustaining of a mood is prized above all things. It originated a vibe, suspended somewhere between sensuality and foreboding, which is the room temperature of so much music made in the twenty-first century. It's for that, the way its message dropped on the ear, rather than the message itself, that it's remembered. The ghostly samba of the music and the pained majesty of his voice lives on, almost fifty years later.

Those looking for musicians who act out the promise of their songs in their own lives are usually disappointed. Marvin Gaye was more conflicted than most when it came to this. He preferred the lush life. He couldn't even bring himself to dress funky for the cover of *What's Going On*, looking instead like a man who had been caught in a sudden downpour while waiting for his limousine. His concern for the decaying inner city and its problems didn't keep him in Detroit. Within a year of making *What's Going On* he was living in Hollywood and had left the older woman for a girl almost exactly the same number of years younger. The first thing he did after *What's Going On* was a violent grindhouse film called *Chrome and Hot Leather*. Such a move was every bit as much Marvin Gaye as *What's Going On*.

At the same time as *What's Going On* was enjoying its reign at number one, another Motown superstar, ten years younger than Marvin Gaye, left Detroit and relocated in New York with his new wife Syreeta Wright. Stevie Wonder could finally afford this move because he was turning twenty-one in May 1971 and this meant he was at last about to come into the large sum of money Motown had been holding in trust for him. At the same time he was in a position to negotiate a new deal with the company who had been in charge of his life since he was ten years old. He threw a party in Detroit to celebrate his coming of age. Berry Gordy was a guest. Stevie didn't give him any inkling of what was coming. When Gordy returned to Los Angeles he was faced with a letter from Wonder's attorney disavowing his Motown contract and announcing his intention to move elsewhere. To Gordy's mind this was a betrayal of Shakespearean dimensions.

Whatever Stevie did next, whether it was to be on the same label or a different one, he was determined it would be outside the Motown studio system. Moving away from Detroit was an important step in this direction. Then there was a further, fateful accidental meeting. In New York he had a bass player called Ronnie Blanco who engineered a meeting which would move Stevie Wonder to higher ground and change pop music at the same time.

Blanco had spent a lot of time at Media Sound, a studio housed in an old Baptist church on 57th Street. Here he'd made the acquaintance of a middle-aged British jazz musician called Malcolm Cecil and his partner, a former filmmaker called Robert Margouleff. Cecil, who had played jazz with Tubby Hayes and blues with Cyril Davis, was working as Media Sound's night maintenance man, beavering away in the basement to keep the first generation of electronic equipment operating. Since Margouleff had been an early adopter of the Moog synthesizer – the rudimentary, monophonic electronic instrument popularized in 1968 by Wendy Carlos's *Switched-On Bach* – he was Media Sound's boffin. The two became friends and collaborators. When the studio was not in use they busied themselves constructing a machine which would combine the music-making products of various manufacturers – Moog, Roland, Arp, Oberheim and others – and building an interface that allowed these technologies to talk to each other. They called it The Original New Timbral Orchestra, TONTO for short.

TONTO looked more like the control room of a power station than a musical instrument and had to be operated by experts. Nevertheless it was the single most dramatic technological advance to hit pop music since the electric guitar. Because it had such a wide range of tone colours the sounds TONTO produced could not be matched by any conventional instrument or machine. Looking back at these events from the far shore of the great digital transmigration it is almost impossible to recapture a time when the very idea that so many unusual noises and voices could be coaxed from something that looked like a telephone exchange merely by connecting the right leads and turning the appropriate knobs seemed like witchcraft.

Cecil and Margouleff made an album called *Zero Time* by Tonto's Expanding Head Band to demonstrate their invention. It was released on a label run by jazz flautist Herbie Mann. In an era when it was impossible to get involved with electronic keyboards unless you could read a circuit diagram and had your own soldering iron, *Zero Time* was the kind of record that only musicians and technophiles enthused over. Ronnie Blanco played *Zero Time* to Stevie Wonder and told him that all these sounds he was hearing, all these slurring, slithering, spectral noises, were coming from one instrument. Stevie was impressed and asked Blanco to take him to, in his words, 'see it'.

The two of them turned up at Media Sound on the last Sunday in May 1971 and rang the bell. Cecil, busy at the time fixing Felix Pappalardi's Mellotron, looked out of the window and saw his unexpected visitors, one of them a young black man in shades wearing a pistachio jumpsuit. They brought Stevie into the studio, sat him down at TONTO's keyboards and began putting the instrument through its paces. Cecil and Margouleff ran round making connections and turning switches while Stevie rejoiced in the unprecedented freedom of being able to actually make the music he heard in his head without having to do it via instructions to other musicians. Margouleff and Cecil in turn enjoyed having the undivided attention of a name musician who would quite happily sit at the keyboard and play for hours. As they later recalled, 'Stevie came and didn't leave for over a year. We worked weekends, birthdays, holidays, even Christmas Day.' With Cecil playing the role of boffin, Margouleff engineering and Wonder giving free rein to his musical imagination, which in its extraordinary fecundity was the diametric opposite of Marvin Gaye's, they recorded seventeen songs on that one weekend.

By the time he went into Media Sound Stevie Wonder had already lost interest in the last album he had released on Motown. *Where I'm Coming From* had come out on 12 April. It was a step forward from its predecessor, *Live At The Talk*

Of The Town, but the new music he was making would make it seem every bit as stiff. *Where I'm Coming From* is a solemn declaration of independence, as exemplified by 'I Wanna Talk To You', in which he takes on the role of a poor sharecropper asking his master to cut him a little slack. Although it features the same Hohner clavinet which he would later use to great effect, it's employed in a rather stagey fashion as if it's always trying to quote from some more respectable kind of music. But it had a hit, 'If You Really Love Me', written, like the rest of the songs, with Syreeta Wright. It sounded like the work of a man reluctantly working through other musicians.

In 1971 a handful of artists had already had a try at making a record single-handed, a record on which they would play all the parts themselves. *Runt*, the second album by Todd Rundgren, came out in March 1971. For this recording Rundgren had played most of the instruments, taking advantage of the fact that he was the resident producer and engineer at Bearsville, the studios owned by Dylan's manager Albert Grossman, and could therefore use studio downtime without payment. Paul McCartney had done much the same the previous year with his first solo album, recording at home on a four-track tape recorder with no way of monitoring input levels. The resulting rawness was part of the charm but the method didn't seem to have much of a future.

It would be difficult to imagine a way of working further removed from Motown's process-oriented system, which worked like the big Hollywood studios with committees for vetting material and an owner who thought of himself as the person best qualified for deciding which artist would go best with which material, than the hands-on work Stevie Wonder started doing at Media Sound. Over the next two years he moved his entire operation over to New York's Electric Lady before joining the inevitable trek westward to end up three hit albums later at the Record Plant in LA. Here he spent months in a room with three middle-aged white nerds, Margouleff, Cecil and Johanan Vigoda, an eccentric lawyer he had hired to sort out his business affairs. Vigoda looked like an unmade bed, which may have led Gordy to underestimate him. That underestimation cost his company $13,000,000, which was the eventual price of re-signing the former boy wonder. Vigoda's vision saw Stevie succeeding far beyond the narrow horizons of Motown. He was the first person to recognize that his client's future lay in the same album market as the big white acts. He was the one who had the idea of getting him a support slot on the Rolling Stones tour of 1972, an unprecedented move at the time.

It's tempting to speculate that Stevie Wonder's attitude might have been different had he been sighted. Because he didn't have to explain to other musicians what he wanted or to get them on the same beam he was on, a lot of the music on *Music Of My Mind*, which was made in 1971 and came out the following year, seems attractively rough-edged and unfinished, full of odd turns, digressions and fantastical spoken passages, all of which seem to come out of one imagination. Those sessions blurred into those for *Talking Book*, *Innervisions* and *Fulfillingness' First Finale*. From then on they were on what Cecil called 'Stevie Time', dictated by a man who really didn't want to do anything but play music and was delighted to be able to play it on an entirely new machine. This state of affairs couldn't last for ever and inevitably didn't end happily. By the year's end he had separated from his young wife Syreeta. Margouleff and Cecil were so thrilled about the use to which their invention had been put that they carried on working for a day rate, in the hope that a royalty share would one day be sorted out. It wasn't. They stopped working with him in 1974 after *Fulfillingness' First Finale* and sensed that one of the reasons they were no longer wanted was that by then Stevie's people didn't like him being beholden to honkies.

The music that arose from the partnership initiated on that hot weekend in 1971, the records which eventually spawned 'Superstition', 'You Are The Sunshine Of My Life', 'Living For The City' and scores more, were the purest expression of Stevie Wonder's genial cool. They also shaped the popular music made by everyone else just as surely as the Beatles had shaped it a decade before. This music came out of a room full of wires and plugs, a room reeking of solder and overheating machines, more a workshop than a conventional studio, a room where a visually handicapped young black man could work with three middle-aged white men, none of whom could in all honesty have been accused of knowing the first thing about funk. It was nonetheless the dawn of a new way of doing things.

Don Cornelius was a thirty-five-year-old black presenter working for a Chicago TV station when, in 1970, he persuaded his bosses to let him try launching a music show. To his amazement they didn't insist he give up his rights to be the show's owner. Cornelius wanted his programme to do for black music and black kids what Dick Clark's *American*

Bandstand had been doing for white music and white kids since the fifties.

There were scarcely any black faces on television either side of the Atlantic. Black youth had more chance of appearing on screen as threatening elements in news reports about urban strife than as on-screen talent. In April 1971, when *Ebony* magazine published its list of the one hundred most influential black Americans, there wasn't a single TV presenter on the list.

Initially Cornelius put most of his efforts into persuading acts to appear on *Soul Train*, leaning on locally based talent like Curtis Mayfield and B. B. King. Like everyone who ever started a music TV show respectability was the thing he craved most, but he found the excitement coming from an unexpected direction. As the show gained momentum and, thanks to a tie-in with America's biggest manufacturer of black hair products, was taken up by more stations, it became clear that the musicians were not as important to the TV audience as the young people who danced to the hits in the TV studio.

In 1971 Cornelius took *Soul Train* national and joined the exodus taking the rest of the music industry to Los Angeles. In California the show's vibe was immediately different. It was now shot in colour, the dancers recruited from the rich supply of exhibitionists who hung around the city's various arts initiatives, and Cornelius's show, which he hosted himself with the decidedly self-important air of a well-dressed young Congressman, was suddenly America's first interesting TV music show.

The dancers, who were unpaid and expected to sustain themselves through marathon taping sessions on a diet of soda and fried chicken, were what made it great television. The young men were snake-hipped and tall, with massive penumbras of natural hair treated with Afro-Sheen. The girls were slender and dressed to ensure the maximum camera time. There was nothing vampish about their appearance, due partly to American TV's traditional prudery and partly to the atmosphere of the show, which was as much church social as discotheque. In their home-made jumpsuits and hot pants the girls exuded the breeziness of *Sesame Street* rather than the stickiness of *Top of the Pops*. Cornelius was keen to make sure his people were shown in a good light. There was a regular feature in which the studio guests had to rearrange letters on a board to spell out the names of distinguished African-Americans. To guarantee that nothing went wrong which might reflect badly on the people he was pledged to represent, he made sure this part of the show was fixed.

The sweet spot of *Soul Train* was the soul train line. For this the dancers formed a guard of honour down which couples took their turn to parade, showing off the moves they had spent the week perfecting in the hope that all over the nation kids in schoolyards would be attempting to imitate them over the following week. These dance moves, which took the generic frugs and twitches of pop dance and reclassified them into an entirely new terpsichorean taxonomy, swept the nation. They reached black kids in the cities and allowed them to feel validated for the first time in their lives, and they reached white kids in the suburbs who for the first time saw a different and exciting way to move and to carry themselves.

Music is as much about how you move as anything else. The *Soul Train* kids took the lead and the music business began to follow. The musicians seemed to recede into the background. The cameras didn't go in for admiring low-angle shots. Instead they pulled back from the acts to show the dancers who were elbowing their way in front of each other as if their lives depended on it. For some of them it did. *Soul Train* made the names of many people who didn't make records but instead danced to them. It made display a central part of popular music. In that sense it changed popular music even more than Stevie Wonder did.

While Marvin Gaye was re-mixing *What's Going On* in Hollywood, twenty-eight-year-old Sly Stone was down the road in Bel Air, living in a rented mansion which had formerly been the home of musical comedy star Jeanette Macdonald. It's unlikely that under the previous occupant the house ever had a safe full of drugs in a basement, as it did during Sly's eventful tenure. In it he kept, according to one of the many musicians who passed through and briefly lived at 783 Bel Air Road in that time, 'pounds of cocaine'.

Sly Stone was as big a musical star as you could find anywhere in the United States in 1971. A DJ, producer and hustler from northern California, with his revue-style band the Family Stone, Sylvester Stewart had provided a string of hit singles such as 'Dance To The Music' and 'Everyday People', records which cleverly combined Aquarian Age sentiments with the demands of the discotheque, records which everyone related to, from the bookers of TV shows to the editors of hip magazines; furthermore he had beaten off all comers when it came to stealing the show as *Woodstock* hit the cinemas.

But for all his shrewdness, charisma and talent, Sly was arguably the least reliable superstar in the history of popular music. He was two years late delivering a new record, so late that Clive Davis, the boss of Epic and Columbia, withheld his back royalties until he delivered it. The Black Panthers, rarely far from the door of any brother with access to cash and prominence, were leaning on him to get rid of the two white members of his band and his white, Jewish manager. Meanwhile the manager was threatening that if his client didn't deliver the record he would set his own enforcers on him. The many women in his life were giving him grief about the many women in his life. The people who sold him the drugs were keen to sell him more. On top of all this he was experiencing the traditional musician's fear of actually delivering the record, and the judgement that would inevitably follow.

A twelve-track console had been installed in the basement of the house in Bel Air and here Sly worked, calling in members of the band to play occasional parts. Because he was less a musician than a conceptualist, Sly preferred to start with the MRK-1 rhythm machine and build from there. This way nobody could ask him whether he had any idea what he was driving at and he was free to just potter around until the music fell into an appealing pattern. The argument for working this way is that what's lost in abandoning the natural sound of a live band is made up for in control.

More in hope than anything else, the record company was promising that the album would be called *The Incredible And Unpredictable Sly And The Family Stone*. They were presumably expecting more of the buckskin-fringed happy-clappy music with which Sly had electrified Woodstock just a year before. Sly was one of the few black performers who was a hot ticket with the rock crowd and they wanted an album that would sell to them. The cover with the star-spangled banner on the front and the saturated colour shot of Sly performing for a massive crowd of Caucasians in the fold-out seemed to be anticipating a certain kind of record. It was far from the one that turned up.

What Clive Davis would have heard that spring would not have filled him with confidence. Lots of it was downbeat. All of it was difficult to decipher. Sly had even taken his band's upbeat hit 'Thank You (Falettinme Be Mice Elf Agin)', slowed it down to a stumble and called it 'Thank You For Talking To Me Africa', which seemed plain bloody-minded. The single 'Family Affair' had only been made acceptable after engineering consultant Richard Tilles had come in, muted most of Sly's guitar parts, edited the rhythm box to make it sound like a heartbeat and accentuated the electric piano. This was played by Billy Preston, fresh from providing the same sound on the Beatles' last single. What nobody could get rid of was the tape hiss accrued through Sly's endless overdubbing. It lay on the surface of the finished record like the glaze of ages on a Rembrandt.

Apart from 'Family Affair', which is not only the perfectly realized pop single but also the kind of thing whose meaning people interpret for themselves and then take to heart, the bulk of *There's A Riot Goin' On* is opaque. When it was released in November 1971 it sounded like a collection of demos with placeholder vocal parts and riffs that often trailed off into incoherence. It remains the least pat, least tidy, least house-trained album that ever dominated the number one spot on the *Billboard* pop and soul charts for weeks on end. It's incomplete, it's unsettling, it's full of loose ends. The songs aren't so much sung as narrated or remarked upon. It's the sound you hear in your head when you've done lots of drugs and haven't had enough sleep. The groove is pushed to the front. The songs have to take their chances in the space remaining.

Amazingly, it would turn out to be the future for lots of music, although none of it would be made by Sly, who was clearly wrung dry by the effort. Some of that music would be made by Miles Davis, who changed his style under Sly's influence. Miles, who was one of the people called in to talk sense to Sly during these years, couldn't help observing that Sly took a lot of cocaine. Although Sly made and continues to make records, he never wrote anything significant again.

He didn't need to. *There's A Riot Goin' On* made all sorts of things possible. Forty years later its fingerprint is discernible all over hip hop. And Sly didn't have to wait that long to see how influential it was. As Greil Marcus has written, the great records that came out in its wake, by Curtis Mayfield, the Staples Singers, the Temptations, War and others, records which it would be patronizing to call 'conscious', were suddenly 'all of one piece; one enormous answer record'.

*

On the morning of 12 April 1971 a film crew was working on Mott Street in New York's Little Italy. In the scene they were filming was an elderly man in a shapeless suit and a voluminous greatcoat buying fruit from a kerbside vendor. As he turned away from the stall to make his way to the car waiting for him two gunmen appeared and shot him repeatedly. He collapsed on the hood of the car. The gunmen got into their car, which screamed away.

The elderly man was being played by Marlon Brando, doing his first day's filming on the Paramount picture *The Godfather*, based on Mario Puzo's book which had been a best-seller when it was published in 1969. It had taken a lot of careful diplomatic work by Albert Ruddy, one of the film's producers, to win permission to film on the streets of New York, particularly in a district like Little Italy. The people who were either in the Mafia or were happy to have people think they were in the Mafia didn't know whether to feel flattered or traduced. Ruddy had had to present himself before a meeting of 1,500 members of the Italian-American Civil Rights League and Joseph Colombo Senior, one of its leading figures and a head of one of the five families that controlled much of the illegal gain in New York. It was only when Ruddy persuaded them that the film was simply a study of corruption rather than an attempt to slander an entire community that the film's crews found they could get on with their work free from petty obstructions and the intrusions of bureaucracy. The film wrapped that summer, and by the time it had been made ready for its launch on Christmas Day 1971 (it was later delayed until March 1972) Paramount were feeling bullish enough about its prospects to be thinking about another one to be called *Son of Godfather*.

In 1971 the major movie studios were floundering. The big stars were still cowboys like John Wayne and Clint Eastwood. Their key projects were adaptations of Broadway smashes like *Fiddler on the Roof* or best-sellers like *Love Story* and they had few franchises, which left a bit more room on the screens for smaller-budget productions. On 23 April a movie called *Sweet Sweetback's Baadasssss Song* premiered in New York. It was almost entirely the work of Melvin Van Peebles, an African-American writer who had taught himself how to make a film. He had even composed the music himself and had hired the then unsigned Chicago band Earth, Wind and Fire to play it. 'I had a tiny little chance,' he recalled later. 'But for a coloured man that was a big chance.' Realizing he needed to use any means possible to promote his film, he took the music to the Memphis-based independent record label Stax and per-suaded them to release it.

Van Peebles' film did well. It appealed to an African-American audience understandably pleased to see their own on screen and every bit as keen on sex and violence as the audience in the white suburbs. That same audience iden-tified with heroes who were speaking on their behalf. The characters in *Sweet Sweetback*, twenty feet high, said what had previously been considered unsayable. For instance, 'Every dollar we make the guineas get twenty, the police gets forty and Goldberg gets fifty. Anybody can tell you that don't add up to a dollar.'

In the week of *Sweet Sweetback*'s release Gil Scott-Heron, who was hailed as 'a new black poet', went into RCA Studios in New York and recorded his second album, *Pieces Of A Man*, which began with the proto-rap 'The Revolution Will Not Be Televised'. This was not as outlandish a signing as it might appear since *This Is Madness*, the second album by the Last Poets, was between Bobby Womack and Wilson Pickett on the soul album charts, even though, as their record company pointed out, there was nothing on it that you could play on the radio. Sometimes black consciousness took the form of political action. More often it expressed itself in consumerism. The entertainment companies were beginning to notice this.

MGM were already looking to make the move into what later became known as 'blaxploitation' with a movie by fashion photographer Gordon Parks. This was to star Richard Roundtree as John Shaft, a handsome black private detective having trouble with the Mafia. They tapped Isaac Hayes to come up with the music which they thought would be a vital part of the package. Hayes, along with David Porter, had written and produced some of Stax's biggest hits of the 1960s. In 1970 he had emerged as a solo act. He specialized in bookending well-known standards like 'Walk On By' and 'By The Time I Get To Phoenix' with lubricious spoken passages wherein he would list the many varieties of sweet love he would make at the end of his journey. These went well with his shaven-head love god persona. Since he always copyrighted his raps, that also meant he made as much out of his reading of 'By The Time I Get To Phoenix' as Jimmy Webb, the man who wrote the actual song.

While *Shaft* was being shot and edited in Hollywood, Hayes and his band, who were heavily based on the Stax house band the Bar-Kays, spent the weekend playing lucrative gigs on the East Coast and then flew to Hollywood for the week to add their music to the film's scenes. They did this entirely in their heads, confounding the soundtrack specialists with their ability to start and finish on cue. The theme from *Shaft*, the lyrics of which Hayes had composed after hearing some backing singers cooing about Roundtree, won him the Best Original Song at the 1971 Oscars, where he triumphed over Henry Mancini and Marvin Hamlisch.

It's doubtful that the latter pair would have recognized how the theme from *Shaft* came to be composed. The drummer was told to play at the same tempo as the actors were walking on the screen. The guitarist was just testing his wah-wah pedal when Hayes told him to repeat what he'd just been doing. It was one of the first number one records that was narrated as much as it was sung. Hayes only put a vocal on it in the end in order to be able to enter it for Best Original Song at the Oscars. The signature line 'hush your mouth' was performed by Telma Hopkins. At the time she was also a member of Tony Orlando's Dawn whose 'Knock Three Times' had been a huge international hit in January. Thus she featured prominently on the most white bread hit of the year as well as the one that was, ostensibly at least, the nearest to the sound of the street. It was also the sound of the future.

APRIL PLAYLIST

Marvin Gaye, 'What's Going On'
Isaac Hayes, 'Theme From *Shaft*'
Gil Scott-Heron, 'The Revolution Will Not Be Televised'
Tonto's Expanding Head Band, 'Cybernaut'
Sly and the Family Stone, 'Family Affair'
Curtis Mayfield, 'Get Down'
The Supremes, 'Nathan Jones'
Al Green, 'Can't Get Next To You'
Aretha Franklin, 'Oh Me Oh My (I'm A Fool For You Baby)'
Santana, 'Toussaint L'Ouverture'

MAY:
BROWN SUGAR

On 4 April 1971, an eighteen-year-old from Santa Monica called Glenn Cowan was competing for the US table tennis team at the World Championships in Japan. After the day's practice session he was unable to find the team bus to take him back to the hotel. Spotting another bus bearing the competition's logo, he climbed aboard. There were no free seats so he stood.

The bus's occupants stared at their exotic new passenger with undisguised disbelief. Cowan was used to this. His long hair, tie-dyed pants and floppy hats, which attracted attention even at home in southern California, had drawn crowds in the Japanese city. But there was a different quality to the scrutiny on this bus, because the occupants were members of the table tennis team of the People's Republic of China, the vast, unknown nation that had shut itself off from the rest of the world in 1948.

Cowan's appearance was no more extreme than that of any other young American of 1971 hoping to be taken for Keith Richards, but in the Far East of the time it was an outlandish form of fancy dress which demanded an explanation. Cowan asked the team's interpreter to assure the Chinese players that in America many people looked the way he did. This relieved the tension a little.

Eventually the top player of the Chinese team, Zhaung Zedong, a thirty-year-old who was the star of the world game, came forward and presented Cowan with a silk weaving depicting the Huangshan mountains. Feeling he should reciprocate, Cowan went through his own bag for a gift. He could only manage a comb. He handed it over. When the bus got back to the hotel the Californian went directly to a shopping centre and bought two T-shirts with a design that combined an American flag with a peace symbol and the words 'Let It Be'. It was the kind of item just becoming available in the world's alternative bazaars, a muddled expression of right-on sentiments you could send away for via the small ads in *National Lampoon* or *Rolling Stone*. He presented one to Zedong and kept one for himself.

Following these spontaneous overtures there appeared out of the blue an unprecedented invitation for the American team to finish their visit to the Far East by spending a few days in China. This was big news far beyond the world of table tennis because it represented the first official contact between the world's most populous nation and its most powerful one since China's self-imposed isolation almost a quarter of a century earlier. The invitation was eagerly accepted, and on 10 April nine American table tennis players accompanied by four officials and two spouses crossed a bridge from the British colony of Hong Kong into the People's Republic of China.

It was, as one of them later recalled, like going to the moon. Their organized visits to the Great Wall, the ballet and the stupendous republic's handful of tourist must-sees were given prime-time coverage on nightly TV in China and relayed, with scarcely less pride, into American homes by American networks. It was the most significant piece of sporting diplomacy of the twentieth century. *Time* magazine called it 'the ping heard around the world'. Within a month of the visit a poll conducted in the USA found that more than half of the population were suddenly in favour of China's admission to the United Nations. Its effects were felt far beyond sport. It led to a fundamental realignment of world power and also, eventually, the iPod.

This apparently impromptu visit had been facilitated at a high level. The green light for the American players' arrival had come from Chairman Mao himself. A keen table tennis player since the 1930s, he had been responsible for making the game the Chinese national sport. In 1971 he knew that President Richard Nixon was sending out diplomatic feelers. Messages from his consigliere Henry Kissinger to the Chinese Premier Zhou Enlai were routed through Pakistan. On the face of it the two countries were implacably committed to each other's destruction. As the players were being driven down Chinese streets plastered with posters reading 'People of the world defeat the US aggressors and their running dogs' they were unaware that a handful of people at the head of both nations were playing footsie.

Nixon's problem was Vietnam. It was the baby boomers' big issue as well. The draft was an immediate threat to the life of every young man of military age in the country. In 1971 a twenty-seven-year-old former naval officer and Vietnam veteran called John Kerry faced a Senate committee and asked them how many young men had to die in order for Richard Nixon not to be the first American President to lose a war.

With his stiff bearing and glowering look of disapproval, Nixon was the stereotypical straight of every alternative paper illustration, the butt of every Woodstock nation wisecrack, the only cloud in their clear blue sky. The President cordially returned the favour. The tapes of his conversations with aides in the Oval Office from the spring of 1971 abound with references to longhairs, freaks, drugs, even hot pants, and the part each may be playing in the imminent breakdown of civilization.

As is often the case in politics, the more Nixon was seen to lean towards one wing the freer he was to reach out towards the other. His conservative credentials made him the only president who could open up lines to China without being accused of being soft on communism. China needed an outlet for its goods. The US needed to find a way to get American troops out of Vietnam. Nixon knew the admittance of the table tennis players indicated that his offer of talks would be accepted and hoped that he would be able to make the huge step of actually visiting China in the not-too-distant future. 'If we get this thing working,' he told Kissinger in the spring of 1971, 'we will end Vietnam this year.'

Nobody knew this on 1 May, when thirty thousand hippies descended on Washington, intent on stopping the work of the government. They were entertained on their first day in West Potomac Park by Linda Ronstadt, Charlie Mingus, NRBQ, Mother Earth, Phil Ochs, Mitch Ryder (whose pelvic thrusting so offended some of the newly radical feminists that they demanded the right to speak afterwards) and the Beach Boys. David Fenton, who reviewed the event for the alternative paper *Ann Arbor Sun*, knew the freaks among his readership would be surprised to see the last-named on the bill but reassured them 'they're freaks now with really long hair and bushy beards . . . That's an indication of how widespread the changes in this generation have reached.'

On 2 May the President withdrew the protesters' permits and ordered the army into the city. So many troops were airlifted into the nation's capital that at one stage troop transports were arriving at Andrews Air Force Base every three minutes. Over ten thousand people were arrested or detained. It was the largest mass arrest in American history.

Three days later, on 5 May 1971, the five members of the Rolling Stones assembled at Nellcôte, the eight-bedroom mansion above the town of Villefranche-sur-Mer on the Côte d'Azur which Keith Richards had recently begun renting. The tear gas was still hovering over the Washington Mall but the men who wrote 'Street Fighting Man' were settling down to a new life in a millionaires' playground.

1971 was a huge year for the Rolling Stones. In March they had toured the UK for the first time since 1966, back in the days when the screaming made them impossible to hear.

This seventeen-night swing through city halls and theatres was informally known as the Goodbye to Britain tour. As it began at Newcastle City Hall on 4 March they announced that when it was over they would be leaving to become tax exiles. It was the first time those words had been used in the context of the music business. They finished with two nights at the Roundhouse in London and then on 26 March performed at the four-hundred-capacity Marquee Club in Soho, the first of the 'back to the clubs' shows which were to become a feature of their career. This sentimental homecoming was marred by an incident during which Keith Richards attacked the club's owner with a guitar for insisting they perform in front of the venue's traditional branding. They did further promotional chores such as recording a performance of their new single 'Brown Sugar' for the BBC's *Top of the Pops*, with Jagger wearing a pink satin suit and baseball cap while singing live over a pre-recorded instrumental track.

At the beginning of April, just as the new tax year began, they and their families and retainers left their homes in England and flew out to new ones in France. Charlie Watts and his wife found one in the Vaucluse. The new guitarist, Mick Taylor, whose girlfriend, Rose Millar, had just given birth to their child, stayed in the Byblos Hotel in St-Tropez. Mick Jagger, who spoke French and had a new girlfriend who had lived in Paris since her teens, took a house in the picturesque hilltop town of Biot. They were not exactly close neighbours.

In 1971, very few Englishmen followed their work overseas. Bill Wyman, who rented a house near Grasse, was old enough to realize the move to France might have long-term consequences, though like the rest he had no inkling of what long term might mean. He was thirty-five and already had one divorce behind him. Charlie Watts was just on the safe side of thirty. Despite having been at the top of their tree for seven years, Mick and Keith still had their twenty-eighth birthdays in front of them. Mick Taylor was just twenty-two.

The Stones' move to France was made at Mick Jagger's urging. In the world of rock stars, where the ability to balance a chequebook attracts both awe and suspicion, Jagger is often cited as a financial genius. His brief attendance at the London School of Economics rarely goes unmentioned. In fact what Jagger did in 1971 was no more than what any other bright CEO would have done if he suspected his company was on the brink of falling apart. In doing so he gave the Rolling Stones an entirely new focus.

Jagger had learned many bitter lessons in the music business, the chief being that success is only the beginning of a band's problems. In 1965 they had hired the American accountant Allen Klein to bully royalties out of their sleepy British record company. When the contract with that company expired with *Let It Bleed* in 1969 they found to their dismay that Klein had bought the US rights to their catalogue of sixties hits for his own company, ABKCO. The rights they thought they had been signing over to themselves they had actually been signing over to a company controlled by him, which is the kind of thing that causes iron to enter even the most forgiving soul. Jagger was determined that none of this was going to happen again. By moving the band to France he was doing what no sixties band had managed to do, which was to start again without breaking up.

Mick and Keith, the clear leaders of the group since the departure of Brian Jones, had been laying the groundwork for Rolling Stones mark two for the previous year. This involved a few different steps. They would sign to a major international label, not one of Britain's pinstriped and risk-averse old firms. This would be a company that would give them a large advance and better royalty rates, spend large sums on promoting their releases and generally treat them in a manner befitting their self-proclaimed status as the greatest rock and roll band in the world. And they would no longer rely on a manager to lead them. Most of the bands who had become successful in the sixties had needed managers to negotiate their fees and operate as an executive nanny service. In Mick Jagger the Rolling Stones had a leader who realized that the price of remaining in control was a willingness to pay attention in meetings, a skill few of his contemporaries ever acquired. Doing without a manager had an immediate fiscal benefit. A manager's cut turns any five-piece group into a six-piece. The Rolling Stones mark two had no intention of doing that.

Instead of finding a replacement for Andrew Oldham, who had ceased being involved with them in 1967, Mick Jagger had gone to see Prince Rupert Lowenstein. Lowenstein was at the time the managing director of merchant bank Leopold Joseph. The introductions were made by Jagger's art dealer friend Christopher Gibbs. Lowenstein's background as a man steeped in the specialist science of wealth management sent a strong message to anyone seeking to take advantage of them. He signed on as their business adviser.

Once he was in post in 1970, Lowenstein, already in his late thirties and healthily incurious about either the music or the celebrity of his new clients, was amazed at how little money the Stones had managed to make out of their fame and how small a proportion of that they'd hung on to. The old saying goes that most people in the music business are either poorer than you'd think or richer than you could possibly imagine. At the time the Stones were in the former category.

A combination of low royalty rates, non-existent merchandising revenues, and a career which had been stalled by legal problems followed by the slow unwinding of Brian Jones had seen them not earn as much money as they might have. For the latter part of the sixties their revenues had been routed through Allen Klein's organization, which reduced them further, and whatever profit they made was being assessed for income tax and surtax at a figure which amounted to anything between 83 and 98 per cent. On top of that they found that they owed back taxes. Bill Wyman alone, who didn't participate in songwriting, the most lucrative seam, owed almost $200,000. This was in 1970, when the average cost of a new car was $2,500. Lowenstein argued that the only way the Stones could pay the back tax they owed was by moving to a jurisdiction where the lower rates gave them a fighting chance of hanging on to more of what they earned in the future. And in 1971 the place to go was France.

While there they would make a record. In 1971, France had the same reputation for fine recording studios as London had for fine dining. The only decent ones were in Paris. The Stones wanted to live somewhere warm like the Côte d'Azur. The compromise was that the Stones' mobile truck, which had already been used to record at Mick's English country house Stargroves, could be driven down to the South of France and parked at Nellcôte, where Keith, who was emerging as the member who had to be pleased at all times, could record without getting out of bed.

On 1 April 1971, after months of flirtation with Columbia who were the only realistic alternative, the Rolling Stones announced they had signed with Atlantic Records. A week later their single 'Brown Sugar' was released for the first time on their own Rolling Stones label. There was a party at the Cannes Yacht Club to make sure that the business took notice. The man paying for that party, enjoying his share of the limelight and providing both prestige and cash, was, like Lowenstein, a well-dressed individual from an older generation.

Ahmet Ertegun had sold his R&B company Atlantic, once the home of Ray Charles, Big Joe Turner, the Coasters and scores of other great African-American acts, to Warner Brothers in 1967. The forty-five-year-old, impeccably sophis-ticated son of a Turkish diplomat was, like all the men who built the record business, every bit as excited by money as he was by music. Ertegun recognized that something fun-damental was changing in 1971 and that the future was in big-selling, high-margin long-players aimed at the white market rather than low-margin 45s for the urban market. What had been about selling to kids was now about selling to adults. What had been about hits was now going to be about careers.

Columbia Records, who had been making the running in the rock album market by signing West Coast acts like Janis Joplin and Santana, were the perceived leaders but they couldn't quite land the Stones. Clive Davis, who ran

Paul and Linda McCartney (**left**) attend the High Court in London in February 1971. McCartney's legal action triggered the winding-up of the Beatles. John Lennon's *Rolling Stone* interview (**above**) the same month ensured there would be no going back.

Alfred Hitchcock returns to London's Covent Garden to film *Frenzy* in January, just as developers are planning to flatten the old market.

David Bowie (**above**) performs at a Hollywood party wearing a Michael Fish gown during his first visit to the USA in February. In June he and Angie and their baby Zowie (**left**) pose for the *Daily Mirror*. The headline reads 'Which one is Dad?'

Right: Tower Records' newly opened Hollywood store is a temple to long-playing vinyl albums, the one product young people truly desire.

Below: At the same time as Carole King records *Tapestry* in Hollywood in January, Joni Mitchell is making *Blue* in the studio next door and James Taylor is cutting 'You've Got A Friend' round the corner.

NOTTINGHAM BOAT CLUB
trent bridge. . . . nottingham

★   ★   ★

LED ZEPPELIN

SUNDAY, 21st MARCH   7.30p.m. to 11.0p.m.

MEMBERS ONLY ADMITTED   Nº 326   MEMBERS MUST SHOW THEIR MEMBERSHIP CARD AT DOOR

ADMISSION IS STRICTLY BY TICKET ONLY

Above: Led Zeppelin's 'back to the clubs' tour during the spring allows them to unveil new songs like 'Stairway To Heaven' in small venues months before they were to come out on record.

Right: Nick Drake's reluctance to stir from his room to promote his records means the release of *Bryter Layter* in March goes unremarked. Later in the year he drops off the tapes of *Pink Moon* at his record company and disappears.

Left: The Rolling Stones follow Led Zeppelin into many of the same university halls on their 'farewell to Britain' tour. Mick Jagger and his girlfriend Bianca let the train take the strain.

Below: Before credit-card booking, rock audiences comprise those willing to stand in line. Stones fans in Manchester show their prized tickets.

Right: 1971 is the year in which Stevie Wonder turns twenty-one, marries Syreeta, renegotiates his Motown contract and begins working with TONTO, the revolutionary synthesizer invented by Robert Margouleff and Malcolm Cecil (**below**).

Below: The true stars of *Soul Train*, the TV show that Don Cornelius takes national in 1971, are the self-taught dancers in the programme's trademark 'line'.

Above: In April Francis Ford Coppola finally begins shooting *The Godfather*, with the gunning-down of Marlon Brando on Little Italy's Mott Street.

Above: Motown boss, Berry Gordy, doesn't think *What's Going On* is the kind of material his leading man Marvin Gaye should be recording but is too preoccupied to prevent it.

Left: 'Spanish' Tony Sanchez and dancer Madeleine D'Arcy board the plane sent by Mick Jagger to convey the beautiful people from London to France for his wedding to Bianca Pérez-Mora Macias.

Below: Ahmet Ertegun is at Mick Jagger's right hand when he marries Bianca in St-Tropez in May. Keith Richards skulks in the background, muttering dissent.

Bottom left: Unprepared for the level of interest, Jagger makes his wedding vows inches from a battery of cameras. It's the last time he gets married.

Bottom right: Julie Christie, fresh from *The Go-Between* and *McCabe & Mrs. Miller*, dances to the hastily convened wedding band at the Café Des Arts.

Left: The August *Rolling Stone* cover that began the cult of Keef, inspiring Patti Smith and many others to take scissors to their own hair.

Right: US table-tennis star Glenn Cowan stops traffic in China during the 'ping-pong diplomacy' that eventually opens up relations with the USA.

Below: Over ten thousand are arrested or detained during the 1 May Washington protests against the Vietnam war, the largest mass arrest in American history.

Above: The pyramid stage is built for the first Glastonbury Festival in June, which is blessed by good weather and sparse attendance.

Below: During the same summer solstice, hundreds of thousands of young Americans troop to the inhospitable wilds of Louisiana for the misnamed 'Celebration of Life'. Some don't come back.

Above: The three defendants in the
Oz magazine trial are ritually sheared
while awaiting sentence in June over
their controversial 'school kids issue'
seen inset in a benefit issue (**below**).

Right: The 'shag' hairstyle that Jane Fonda
sports in the hit *Klute* is widely copied. In
1971's movies, all big cities are dirty and
dangerous.

Columbia, might have been a good businessman, but Ahmet Ertegun wrote 'Mess Around' for Ray Charles. In the world of the Stones this counted for a lot more.

Ertegun used the credentials earned in a world which had vanished to put himself at the head of one that was yet to be born. He knew how musicians' minds work, that their motives are coloured by sentimentality and ego as well as money. 'I think Mick would have liked to sign with Excello,' he recalled, talking of the tiny R&B label on which Slim Harpo's 'I'm A King Bee' had been released. 'We were the closest he could get to Excello and still get five million dollars.'

The Stones' own label deal was the template for the record business of the future: funky on the outside, fiscal as hell below. In the corner of the label on 'Brown Sugar', unnoticed by most fans who were too busy smirking at the new jutting tongue logo, were the words 'Promotone B.V.'. This newly founded company, which was owned by the Stones and based in the Netherlands, would own the copyright of any records they put out in the future and license them to the major record companies whose job it was to exploit them. The Stones had resolved that henceforth they would own their own recordings. They would take advances from record companies for the privilege of distributing them but at the end of each relationship they could take their catalogue elsewhere. The Netherlands was attractive as a place to base the company because it didn't tax royalties. In every respect the Rolling Stones were moving upmarket.

This pivotal month in the transfiguration of a scruffy beat group from south London into a grande luxe international attraction was further marked by an occasion which is traditionally every bit as concerned with prestige as it is with romance – a wedding. The 12 May marriage between Michael Philip Jagger and Bianca Pérez-Mora Macias marked the establishment of rock and roll as a viable branch of high society and a recognition on the part of the Establishment that the money, fame and status the newborn pop industry had brought with it during the sixties was only going to increase in the seventies.

The day before the wedding Jagger chartered a Dan Air Comet to fly seventy-five UK-based friends to the wedding in St-Tropez. These people had only been informed of the impending nuptials twenty-four hours earlier. The newsreel cameras were there to see them off. Old mates from the package tour years such as Ronnie Lane, Kenney Jones, Ronnie Wood, Ringo Starr, Doris Troy and Peter Frampton sashayed across the tarmac at Heathrow in their white suits, clutching amusing presents for the happy couple, trailed by wives and girlfriends in wide-brimmed straw hats and hot pants, some of them hitching newly arrived infants on to their hips, all still giggling at their great good fortune and appearing to the rest of the workaday world like the avatars of a blithe new species.

Ossie Clark, who was enjoying a new eminence thanks to David Hockney's recently unveiled portrait *Mr and Mrs Clark and Percy*, strode through the terminal wearing a particularly challenging outfit of lemon shorts and knee-high suede boots, carrying both a doctor's bag and what in years to come would be known as a man bag. Paul McCartney, accompanied by Linda and daughters Heather and Mary, was no less courageously attired in three-quarter-length trousers of the kind that would subsequently become familiar via the Bay City Rollers. He was tight-lipped while boarding the plane, worried that he might be seated near Ringo, with whom he was locked in a bitter legal fight. This had been foreseen and they were kept apart.

At the Hotel Byblos they mixed with their new friends, some of whom, such as the Earl of Lichfield who gave the bride away, were aristocrats. There were no fewer than three people on the guest list from the Ormsby-Gore family. One of them, the eighteen-year-old Alice, was the fiancée of Eric Clapton. The daughter of Lord Harlech, the former British Ambassador to Washington, she was a member of that group of aristocratic hippies who now found themselves moving in the same circles as the superstars. The old landed gentry was mingling with the new and dealing with some old afflictions. Clapton's main concern while attending the wedding party was keeping himself topped up with heroin.

1971 was the high watermark of rock's over-indulgence in drugs. Al Wilson of Canned Heat, Jimi Hendrix and Janis Joplin had all died within four weeks of each other in the autumn of the previous year, their deaths caused by accidentally miscalculating how much they or their bodies could stand. At this stage it was still considered unnecessary to keep an eye on anyone who was using. Rose Millar, who was at Nellcôte almost every day because she had to drive her husband Mick there and drive him back, doesn't recall seeing Keith take anything more than Jack Daniel's or marijuana during that summer. 'I suppose they were geniuses at concealment,' she told journalist and author Robert Greenfield. Keith was using in a big way, as was his partner Anita

Pallenberg. He moved to France a week ahead of her while she was undergoing the latest of many attempted cures. They weren't the only ones. When John Lennon visited Nellcôte later that week while in Cannes for the Film Festival he drank too much red wine and threw up on the steps, which was attributed to the fact that he was being weaned off heroin via methadone.

Among the wedding party there were drug dealers like 'Spanish' Tony Sanchez, who dressed as if he wished to be taken for Keith Richards – an affliction which eventually affected hundreds of thousands of young men and women – accompanied by his girlfriend Madeleine D'Arcy, her dancer's body introduced into hot pants, sporting a straw hat and bug-eyed shades like Jane Fonda as Bree Daniels in *Klute*, one of the films of 1971. Hanging around Nellcôte and also supplying the Stones' friends the Gettys back in London was Jean de Breteuil, a French aristocrat whom Keith called 'Johnny Braces' to get round the fact that he couldn't pronounce his name.

A few guests, like the art dealer Robert Fraser, had made their names by greasing the adjoining doors between the high life and the low life, while others, such as the model Donyale Luna, were creatures entirely of their own invention. Bianca Pérez-Mora Macias was a member of that group. She had come to Europe from Nicaragua as a teenager to study at the Institut d'Etudes Politiques in Paris. She took strategic advantage of the blurring effect that often attends the swapping of continents. Her parents had broken up and her mother ran a shop to make ends meet. She liked to say her father was a well-to-do coffee planter or a diplomat. In fact the diplomat was an uncle, who was a cultural attaché at the Nicaraguan Embassy in Paris and therefore in a position to keep an eye on his bright, wilful and perilously beautiful niece. 'I studied hard and remained a virgin until I was eighteen and a half,' she recalls with telling precision.

By 1968 the studying had become less of a priority. She was living with Michael Caine – not the sort of thing that happens to most overseas students. She was introduced to the actor, already a star, by his tailor Doug Hayward, a key figure in smart London who was the model for the Caine character Alfie and later written into fiction by John le Carré as *The Tailor of Panama*. Bianca's beauty opened doors and allowed her to present herself as rather grander than she was. The fabled egalitarianism of Swinging London was always prepared to make exceptions for physical attractiveness. In 1970 she was twenty-two years old, spoke five languages and was already accustomed to the attentions of wealthy, powerful and significantly older men. She was introduced to Mick Jagger by another of her lovers, the fifty-year-old French record mogul Eddie Barclay.

Like the other members of this longhair aristocracy Mick Jagger had grown up in the fifties. Like them he had traditional expectations of women and a feeling that it was bad form to be without a girlfriend for even a short time. This inevitably resulted in periods of overlap which could be fraught. Open cohabitation, or 'living in sin' as it was known, was still very rare, even among the young and famous. Paul McCartney only got away with living with Jane Asher outside wedlock because it was under her parents' roof and therefore considered somehow chaste. The eighteen-year-old

Marianne Faithfull, who only started making records to get out of doing her A levels, married the art dealer John Dunbar in 1965 because she was pregnant with their child. In the wedding photos she poses with a soft toy in her lap to conceal her pregnancy. After the child was born she embarked on a high-profile affair with Jagger, who was still notionally with Chrissie Shrimpton at the time. The four-year affair with Faithfull, which made them the iconic couple of the decade, ended in a miscarriage and a suicide attempt while he was filming *Ned Kelly* in Australia.

After she moved out Jagger had considered marrying the actress and singer Marsha Hunt when she became pregnant with his child. He already had a live-in chef called Janice Kenner at his London house in Cheyne Walk who slept with him from time to time, on the basis that in those days it would have been impolite not to do so. At the same time he conducted an affair with Catherine James, an ex-girlfriend of Eric Clapton's who had a child with the Moody Blues' Denny Laine. When he met Bianca he was impressed and, if it's possible, flattered that on their first meeting she was prepared to ditch Eddie Barclay to go with the younger and more glamorous man.

There was talk of an alternative society in 1971. The enduring alternative was the society inhabited by the rich and famous. While the people in West Potomac Park, the editorials in the underground press and pockets of dreamy rock fans all over the world mused at what sort of new world might be in the process of being born in 1971, Mick Jagger was determinedly burrowing his way into the old one. Having already seen more sex than a policeman's torch during his years as a pop idol, he understood that fame finds money and becomes glamour.

More than any other sixties act the Rolling Stones had always evoked the exotic world of St James nightclubs which the rest of us merely read about in the music papers. Their songs conjured up dreams of models, photographers and fast cars, of sunglasses worn indoors, of the workaday world surveyed with exquisite boredom through the steamed-up window of the car from the airport. This fabulous world of spoiled girls who had grown up in circumstances the rest of us could only dream about, of frisky journalists who needed taking down a peg or two, the heiress who got her kicks in Stepney not in Knightsbridge any more, the girl who once had him down but is now under his thumb, sounded far more exciting than the one the rest of us had to live in. At one time the Stones had merely sung about it. Now, like a few of their peers, they were living it out.

Almost without exception, the rock stars of the sixties married women who would never have looked at them twice had it not been for their wealth and fame. Beneath the veneer of the Aquarian Age the world beyond the red rope operated according to rules that would have been familiar to Edith Wharton or Thackeray. Here young bucks competed to see who could bed the toniest, the most alluring, the most enviable girl in the rock and roll high school, and when they did they wished to advertise the fact on the biggest stage. That's why everyone was invited to St-Tropez. Mick felt he had won the prize and wished it to be known.

That wedding day, 12 May 1971, marks both the last point at which he underestimated the power of his own fame and the point at which he discovered the limits of his own power. The ceremony almost didn't go ahead at all, when Bianca discovered on the morning of her big day that French law, as unsentimental in this respect as it is in all others, required that the couple make it clear what property they held in common. Having learned how little this was, she threatened to call it off, presenting Jagger with the prospect of a most humiliating reverse in front of his peers. She eventually relented.

Mick, nominally Anglican, had prepared himself for the service, which was to take place in the picturesque fisherman's church of Ste Anne, by attending meetings with the pastor. He reckoned without the fact that the civil ceremony, which had to take place first, would be conducted at the Town Hall and, by French law, had to be open to anyone who wished to witness it. That meant that hundreds of photographers, many of whom had come over on the flight after the superstar airlift, installed themselves in the room where the ceremony was due to take place, forcing Les Perrin, the Stones' sober-suited, old-school PR man, to ring Jagger to warn him what to expect. Jagger said he wouldn't get married in a goldfish bowl. This was one of those occasions when the rock star's flounce was countered by the bureaucrat's shrug. Mariu Estevan, the Mayor of St-Tropez, said there was nothing he could do about it. If Monsieur Jagger wanted to get married in France he must do it the French way. When the bride and groom eventually arrived, late and already perspiring, pushing their way as best they could through the crowds of pressmen, holidaymakers and rubberneckers, they appeared harassed and faintly shocked. The only security for the whole day was provided by Alan Dunn, who worked for Mick, and

Jerry Pompili, former house manager of the Fillmore East. It wasn't remotely adequate.

Brides tend to float through their wedding day in a trance of delight, while their grooms are nervous and unsure. This occasion was no different. Jagger appeared more thrown by the chaos than his bride. She was wearing a skirt and jacket specially designed by Yves Saint Laurent, the décolletage of which had clearly been chosen with the express intention of getting on to every front page in the world, and also subliminally advertising what nobody but the groom knew, which was that she was already four months' pregnant. Jagger wore a suit and shoes which were not yet known as trainers. This was an unprecedented combination of formal and informal which was to be widely copied. They rushed through the civil ceremony to the accompaniment of shutters that were never more than feet away. Their union was witnessed by the film director Roger Vadim and model-actress Nathalie Delon. Jagger's parents, for whom he was always 'Mike', stood in the middle of this mayhem, looking unsurprisingly like people who were watching their son disappear into a mad new world. Their place at their son's right-hand side had been usurped by Ahmet Ertegun. He was the daddy now.

That ceremony alone would have been enough to put most people off public pledges of affection for life. When it was over, Monsieur et Madame Jagger still had the religious one to come. By the time they reached the pretty church at the top of the hill, Les Perrin, who by now had added the role of wedding planner and sole responsible adult to his duties as press officer, had decided that the only way he could stop the thing degenerating even further was by instructing Father

Lucien Baud to lock the doors and not admit anyone else. Thus the least forgiving section of the world's press found, to their delight, that they got a close-up view of the world's number one rock god having to bang on the door and beg admittance like anyone else whose name has been left off the guest list at an exclusive club gig.

Inside the church, rock stars and their molls in their diaphanous finery lolled around sniggering and bitching, to the understandable discomfort of the priest. Each stage of the ancient Catholic rite was punctuated by a flashbulb broadside from feet away. Nobody could take their eyes off Bianca's cleavage. Keith couldn't disguise his disapproval of the fact that his singer had done something as retrograde as getting married in the first place. Anita Pallenberg couldn't disguise the fact that she loathed Bianca and regarded her as a threat to her role as queen of the court of the Stones. They both sneered at the fact that Bianca, who had even less interest in the music of the Stones than Prince Rupert, had asked the organist to play the theme from *Love Story*. It would prove to be the first and last marriage for both of them, although not in the way anyone thought.

Their union finally consecrated, they stumbled on to the party at the Café Des Arts where Terry Reid, Steve Stills, Doris Troy and Michael Shrieve from Santana jammed while the likes of Julie Christie, then at the zenith of her beauty, and Brigitte Bardot, a star so long-established that her presence even impressed the Stones, frugged listlessly. Keith Richards would have joined the band, reported *Rolling Stone*, but by the time the jam had been organized he had passed out flat on his back with his mouth open. Mick Jagger's father Joe, a mere fifty-eight at the time, looked and felt like a stranger at his eldest son's big day. When he left the Café Des Arts late that night he was still carrying the wedding present he had had no opportunity to present to his son and bride throughout the long, trying day, and confided feelingly to a reporter, 'I hope my other son doesn't become a superstar.' This last wish was to be fulfilled. Les Perrin later described 12 May as 'the most difficult day of my professional career'.

Back in London that same night the groom's forsaken partner Marianne Faithfull was in a cell at Paddington Green police station, sleeping off the effects of a shot of Valium administered by a Harley Street specialist and the three vodka martinis she'd drunk to deal with the fact that Mick was marrying someone else. In her memoirs she waspishly points to the close physical resemblance between the bride and groom and ascribes the match to his narcissism. 'Mick married himself,' she wrote.

By the morning the agreed facts of Mick Jagger's wedding day had already begun to splinter into a hundred, often contradictory accounts. It's such a mess that three men – Keith Richards, the saxophonist Bobby Keys and Roger Vadim – all claim to have been best man. A guest assured me that Keith had decided to liven up proceedings by wearing a Nazi uniform. If so that's one of the few things the press didn't record. Bianca claims that later that night the bedroom of the happy couple was invaded by Keith Moon. He was actually on his way to play with the Who at the Kinetic Circus in Birmingham.

The Jagger wedding was the shabbiest bun fight in the history of both rock and marriage and clearly skin-crawlingly embarrassing for all the key participants. It apotheosized the sixties generation's genius for dismantling all the old formality and putting little but inebriation and self-indulgence in its place, perfectly framing the moment at which those who had come to tear down the temple of society were actually caught groping at its open blouse, taking their celebrity and their power and their beautiful girlfriends and their drugs and their tax exile and flaunting it in front of everyone from the World War Two veterans looking at the pictures in the *Daily News* to the sixteen-year-old Black Sabbath fans reading all about it in *Rolling Stone*. It ought to have been a *Titanic* meets iceberg moment. It should have been the end of the affair.

It wasn't. It was actually a beginning. In a sense this misfiring spectacular was the perfect launch pad for not only Stones mark two but also a whole new lease of rock life, one that none of the participants would have been able to imagine. This was down to two things. The first was a record.

Sticky Fingers, the group's ninth album in the UK and their eleventh US release, came out in the USA in the week of the wedding. It had appeared in Europe earlier and it was already number one in the UK chart while 'Brown Sugar' was in the same position on the singles chart. The week after the wedding the album went to number one on the US chart and stayed there for four weeks.

Both album and single dominated the early summer of 1971, outshining other superstar releases in May like James Taylor's *Mud Slide Slim And The Blue Horizon*, Paul McCartney's *Ram*, Crosby, Stills, Nash & Young's live double

Four Way Street and Jethro Tull's *Aqualung*, which came out on the day of the wedding. It also overshadowed cult contenders which came out in the same month like Roy Harper's *Stormcock*, Caravan's *In The Land Of Grey And Pink*, the Flamin' Groovies' *Teenage Head* and the first stirring of what would later come to be called 'world music', the debut release by Osibisa.

Also that May *All Things Considered* was launched as the flagship news programme of National Public Radio in America. Woody Allen stood in for Johnny Carson on the *Tonight Show*, plugging his recently released movie *Bananas* and welcoming Bob Hope as his guest. Hope joked that he couldn't stay long because he had to entertain the troops in Washington. The cover of *Newsweek* wondered if J. Edgar Hoover, director of the FBI since Prohibition, should retire. *Playboy* published a major interview with John Wayne in which he defended his involvement in the expulsion of alleged communists from Hollywood in the fifties and described films like *Midnight Cowboy* and *Easy Rider* as 'perverted'.

The hot book was William Peter Blatty's *The Exorcist*, which was at number one on the *New York Times* best-seller list for seventeen weeks. Also Frederick Forsyth, a journalist with no previous thriller-writing experience, was getting rave reviews for *The Day of the Jackal*. The *NY Times*, while enthusing, commented, 'if there is anything to cavil at it would have to be the author's graceless prose style which shapes up as a lot of récitatif and very little aria'. *THX 1138*, the first feature film by a recently graduated George Lucas, was released that May in the USA. The surprise hit of the month was *Summer of '42* starring Jennifer O'Neill as a beautiful woman widowed during the war who introduces the fifteen-year-old hero to sex one wartime summer in Nantucket.

In Britain, *Sticky Fingers* was the first Rolling Stones album not to be priced in pounds, shillings and pence. In the USA the list price was $5.98, but even at the discount price of $3.39 being offered by Gary's on Fifth Avenue only the wealthiest fans could go straight out and buy it. Most would go and visit it in the record shop where they might be able to listen to a couple of tracks and certainly gaze in wonder at its cover, which is the thing that really made it a star.

Like *Sergeant Pepper's Lonely Hearts Club Band*, *Sticky Fingers* is one of the handful of records which are as famous for their covers as for what that cover contains. It remains probably their most charismatic album thanks to the halo effect provided by the sleeve. This was dominated by a black and white picture of the business section of a male stud wearing Levi's jeans, the fly of which had an actual zipper that could be pulled down to reveal an inner card showing a pair of white briefs and a male torso. The card was added late in the design process after it was realized that the zip would otherwise damage the record. The sleeve, a play on the idea of 'packaging' which went over most heads, was designed by Andy Warhol. Billy Name, who was a resident photographer at his Factory, took the picture. Many members of his Factory, including the actor-model-stud Joe Dallesandro, claim the credit for modelling for the picture. (In Spain, which was still ruled by the illiberal General Franco, it was replaced by a photograph of disembodied fingers reaching out of a jar of treacle.)

For the Rolling Stones the cover was the outward sign of a new confidence, a determination to answer to nobody but themselves. Warhol had originally been contacted by Mick Jagger in 1969 with a view to his doing the cover for their second greatest hits album *Through The Past Darkly*. Jagger's letter said 'do whatever you want and please write back saying how much money you would like'. It's unlikely that Decca, the record company at the time, would have signed the purchase order arising from such a brief. They similarly baulked at Jagger's wish to have a lavatory wall on the cover of *Beggars Banquet*. But with the new label, backed by Atlantic, which was in turn part of Warner Brothers, which was ultimately bankrolled by the Kinney Group's car park and funeral homes millions, money was less likely to be a problem. Questions of taste, which had previously been ruled on by their elders, were all theirs. The Man no longer appeared to be in charge.

Sticky Fingers was a transitional record in every respect. When their contract expired in 1970 Decca claimed that they were still owed a single. The Rolling Stones provided one called 'Cocksucker Blues', confident that company head Sir Edward Lewis would never release that. He didn't. It was the first one made without any input from Brian Jones, the difficult young man whose band they had originally been. In his place they had Mick Taylor, an orthodox lead guitar virtuoso who had come to their attention as the latest and youngest of a succession of featured soloists with John Mayall's band. Taylor made no contribution to the group's image, which may have been one of the reasons they chose him. When difficult employees are replaced it's often by someone from the opposite end of the difficulty spectrum. The soft-featured Taylor was unlikely to get into anyone else's light. He was biddable, and when he left the band in 1974 he had just one joint-writing credit to his name.

Sticky Fingers straddled two decades. It was made up of material that had been left over from the previous albums – 'Brown Sugar' and 'Wild Horses' had been recorded at Muscle Shoals not long after Altamont in late 1969 – and during the sessions which took place at Olympic in west London in early 1971 they recorded some tunes that they would hold over for 1972's *Exile On Main Street*. Two of the songs had come out in other people's versions before the release of the album. 'Sister Morphine', which was co-written by Marianne Faithfull, first emerged as the B-side of her single in 1969, but then was pulled two days after release when Decca realized what it was about. When the *Sticky Fingers* version came out her writing credit wasn't on it, a state of affairs Jagger attributes to the desire to keep the publishing out of the clutches of her former manager. Gram Parsons, who had been sent a tape of 'Wild Horses' by his friend Keith Richards with a view to getting the Flying Burrito Brothers' Sneaky Pete Kleinow to put pedal steel on it, had realized the appeal of the song, recorded his own version and then twisted Jagger and Richards' arms to allow him to put it out a full year before the release of *Sticky Fingers*.

Sticky Fingers has more musical range than any other Rolling Stones album thanks to the input of a lot of people who weren't strictly in the band, or were new to it: saxophonist Bobby Keys on 'Can't You Hear Me Knocking', Memphis maestro Jim Dickinson's honky-tonk piano on 'Wild Horses',

Billy Preston's churchy organ solo on 'I Got The Blues', slide guitar on 'Sister Morphine' left over from Ry Cooder's controversial contributions to *Let It Bleed*, and on 'Can't You Hear Me Knocking' a Latin-flavoured guitar solo from Mick Taylor that suggested he'd been listening to Santana's *Abraxas*, which had been a huge hit in 1970.

Nobody can remember precisely how the lyrics came along: Marianne Faithfull reckons Jagger had the chords for 'Sister Morphine' for six months before she wrote the words; some reckon 'Wild Horses' was written by Keith about Anita Pallenberg, Marianne says it was something she said during a domestic exchange with Jagger; Claudia Linnear and Marsha Hunt have both claimed to be the inspiration behind 'Brown Sugar'. All the women involved have in their different ways been forced to accept that they owe their fame to their association with a bunch of young men who, almost without exception, traded them in for younger models. As Faithfull has reflected, it's all very flattering being the paramour of the star and being quoted as the inspiration of his material but eventually your life is no longer your own and you end up as the punchline of a piece of rock trivia. At the time few people pointed out that the exasperated, up-for-days tone of the lyrics could mask a streak of something called sexism. The word was scarcely ever in use, and anyway, as Spinal Tap were later to say, 'What's wrong with sexy?' The songs of the Stones might have depicted a world of predatory women, sleazy businessmen and straights who weren't with the programme, but the message of the music was that you can escape all this in the everlasting adolescence offered by the sound the band makes.

Although there are tracks such as the closer 'Moonlight Mile' which are grander and more gothic than anything they'd done before, the record's heart is in 'Brown Sugar', 'Bitch' and 'I Got The Blues', in which they still sound like the rock and roll dance band who made 'Around And Around'. Anyone seeking to advance the argument that the true leaders of rock bands are the rhythm sections doesn't have to look much further than the push and pull between Bill Wyman and Charlie Watts, the two members who learned to play rock and roll after they'd already mastered other styles, on these tracks.

'Brown Sugar' was the key single of 1971. I recall Saturday nights that summer turning up to shabbily furnished north London firetraps lugging a Party Seven of sticky sweet Watney's Red, twenty Benson & Hedges and a copy of that yellow-labelled mono single with the protruding tongue on it, nights that would climax with the sound of 'Brown Sugar' rasping and rattling from somebody's lovingly assembled and nervously guarded component stereo, trainee teachers thrusting their hips in each other's direction with unmistakably carnal intent while studiously avoiding anything as telling as eye contact, cigarettes held aloft, each recapitulation of the chorus lasciviously lip-synced, temporarily transported to the Dionysian state of peak horn which the Stones achieved more often than anyone else, the rented room gravid with lust and throbbing with abandon. If records do change lives, as section editors are always insisting they do, then they tend to do it for only as long as the record runs. 'Brown Sugar' changed lives for three minutes fifty seconds, which is the most you can ask of even the greatest record.

In a sense it was the Rolling Stones' last proper pop hit. 'Brown Sugar' was an old-fashioned juke box record. It worked because it had the power to move a room, any room. Since most 45s tend to be bought by people who like the record more than they like the band, singles sales measure the popularity of the music, whereas album sales measure the popularity of the act. Among those people who laid down their money for that single – effectively an EP with the addition of 'Bitch' and a brilliant live recording of 'Let It Rock' which may actually have been the best of their many Chuck Berry covers – there was little debate about the subject of the song, a scarred old slaver who whipped and went down on the women in the slave quarters. The whole song, riff and all, was composed by Mick Jagger, who wrote it while killing time between shots on the Australian set of *Ned Kelly* in 1970. It's still a staple of the Stones' live set, but when he sings it he often changes the line 'hear him whip the women just around midnight' to 'you should have heard him just around midnight'. 'I never would write that song. I would probably censor myself,' he says nowadays.

Sticky Fingers is also the Rolling Stones' most influential album. The boho cowboy pose that people associate with the many heirs of Gram Parsons, that frayed country sound that is apologetically referred to as alt-country, begins with 'Dead Flowers' (which has been covered by New Riders of the Purple Sage, Cowboy Junkies, Steve Earle and anybody else who ever wore buckskin) and 'Wild Horses', which became one of Jagger and Richards' most covered songs with versions by Guns N Roses, Jewel, Bush, Alicia Keys and Susan Boyle.

Then there are the groups whose entire careers seem to come in the form of love notes to *Sticky Fingers*. When in 1991 Primal Scream hired the album's producer Jimmy Miller the result was 'Moving On Up', to all intents and purposes a postdated fan letter to this era of the Rolling Stones. Everything the Verve tried to do is in Paul Buckmaster's strings at the end of 'Moonlight Mile'. Groups as far apart in time and space as the New York Dolls, Aerosmith, the Black Crowes and the Kings of Leon have at the very least started their careers as humble footnotes to the Rolling Stones as they were in 1971, at the very peak of their glory.

The fact that the Stones also embodied the look of the year indicated how far they had bent the world to their will. Mick Jagger had never been considered particularly handsome. When the Stones first emerged the newspapers liked to contrast them unfavourably with the well-groomed Beatles. Adult eyes failed to register that the Stones put just as much care into their appearance as the Beatles did. In addition their front man with the wanton, parted lips and the sleepy, insolent eyes had one of those faces the gaze was quite happy to feast on. Chrissie Shrimpton remembers her boyfriend having vegetables thrown at him in the street in the sixties. In those days the very way he carried himself seemed like an affront to some people's ideas of maleness. His movements in performance were said to be stolen from James Brown or Tina Turner but they were transformed by a fresh layer of knowingness, by flickers of camp and the additional dimension of being a member of an outfit that like all great groups carried with it its own internal narrative, a narrative that made everyone else's seem pale and tired. By 1971, thanks to the work of a new generation of portrait photographers like David Bailey and pop photographers like Gered Mankowitz, Jagger had come to represent a new form of androgynous male beauty. (Also in 1971, a young woman from New Jersey transformed herself into a New York scenester by clipping some Keith Richards pictures out of the newspaper and cutting her own hair in imitation. 'Macheteing my way out of the folk era,' as Patti Smith later recalled.)

Carly Simon, who is two years younger than Jagger, was in 1971 homing in on the same look from the other side of the spectrum. Carly was regarded as the least beautiful of the three daughters of the prominent New York publisher Richard Simon, one of the partners of Simon & Schuster, and grew up acutely aware of it. However, as she got older she was also aware that people were beginning to remark that she had a quality of raw sexuality, often attributed to her long legs and wide mouth. In addition she also had that property which Jagger had of appearing to light up when performing.

The young folkie Simon was fortunate to be signed to Elektra Records in 1970 rather than CBS. Elektra was run by Jac Holzman, who of all the old record business men understood best that the most powerful marketing tool at his disposal was the twelve-inch-square cover of the album. Album covers had the effect of making their contents seem more important than they were, and Elektra's album covers, which included works by Love and the Doors, looked more important than anyone else's. Which is why Simon's first two albums, both of which came out in 1971, put her picture front and centre: on the first she is reclining on an old couch, her dress pulled taut across her parted legs; in the second she's standing framed by a gate in Regent's Park, the light from behind silhouetting her legs through a diaphanous peasant skirt. When she appeared on the bill at a televised concert in Central Park in July she out-dazzled the rest of the bill, which included Boz Scaggs and the Beach Boys, in a clinging red dress slashed to reveal her interminable legs.

In the week of Jagger's wedding she was making her first New York appearance, supporting the equally glamorous Kris Kristofferson at the Bitter End. They were both performers you were as happy to gaze upon as you might be to hear. People remarked that Carly looked like Mick Jagger. She was sufficiently connected in New York society to make something of this resemblance. A few days before Jagger's wedding she interviewed him by phone for the *New York Times*. Their exchanges were flirtatious. It seems reasonable to assume that this didn't come about via the standard PR approach. Jagger probably knew that in the last year Simon had been romantically linked with Kristofferson, Cat Stevens and Warren Beatty and probably wondered what he'd done to be left out.

A year later the two hooked up at a party thrown for the Stones. She was seeing James Taylor by then and Jagger was married but vows rarely get in the way when two centres of ego and beauty wish to merge. They're even more bootless when they appear to be in some senses the same person. Against such forces the battlements of feminism and hippy culture cannot endure long. They say swans mate for life. Stars mate for glory and their glamour's increase. The spur for Carly Simon's marriage to James Taylor was Bianca

Jagger ringing him up and suggesting his fiancée was having an affair with her new husband. It seems Bianca was no less persuaded by Jagger's distinctive backing vocals on Simon's huge worldwide hit 'You're So Vain' than the rest of us. That record, intoxicating precisely because of the things it supposedly satirizes, comes from inside the new world that was being born in 1971. In this song and its attendant hoopla the world of pop music met the world of Lear jets and yachts and an entirely new sort of glamour was born. As the decade went on it would come to make the Hollywood kind look shabby and old.

Following their wedding, Mr and Mrs Jagger began their honeymoon on a yacht. Since his new wife had little use for seclusion they ended up in Venice – never the best place to avoid photographers. The couple were discovering that there is a peculiar mathematics of fame whereby if one famous person marries a slightly less famous but glamorous person then there is no limit to the amount of fame they can jointly generate or the quantity of publicity they will attract. Modern multi-media power couples like Kim Kardashian and Kanye West, Brad Pitt and Angelina Jolie, Beyoncé and Jay Z and David and Victoria Beckham are the contemporary heirs of Mick and Bianca. The photographers who had tussled for access had a limited market for their pictures. Neither the UK nor the USA had any kind of celebrity magazine at the time. Many of the newspapers thought the marriage of a rock star was beneath them. The counterculture publications treated it with lofty disdain.

Meanwhile the Stones' mobile recording truck had arrived at Nellcôte. A week later the band started playing in the basement. This was the same basement where, according to myths happily promoted by Keith, the German occupiers would keep those they wished to interrogate. It was damp, acoustically poor and far from ideal for recording, which meant that a process which was always likely to be long and drawn out was even more so. Unwilling to pay the normal tariff for electricity, somebody shinned up a pole and tried to run the mobile off the town's power supply. What they found was that the town was susceptible to the same sudden losses of power as many southern European communities in those days. This is mildly inconvenient if you're shaving. If you're painstakingly adding a guitar solo on a multi-track recording it can be catastrophic. This was classic Stones: an act of rebellion which ends up making life more difficult for the rebels.

On top of Nellcôte's shortcomings as a place to make music were overlaid intrigues worthy of a Jacobean court as the usual Stones cast of retainers, petitioners and villains drifted in and out at the pleasure, often abruptly withdrawn, of the house's tenant. The true power centre was in the upstairs rooms to which both Keith and Anita would mysteriously repair in order to top themselves up with the heroin which was, thanks to the proximity of Marseilles, in ready supply. Even Mick Jagger didn't dare go upstairs to find out why the guitarist had withdrawn from the session and left everyone else twiddling their thumbs.

Jagger had agreed to site the recording truck at Keith's place because at least it meant nobody would have to get him to the studio. However, he underestimated how difficult it could be to get him out of bed, and once he was out to get him to work on a song. The band were hardly ever all present at one time. Charlie lived too far away. Bill didn't like the atmosphere. Mick Taylor could only get there when his wife was available to drive him. The singer was on honeymoon. Jimmy Miller, who had produced *Sticky Fingers*, was heard to plead 'Hasn't anyone got a song?' as the sessions stumbled on as if without end. The record only started to sit up and take solids in the autumn of 1971 when they moved to Los Angeles and added the vocals.

Exile On Main Street came out in 1972. Like most double albums it took a while to digest. Even if you could decipher the lyrics through the density of the mix you couldn't really say that they made a great deal of sense. This no longer mattered. From here on Stones records seemed to be about themselves, designed to sustain and boost the mystique of the Stones brand, which was to become more important than any individual record. Henceforth they lived in a position of gilded statelessness. Their records no longer seemed to refer to London, New York, Los Angeles or anywhere in the known world but instead to emanate from a Guy Peellaert illustration come to life.

The people who loved *Exile On Main Street* were not the pop pickers who'd picked up *Sticky Fingers*. Instead they were the people who loved the Stones most. It appeared in the wake of Keith Richards' 'Lennon remembers'-type interview which got him on the cover of *Rolling Stone* and established the idea that he somehow was the true spirit of the Rolling Stones, an idea he has never been in a hurry to discourage. 1971 was the year the Rolling Stones became a brand and Keith was elevated to the position of being that brand's key spokesman.

In a sense the pictures taken at Nellcôte that summer by French photographer Dominique Tarlé matter as much to the legacy of the Rolling Stones as anything they recorded there. These images of unshaven young men so confident in their appearance that they can afford to be slovenly about it, their clothing apparently made up of whatever garment had been at the end of the bed when the noonday sun tickled them into wakefulness, drifting around the halls of this antique pleasure palace holding precious Martin guitars by their necks, long cigarettes dangling from their mouths as they reach for the first coffee or cognac of the day and make their way down to the villa's dank cellar to fall in with whatever subset of heavy friends happened to have either got up early or remained there from the previous night – this elegantly wasted look became the new hippy fantasy.

In the background, like so many extras, were their lissom blonde girlfriends and their tousle-haired children. It was a dream of a new form of living, a fantasy in which you could live the life of a hippy on the budget of a banker, like Manet's *Le Déjeuner sur l'herbe* as re-imagined by the advertising department of *Rolling Stone*. It became, through Tarlé's photographs, not just the earthly dream of a whole generation of young men, it also, because it was the most photographed recording session of the era, fixed a visual idea of how creativity should look in the rock era. As Mick Jagger later said, it didn't really happen that way, but the look of Nellcôte couldn't help but make us believe that it did.

It was the year they established the mystique on which the Rolling Stones have run ever since. Very little has happened with the Stones since that summer that is all that interesting musically. If you went to see them today and their repertoire didn't go beyond 1972 you'd still feel you'd got the Stones. The rest is pyros. Since that time the main interest has been in them as a brand, a soap opera, a sitcom, a group of wealthy men fighting the depredations of age, an international attraction which is not, as you might imagine, hanging on by its fingernails but instead remains ready to roll through any frontier you put in front of it and set records wherever records are to be set. The move to France didn't just give them another five years. It gave them another forty-five.

Mick and Bianca divorced in 1978. Mick has never formally remarried. Nixon and Mao have gone to their graves, as have Glenn Cowan the long-haired table tennis player, Ian Stewart, Gram Parsons, John Lennon, Jimmy Miller and many others who drifted through Nellcôte that summer. John Kerry, the young man who addressed the Senate committee, is at the time of writing the US Secretary of State. Nellcôte was recently sold to a Russian who reputedly paid a hundred million euros for it. Prince Rupert Lowenstein died in 2014, having given up looking after the Stones' affairs in 2008. He had proposed the Stones should sell their business, having received an offer which amounted to double their net worth in cash in their pockets. They were going to take it until Mick Jagger changed his mind at the last minute.

We will never know what combination of musician's nervousness and businessman's hard-nosed calculation made him withdraw. One of the reasons his group has now been going longer than most record companies is that they haven't entered into any relationship they couldn't walk away from. Over more than fifty years of trading they have seen the business change to the point where hard-headed investors will pay down many millions of dollars for the rights to exploit in the future songs and likenesses which were once thought to be the definition of ephemeral. In this marketplace the Rolling Stones have a value greater than anyone else's for the simple reason that through all that time, through good times and bad, whether relationships were cordial or poisonous, no matter what waves of musical change threatened the cliffs of tradition, they never broke up. This above all is what made them unique. As they used to say about the Windmill Theatre which stayed open through the London Blitz, they never closed.

The small step that took the Rolling Stones from the home counties to the Côte d'Azur took place at the same time as the People's Republic of China made another small step which led to their eventual emergence as the powerhouse of the global economy and began the tilt that has seen them become the world's manufacturing base, the source of all the expensive toys that keep the youth of the world amused and the world's biggest market for luxury goods. Back in 1971 even Mick Jagger, who's never been one for predictions, wouldn't have dreamed that the band he withdrew across the Channel in order to preserve it would still be functioning over forty years later or that he as a great-grandfather would be leading them.

The music doesn't belong to the past. On 27 July 2013 Taylor Swift introduced Carly Simon to duet with her on 'You're So Vain' in front of fifty-five thousand predominantly teenage girls in Foxborough, Massachusetts. All those girls, whose mothers weren't born when the original came out, knew the words. Meanwhile Georgia May Jagger and the Richards Sisters were lending their version of the Rolling Stones brand to the marketing of Sunglass Hut. Bianca Jagger is fronting the Bianca Jagger Human Rights Foundation. Mick Jagger was on the front page of Britain's biggest newspaper when he was photographed entertaining a twenty-seven-year-old dancer he had met on tour in Switzerland, only a month after the death of his long-time partner L'Wren Scott. The only surprising thing is that we find it surprising.

On 12 March 2014 the Rolling Stones played their second show in China, at the Mercedes Benz arena in Shanghai, in front of a crowd of ten thousand, modest by their standards. Like any other international luxury brand the Stones were building up their business in the world's biggest market for luxuries. They played a few tunes from *Sticky Fingers*, which is probably the album you would use if you wished to explain them to a Martian. The first time they played China, in 2006, they had brought on local star Ciu Jian to sing 'Wild Horses' with them. The censors wouldn't allow them to do 'Brown Sugar'. They didn't complain. They played 'Dead Flowers' instead. As Prince Rupert was clear-eyed enough to see back in 1971, rock bands don't change the world. The world changes without their help. Writing in the British underground magazine *Oz* in July 1971, co-editor Richard

Neville said the Jagger wedding was 'public confirmation of the growing suspicion that Mick Jagger has finally repudiated the possibilities of a counterculture of which music is a part', which was another way of recognizing the same thing. By the time that line was published, Neville and the other *Oz* editors would be in the dock of Britain's highest court.

MAY PLAYLIST

Rolling Stones, 'Brown Sugar'
Serge Gainsbourg, 'Ballade De Melody Nelson'
Carly Simon, 'Anticipation'
Randy Newman, 'Tickle Me'
James Taylor, 'Hey Mister That's Me Up On The Jukebox'
David Crosby, 'Laughing'
Paul McCartney, 'Uncle Albert/Admiral Halsey'
Elton John, 'Tiny Dancer'
Colin Blunstone, 'Say You Don't Mind'
Stephen Stills, 'Change Partners'

JUNE:
WON'T GET FOOLED
AGAIN

O n 1 May 1971 a bomb had exploded in a store-room at the Biba boutique in Kensington High Street. Responsibility for it was claimed by the Angry Brigade. Since the previous targets of England's only home-grown terrorist cell had all been political – ministers' homes and foreign embassies – the decision to extend their campaign to one of London's most popular fashion outlets was particularly puzzling to the generation of pleasure seekers who had grown up in the sixties, a few of whom might even have had some distant sympathy for the brigade's radical objectives.

The Angry Brigade explained it as follows in their communiqué which had a twist on a Bob Dylan song: 'If you're not busy being born, you're busy buying ... the only thing you can do with the modern slavehouses known as boutiques is WRECK THEM. You can't reform profit capitalism and inhumanity. Just kick it till it breaks.'

1971 was the year the loose alliance of groups and individuals who had rallied under the banner of the alternative society de-merged into different factions, ranging from people who wished to bring about the violent overthrow of the state through those who considered themselves in permanent opposition to bourgeois values to those who simply wanted the right to pursue their lives free from post-war strictures. It also saw the severing of what had previously been seen as natural bonds between rock and rebellion. People who'd been reading the Marxist philosopher Herbert Marcuse's *One Dimensional Man*, the paperback of which announced it as 'the most subversive book published in the United States this century', argued it was no use looking to rock to bring down society because this allegedly repressive society used things such as rock to neuter the urge to protest. The record business was clearly happy to deal with anything provided it sold. In May, John Lennon's single 'Power To The People', which had been dashed off in response to reading an interview with the radical Tariq Ali, was still in the charts. The same message from less familiar sources fell on stony ground. In June a full-page advertisement appeared in the *Melody Maker*. It was for a new album by a group called Third World War and the sell foreshadowed the punk rock movement of the late seventies. 'This is class rage, class anguish,' declared the ad. The record didn't sell, and it wasn't for want of trying.

In the film of the rooftop concert which climaxes the 1970 Beatles film *Let It Be* there is a cutaway of an older gentleman climbing up a fire ladder to the roof to find out where the noise is coming from. He is wearing a buttoned overcoat, horn-rimmed spectacles, a trilby hat, and in his mouth is jammed a pipe. Even in the few seconds he is in shot it is possible to read the hint of the military in his bearing and the disapproval he can't help but radiate. The world in 1971 appeared to be run by men like that. They had wives who wore twin sets and kept their hats on while drinking Brown Windsor soup in stuffy hotel dining rooms. There was nothing in their manner or appearance that hinted that they had ever been young. And why should there be? When they were in their late teenage years they had been in some godforsaken barracks or living a stultifying domestic existence in which the best they could hope for at the end of a week was powdered egg. These people had grown up believing that pleasure was something that could only be snatched in tiny increments. It was something that was delivered only when the requirements of duty had been fully satisfied. Like a day of sunshine at an English coastal resort it was the exception rather than the rule and was appreciated as such. Pleasure, like freedom, was far from a right.

During the fifties and sixties these people had worked diligently to ensure that their children, the baby boomers, would have a different kind of life. They then reacted with hurt surprise when their offspring turned out to be an entirely different kind of people. My own father could simply never understand why a generation that could afford to wear smart clothes should instead decide to deck themselves out in denim. This feeling of incomprehension was even more pronounced when we would wear army surplus jackets or long naval greatcoats, the kind of clothing he and his generation associated with getting shot at or shouted at. When he said Bob Dylan 'wasn't music', that wasn't an indication of intolerance so much as a poignant statement of sincere belief. How could he possibly be expected to surrender to this, he who was tuned so differently, he who was built for duty rather than fun? The generation that had grown up since the war had little sense of duty. They weren't particularly interested in jobs, careers, money, security or the future because there was a feeling that this would all magically work itself out.

The thing they asked most of so-called straight society was that it should leave them alone. As soon as they could they grew their hair as long as possible and shacked up with boyfriends or girlfriends in distant cities, often without telling their parents that this was what they were doing. For the majority of baby boomers who were in London during this period, that was how they spent their time: growing their hair and having sex. There wasn't an awful lot else to do, and both activities were free.

In 1971 there seemed to be two separate worlds: one was dominated by serious people who had fought in the war, had short hair and ran things; the other was dominated by pranksters with long hair who just wanted to enjoy things. The idea that those two worlds would not be in permanent opposition to each other seemed far-fetched. The idea that politicians could ever wish to tap into the enthusiasm that attended rock and roll, other than in the clumsy manner Harold Wilson had used to sidle into the spotlight of the Beatles, seemed ridiculous. In fact it wasn't even thought about. In modern parlance, it wasn't even a thing.

On the other hand, these fun seekers weren't wildly interested in material things because there weren't an awful lot of them. Their desires in this direction tended to be focused on two particular areas: records and clothes. On Saturdays it was perfectly normal to go into the West End and just spend the day in the company of records. Shops served as libraries, places of association and churches as well as retail outlets. You could wander around the West End, from the twinkling array of imports at Musicland or Harlequin to the severe-looking old blues and jazz albums in Dobell's on Charing Cross Road, from the soul singles outside Cheapo Cheapo in Rupert Street to the tiny kiosk opposite Finsbury Park station out of which reggae singles would be heard blasting. Music wasn't simply a pleasure. Record shops weren't just a place to buy things or to associate with other people who wanted to buy things. They were an education in themselves.

In terms of fashion, in 1971 some of the names that had become closely associated with Swinging London were starting to take their brands on to the average high street, meaning that you could suddenly get your granny or grandad vests, your suede waistcoats, your gender-bisecting loon pants without having to go uptown. This was the time when shops such as Lord John, Take Six, Harry Fenton, Chelsea Girl, Lady Jane and Ravel started to appear on the main streets of Britain. But for the latest stuff you had to go uptown, and uptown meant Kensington and Chelsea, the Chelsea Drugstore and Biba, where Barbara Hulanicki turned out floaty dresses reminiscent of the flappers and made them all in size eight for young women who had grown up with small portions of food. Biba was a heaven. It was a brand before anyone knew there were such things. Its panda-eyed doll girls, its vampish, silent-film-era Theda Bara look (which was also the logo of the underground newspaper *International Times*) were all part of a mood that was just beginning to enjoy the pleasures of looking back.

In his book *Crisis? What Crisis? – Britain in the 1970s*, Alwyn W. Turner hints that Biba was hit by 'the Angries', as the underground press would matily refer to them, because of pressure from their allies in the nascent women's movement, some of whom felt uncomfortable with how much the shop spoke to their depths. In the June 1971 issue of *Vanity Fair*, socialite and casting director Celestia Sporborg posed in a series of upmarket fashions that ranged from the gamine to the racy. The pictures were accompanied by quotes advertising her enviably emancipated lifestyle – 'Maybe I was just born liberated', says one – while making it clear that this lifestyle wouldn't be available to many people beyond the charmed circles of Chelsea. 'If you have to ask your husband every time you want to buy a pair of tights, you're not going to be very liberated,' she says. Upmarket women's glossies have carried variations on the same pictorial ever since, forever attempting to reach an elegant accommodation between their readers' higher aspirations and their baser consumer desires, between the need to be taken seriously and the desire occasionally to be taken frivolously.

The smart magazines were trying to get a handle on the world of liberated London, to turn revolt into style, and therefore they studied the alternative press, which was enjoying a small boom. In London the products of the alternative press could be found if you knew which specialist store in which area of town to look in. In the provinces it was a lot more difficult. If you wished to buy *Oz*, *International Times*, *Friendz*, *Red Dwarf*, *Rolling Stone* or any of the titles which were broadly described as making up 'the underground press' in 1971 and you happened to be in Yorkshire, you had to get on a bus and travel to the nearest big city. In my case this was Leeds where *Oz* could only be found in a newsagent's in the shadow of a railway bridge near City Station where it would be sitting alongside muscle magazines, nudist titles and other periodicals considered unsuitable for public display in mainstream shops.

Given the limitations of their distribution these titles didn't sell many copies, but since a great deal of the material they published was the kind of thing that would never have made it into print in the standard outlets they were much talked-about. They lived in the netherworld of the media, with all the attendant dangers. A steer too far in one direction or another might attract the attention of some guardian of public morals, a printer demanding to be paid up front or a distributor requiring indemnification against possible legal action.

The subliminal message that came through the damp pages of these titles, a message eagerly devoured by those of us who were too young and provincial to actually take part, was that somewhere in Kensington or San Francisco a handful of privileged souls were living in a kind of saturnalia where the music was the choicest, the whole way of speaking and behaving was being changed from top to bottom, nobody had anything more important they ought to be doing, and the joints were being rolled by beautiful long-haired girls who didn't think it necessary to get dressed because within the next half an hour they were bound to be taking you to bed. These magazines would have hated to be described as 'lifestyle' titles but that's inevitably how they were read.

The people who wrote for them may have prided themselves on their willingness to publish rambling, discursive pieces on drugs, politics and 'the war', pieces which were often rendered illegible as well as unreadable by being laid out in broken type on coloured backgrounds on over-absorbent paper; what they didn't like to talk about was the extent to which their sales relied heavily on sex, whether in the humorous form of Germaine Greer reaching inside Viv Stanshall's loons to grab his penis, the recurrence of the popular cliché of a bare-breasted black girl cradling a machine gun, any of the walnut-nippled hot mamas drawn by Robert Crumb, or the crudely cut-out Amazons who ended up on the cover of the notorious Schoolkids Issue, which eventually landed *Oz* in court and brought the carnival to an abrupt halt.

The *Oz* Trial of June 1971 was the climactic event of Britain's Great Hippy Scare. It marked the point at which tweedy, horn-rimmed, pipe-smoking, car-washing, lawnmowing, hat-wearing respectable Britain decided that it was no longer prepared to tolerate the provocations of a bunch of long-haired, loud-mouthed libertines, many of whom were foreign, dammit, all of whom seemed determined to mock everything they and their good lady wives held dear, and was going to give them the metaphorical and actual short back and sides their behaviour was so clearly crying out for.

Mounted in the august theatre of the Old Bailey, with characters wearing either the fancy dress of hippydom or the wigs and gowns of the age of Pitt the Younger, the *Oz* Trial brought the awful majesty of one of the oldest legal systems in the world to deliberate upon the sexual readiness of a cartoon bear and its likeliness to deprave and corrupt children of school age who would never have heard of the scandal had the law not chosen to intervene. Meanwhile on the streets outside lissom daughters of the gentry in hot pants and mini skirts addressed their supporters through megaphones, bemused bobbies moved in to extinguish half-hearted fires lit by supporters a hundred yards away from where in centuries past enemies of the realm would have been actually burned to death, former members of the Beatles led processions nowhere in particular, and representatives of the popular press, some of them in actual macintoshes, lingered in the hope of an aristocratic nipple while the overwhelming mass of the population of London reacted to the entire hoopla with the grumbling indifference that is their ancient birthright. Clive James memorably described it as 'a fair to middling episode of *Monty Python* running at the wrong speed'.

It made celebrities of everyone involved: counsels like John Mortimer, who went on to become Britain's most famous barrister; witnesses like DJ John Peel, jazz singer and art critic George Melly, drug law activist Caroline Coon and comedy writer Marty Feldman, who started a whole seam of British thinking by describing the judge, Lord Justice Argyle, as 'a boring old fart'; and most of all it made the defendants famous, far more famous than any of them wished to be.

Three very different people, they perfectly represented the range of talents and aspirations that were temporarily cloaked in the common cause of the alternative society. Richard Neville was a handsome Australian closing on the age of thirty and feeling it. Neville had the precious gift of being able to talk a good fight and, as far as the press was concerned, the further advantage of a beautiful girlfriend called Louise Ferrier. Jim Anderson was a lawyer by training and had come over with Neville from Australia where their magazine had been a *succès de scandale*. (One of their friends was Martin Sharp, a gifted illustrator who ended up sharing a flat with Eric Clapton, writing the lyrics for Cream's 'Tales Of Brave Ulysses' and designing the cover of *Disraeli Gears*.) The only non-Australian in the dock was Felix Dennis, a twenty-four-year-old former musician from outer London who had come to the notice of the other two through his success in selling *Oz* and had become the magazine's publisher. Anderson was the organization's conscience, Neville its propagandist and Dennis its engine.

Oz had no particular agenda and its lead times were too long to allow it to cover the convulsions of the scene as the weekly *International Times* did. Consequently it relied to a large extent on stunt issues devoted to themes. The Schoolkids Issue, which came out in 1970, was one such wheeze of Neville's. Noting his thirtieth birthday on the horizon he complained that he was feeling old and irrelevant and therefore it might be a good idea to invite a number of schoolkids in to edit the magazine. They advertised in their own pages and, given the rather narrow nature of their demographic, got a lot of well-connected kids from Notting

Hill Comprehensive, the odd precocious scion of libertarian stock, and from Reading the teenage tyro rock writer Charles Shaar Murray.

Between them they produced an issue which featured among other things the well-loved children's character Rupert Bear, the copyright of Express Newspapers, in priapic engagement with Gypsy Grandma, the copyright of Robert Crumb. The cover, which was ripped from a book that happened to be in Jim Anderson's flat, was originally intended to be a centre spread. Only when Felix, demonstrating the nascent flair that would eventually make him a multi-millionaire as a publisher of men's magazines, insisted that the centre spread be used to sell back issues (of which they presumably had a warehouse-full) was this provocative picture promoted to the cover. Hence the juxtaposition of mountains of naked flesh with the words 'Schoolkids Issue' ensured that any intended subtlety would be lost and the die was cast. It was neither the first nor the last time that a magazine's cover arrived at on a whim would have serious repercussions.

The indictment read: 'The Oz Publications conspired together with Vivian Berger and certain other young persons to produce a magazine containing divers obscene lewd sexually perverted articles, cartoons, drawings and illustrations with intent thereby to debauch and corrupt the morals of children and young persons within the Realm and to arouse and implant in their minds lustful and perverted desires.'

This was the kind of sonorous and rarely used charge which could in theory result in ten years in prison. The argument was that this was a magazine aimed at children rather than one put together by teenagers, who were a bit more than children. In 1971 there wasn't the moral panic about corrupting the young that exists today but it was serious enough to carry with it the threat of real jail time. For all that Neville and his fellow defendants dressed up as schoolboys for the committal or as barristers in wigs, for all that they tried to turn the event into a giant prank at the expense of the Establishment, they knew that this was serious. Had a similar case been brought today more would probably have been made about the piece on student agitation at various London schools being placed opposite a photograph of a uniformed teenage schoolgirl headed 'Jailbait of the Month'. Jim Anderson's time in the witness box was additionally tense because he feared that he would be asked whether he was homosexual. He had decided to answer this question honestly if it was put, even though he knew he would be laying himself open to further suspicion of corrupting minors and would also break the heart of his mother at home in Australia.

After a trial lasting almost two months they were found not guilty of conspiracy but guilty of two lesser charges. Prior to sentencing, their hair was cut for them by the prison authorities, a judicial shearing that sent a shiver of dread through every student in Britain. The sentences were overturned on appeal with everyone from the *Listener* to the National Association of Probation Officers condemning it as heavy-handed and pointing out that nobody had been corrupted. The view outside London might have been different. In his diaries, Michael Palin recalls having dinner with some teacher friends of his wife's in Surrey while the trial was going on and finding them determined to resist what they saw as the permissive ideas they associated with smart London folk.

The magazine boomed on the back of the publicity that attended the trial but by 1973 it had blown itself out and *Oz* was closed. Neville and Anderson went back home. Felix Dennis, stung by the judge's description of him as 'the least intelligent of the three', started on the road to a publishing empire, most of which would be anything but alternative. The people who made their names via *Oz* and *IT* had drifted into academe, the quality press or, like Charles Shaar Murray, were writing about rock in papers like the *New Musical Express* which had shrewdly borrowed some of the rebel swagger of the alternatives. As the *Oz* Trial was going on, Jann Wenner's still black and white *Rolling Stone* was balancing its coverage of politics and youth culture with long interviews with record executives like Warner Brothers' Joe Smith, the kind of people who would in future supply the big-name rock stars that would sell copies together with the advertising that would make the title profitable.

John Lennon helped put together a benefit record for *Oz*, which like most benefit records didn't make enough money to benefit anyone. He also wrote a cheque for the *Oz* Defence Fund and told Neville 'don't ever let lawyers into your life' – clearly the key learning gleaned from the endless meetings which the Beatles' split had mired him in. Lennon, newly shorn and holed up in Tittenhurst Park recording *Imagine*, claimed that Mick Jagger had been on the phone offering to help out if it went wrong. Bands did gigs for *Oz*. The reformed Traffic took their live album *Welcome To The Canteen* from one such.

In the summer of 1971 the alternative press treated rock stars as unpredictable uncles who might occasionally be touched for a donation, but still weren't sure whether rock and roll was part of the struggle or something you amused yourself with after the struggling was over. While the trial had been going on, Richard Neville managed to persuade Jim Anderson that it wouldn't look good if he were to slip away at the weekend to go to a rock festival. This was the case no matter how tempting the prospect of what was being planned for the 1971 summer solstice in Somerset.

In June 1971, Andrew Kerr was thirty-eight. Well born and privately educated, Kerr had spent ten years working with Randolph Churchill, spendthrift eldest son of the wartime Prime Minister, as he penned his father's official biography. Kerr was far from the standard clubman. Coming from farming stock himself, he was one of the bohemian tendency among England's landed gentry. These were people who saw the possibilities of a conjunction between their traditional duty to steward the land and the more nebulous aims of the long-haired tribes who were beginning to leave the cities to establish a new way of life in England's countryside.

Returning from the 1970 Isle of Wight Festival, Kerr felt there ought to be a gathering which did more than draw six hundred thousand people to a massive field to bob their heads in time to Jethro Tull and Johnny Winter. He craved a festival with a nobler purpose. Unlike most people returning from rock festivals Kerr didn't forget the idea after a good bath and a hot meal. The first thing he looked for was a site. He wanted one with significance. He inspected Stonehenge, not yet fenced off from visitors, and rejected it because it was surrounded by arable land. He was eventually directed towards Worthy Farm near the village of Pilton in Somerset. Here the farmer, thirty-six-year-old Michael Eavis, had organized a very small rock festival in 1970 in the vain hope of paying off his mortgage. Entrance on that occasion was a pound, the headliners were Tyrannosaurus Rex and the handful of campers were invited to buy their morning milk from the farmhouse door. This venture didn't clear Eavis's mortgage; it actually left him with more debt to pay off. Welcome to the festival business.

Kerr reached an agreement with Eavis to mount a second festival in 1971 at Worthy Farm and moved in to begin planning. He invested his own money and brought on board Randolph's daughter Arabella, who did the same with a small family bequest. In 1954 *Time* magazine had proposed the infant Arabella as a future bride for Prince Charles. By 1970 she had swapped debutante's pearls for the kind of hippy chic which only a handful of hippies could actually afford and joined the trickle of upper-class dropouts in the direction of the Vale of Avalon. The Irish writer George Bernard Shaw had astutely remarked that it is impossible for one Englishman to open his mouth without another Englishman hating him, and the Aquarian Age didn't change this. Eavis regarded Kerr and Churchill with the inverted snobbery which is the standard English response to those whose speech brands them as toffs. All this was relative. For singer Linda Lewis, who was born in the East End of London and joined the throng, Eavis was by some distance the poshest person she had encountered in her twenty-one years.

Pilton is seven miles distant from Glastonbury, the storied settlement where Joseph of Arimathea is said to have journeyed after donating his tomb to Christ. Kerr decided that was close enough to justify calling the new festival Glastonbury Fayre. In making this kind of stretch he was only following in the footsteps of Woodstock, which actually took place at Bethel, New York. Kerr and Churchill attempted to organize the succession of New Agers, chancers and sundry lost souls who began to arrive. Some were in place months before the festival was due to start on 20 June, at the time of the summer solstice. These pioneers included Bill Harkin, who devised the pyramid stage, a one-tenth scale version of the great pyramid at Giza. This was placed on the site of an ancient spring located by dowsing. It was that kind of festival. People came from all over the world to join the effort. The Brazilian musicians Gilberto Gil and Caetano Veloso who had been exiled to London by the military government in their home country turned up and injected ideas from their national tradition of carnival. Jeff Dexter, former mod and now DJ at all of London's head concerts, used his contacts to secure the services of major bands. He approached Pink Floyd and the Grateful Dead, both of whom seemed well qualified on the grounds that their music seemed to be reaching for some higher consciousness. They also had a reputation for occasionally playing for free, which was bound to help.

A key part of Kerr's plan was that everything should be provided gratis. The idea that musical performances should be available without payment had gained sufficient ground since the fence came down at Woodstock in 1969 that some bands had, at least in public, meekly succumbed to the idea.

This was regardless of the fact that it was clear to any sentient observer that whether you wished to pay the performers or not, rock performances incurred considerable expense. As if to drive home this point Pink Floyd had lined up all their equipment on the runway at Biggin Hill airport for the cover of the 1969 album *Ummagumma*. This seemed like an unprecedented arsenal of gear at the time because it required as many as two roadies to look after it all. In the event neither Pink Floyd (who were touring on the continent) nor the Grateful Dead (who were recording at the Château d'Hérouville) could play Glastonbury, though the latter donated some live recordings to the album that was subsequently released to pay off the inevitable debts incurred by the allegedly free festival.

Glastonbury's infrastructure was very basic. The stage cost £1,100, which seemed like a great deal. However, during the set by Quintessence, who could always be relied upon to arrive accompanied by everyone in Notting Hill with nothing better to do, it was moving so much that the designer was forced to wander among the musicians requesting that those not directly related to the performance get down. The lavatories were holes in the ground above which the patrons perched on scaffolding poles. The stage lighting was inadequate unless boosted by the arc lights that David Puttnam and Nic Roeg's film crew brought along with them. Viewed today, their documentary film *Glastonbury Fayre* appears to depict an event on the same scale as one might find in a suburban park during the summer months. The attendance was sparse by Isle of Wight standards, possibly as few as ten thousand people, which left ample elbow room for idiot dancers to do their thing and adequate parking space for those bikers who wished to drive right up to the stage with their bare-breasted old lady on the back.

In Glastonbury's chaotic fields, among the head bangers, tribal drummers, mud sliders, face painters, geodesic dome dwellers, exotic religionists, naked exhibitionists, boy mystics in patent leather shoes, bewildered children, pert-nippled girls rehearsing their music and movement lessons in the open air, ravishing film superstars and rake-thin models rarely seen more than a few yards from the Chelsea Drugstore, and puzzled musicians surveying the bobbing heads of gibbering loons, their brains fried with acid – here, in one week in June 1971, was born a number of things.

This was the week when, according to the people closest to him, David Bowie ceased his dabbling and got serious. Bowie's stock had been rising since his return from the USA in February. He'd appeared on *Top of the Pops* the week before Glastonbury, miming the piano part on Peter Noone's hit recording of his song 'Oh! You Pretty Things', and had recorded an *In Concert* for BBC radio where he appeared in public for the first time with his new group: Mick Ronson, Woody Woodmansey and Trevor Bolder. Bolder, having only previously seen him as a normal bloke in shirt and jeans and assuming him to be just another band leader, had been amazed to see Bowie get changed into a gown before the show. Bolder came from Hull, where such sights were rare.

Bowie and his wife Angie, who had evidently found someone to park their three-week-old son on, made their way to Glastonbury by train, alighting at a remote country station and then attempting to walk to the festival site. This was made more difficult by the costume he had decided upon for the day, which was Oxford bags, unsuitable shoes and Three Musketeers hat. Bowie was supposed to go on in the early evening of the 22nd but delays and Kerr's fear of the neighbours complaining about noise meant that he didn't appear until dawn the following day. He performed as a duet with Ronson, unveiling most of the songs from *Hunky Dory* for the first time. He had already started recording this at Trident Studios in Soho. He played the song that was a hit for Peter Noone, 'Kooks', the song inspired by the birth of the child they had left behind, 'Changes' and 'Song For Bob Dylan'. Arabella Churchill remembers his performance of 'Memory Of A Free Festival', which unfolded as the sun came over the hill to warm those who had endured a night on the cold hard ground, as a particularly magical moment. The song had been inspired by a far less grand occasion which had taken place a couple of years earlier on a recreation ground in Croydon. That Sunday evening as Bowie was travelling back by train, his platforms no doubt hurting as the feather in his hat was doubtless drooping, Radio One broadcast the *In Concert* show he had recorded the week before. It felt to Bowie and his retinue, which included Dana Gillespie, his manager Tony Defries and his publisher Bob Grace, as though things might be finally falling into place.

Traffic, Fairport Convention, Family and Terry Reid also played that week. In the afternoon sunshine Reid, the man who had left school at fifteen to play with a showband, the man who had turned down the chance to be the singer with Led Zeppelin because he wanted to make a different kind of music with his new band of friends from America, including slide guitarist David Lindley, made the sound which wouldn't be heard for another couple of years, on his album *River*. It was a fervent, passionate strain of jammed-up rock which seemed to be able to do without words or riffs. It seems fair to assume that the most beautiful woman there was Julie Christie and the most beautiful man was Terry Reid. In the full splendour of his handsomeness he carried himself like a leading man, exuding such powerful rays of attraction that Linda Lewis appeared unbidden at his side to add backing vocals, drawn by the powerful need to be in his vicinity. They were both just twenty-one.

In the evening the extended line-up of Traffic played. They were newly energized by the success of *John Barleycorn Must Die* and about to record *Low Spark Of High Heeled Boys*, with Jim Gordon on the drums, Ghanaian Rebop Kwaku Baah on percussion and both Dave Mason and Chris Wood back on the strength. Riding atop the foaming swell of 'Gimme Some Lovin'' was their leader Steve Winwood, who had already known three years as a scream idol, two as a hippy princeling and one as an unhappy member of the first band to be formed largely for lucre, now returning to his first love and still only a few weeks beyond his twenty-third birthday.

Both Reid and Traffic hit the top of their curve in the fields of Glastonbury in 1971.

Although Andrew Kerr was inevitably left with bills which took him years to clear, Glastonbury was deemed a success. This was the week when the sylvan memory on which Glastonbury has traded in the years since was first planted. Not that the media or music business took much notice.

Frank Sinatra had announced his retirement the same week. He was fifty-five, which seemed a sensible age to knock it on the head, even for a crooner. Michael Parkinson hosted the first of his chat shows on BBC television. His guest was the gap-toothed cad of a hundred cosy comedies Terry-Thomas. Glenn Frey and Don Henley played their first show together as members of Linda Ronstadt's backing band. The contract with Disneyland, where it was part of an initiative to attract young people to the park, stipulated that Ronstadt must wear a bra. In the same week the South African Broadcasting Corporation revoked its ban on Beatles records. In his message to Congress, Richard Nixon declared the United States' first war on drugs.

Kerr was fortunate in that the two elements that most govern the perception of a successful festival worked in his favour: the weather was good and not too many people turned up. Neither could be said of Stephen Kapelow, who chose the very same summer solstice to launch his Celebration of Life Festival in Louisiana. This is less fondly remembered than Glastonbury, with good reason.

Kapelow was the thirty-year-old heir to a New Orleans property company who decided to get into the rock and roll business via an eight-day festival in the country near Baton Rouge. There were very few rock festivals in the USA that year because city authorities had seen what had happened at Bethel and Altamont and knew that there would be stiff local resistance to bringing hundreds of thousands of fun seekers to their communities. But Kapelow, who was connected, managed to get permission to promote a festival near the town of McCrea.

Many thousands of young people made their way to this remote corner of rural Louisiana, attracted by a bill featuring the Allman Brothers, the Rolling Stones, the Beach Boys, Miles Davis, Sly and the Family Stone, Pink Floyd and, inevitably, Richie Havens and Ravi Shankar. Most of these names obviously didn't appear. Some of them were never going to. Kapelow further promised a spiritual dimension with teachers, healers and consciousness-raising sessions. What he delivered was hell on earth.

The hundreds of thousands of people naive enough to make the journey to the Cypress Pointe Plantation in the month of June, a time when no sane Louisiana native would ever stray far from a block of ice, found themselves camping on a mosquito-infested swamp with no facilities. The site was more like a refugee camp than a pleasure ground. The temperatures were so high that the few bands who turned up to play couldn't perform until after sundown. Security was provided by the Galloping Gooses, a biker gang from New Orleans, with predictable consequences. During the day the only way the fans could cool off was by swimming in the treacherous depths of the Atchafalaya river. Three deaths were recorded and the suspicion is that others went unnoticed. More than one bather waded out to cool off and was never seen again. A boat was sent out to recover one drowned man and returned tugging a corpse by its arm. When they reached the shore they were surrounded by curious hippies, some of whom were naked. The body was carried away by six African-Americans, a reminder that in this part of the world things were not much touched by hippy culture.

The stage collapsed and one man was taken away with a metal pole right through his body. By some miracle it did not breach any internal organs. Over a hundred kids ended up in local jails. They were the lucky ones.

The myth of Woodstock was that if a large mass of long-haired people gathered in the country to listen to their rock heroes then they would not need regulating, policing, organizing and placating because they would be carried through the experience by dint of their magical cohesion as a group. The argument went that they were qualitatively different from a mass of people gathered to watch football or displays of marching. People from the alternative society were somehow alternative people. Those who attended the Celebration of Life knew this was not the case. When the entertainment got started, three and a half days late, it began with one Yogi Bhajan taking the stage and asking the audience to 'meditate for one minute for brotherhood'.

A voice from the crowd rejoined: 'Fuck you! Let's boogie!'

A week later the Newport Jazz Festival, which had been put on in the tiny coastal resort in Rhode Island since 1954, was visited by a similar crowd. Promoter George Wein, like many middle-aged jazz aficionados, had hopes that the rock fans' apparent taste for improvisation might introduce new blood into the jazz family. In 1971 he had booked the Allman Brothers Band to play on a bill that also included Gerry Mulligan, Dave Brubeck and Dizzy Gillespie. All the longhairs in that part of the country duly headed for the site, aware that the Allmans played loud enough for them to be able to hear even if they were not inside the festival grounds. By the Saturday night they had tired of being outside and destroyed the fence, demanding the entertainment be provided for free. This insurrection took place as Dionne Warwick was on stage warbling 'What The World Needs Now Is Love', a song which proved somewhat unequal to the occasion. Some of them invaded the stage and stamped on the keyboard of the piano, destroying equipment and entertaining the crowd with an interminable bongo-based version of 'Land Of A Thousand Dances'. The festival had to be called off on Saturday night, two whole days before it was due to finish. The following year Wein moved his festival to New York. He didn't return to Newport for ten years.

As all this was happening John Lennon was sitting down at the white grand piano in the garden room of his house at Tittenhurst Park to mime his new song 'Imagine' for the promotional video. Rarely has a song seemed so out of touch with the realities of everyday life. Rarely has an artist allowed himself to be seen singing it in a setting more remote from the ones familiar to the people who were watching. Rarely has it mattered less.

In the same week Joni Mitchell released *Blue*, which seemed better tuned to the times. This was her sparest album yet, full of songs that were either openly autobiographical, such as 'My Old Man' about her former lover Graham Nash, secretly autobiographical, such as 'Little Green', which concerned the child she had given up for adoption five years earlier, or perfectly attuned to the creeping mood of disenchantment in many who remembered the sixties and were already hankering after them. One line in the title song seemed to resound more than most: 'acid, booze and ass / needles, guns and grass / lots of laughs / lots of laughs'.

A week after the festivals at Glastonbury and Grosse Pointe the Who released their new single, 'Won't Get Fooled Again'. The version that was played on the radio was a three-minute edit of a recording which would run for eight minutes on their upcoming record *Who's Next*. The music was the sound of the Who at their imperious best. The message was one that could be traced back to Woodstock, when Youth International Party activist Abbie Hoffman interrupted the Who's set to make a statement about the imprisonment of John Sinclair, an interruption which ended when Pete Townshend attacked him with his guitar and told him to 'fuck off my fucking stage'. The key word in that sentence was the possessive pronoun. What rock stars really resented, and resented far more than people realized, was the assumption that they could be used, their platform appropriated, their music co-opted to serve the purposes of some of the most self-interested exhibitionists who ever drew breath.

The Who held a launch party for the record at Tara, Keith Moon's new home in Chertsey, Surrey. Here Townshend was cornered by Mick Farren and other members of the underground press who demanded that he clarify what, if anything, the lyrics of 'Won't Get Fooled Again' – with its line about meeting the new boss, just like the old boss – said about how the Who related to 'The Movement'. He responded in full in a piece in *International Times*. Talking of Roger Daltrey's climactic scream, he said it 'screams defiance at those who try to tell us what we have to do with money that's not ours, a power that belongs not to us but to our audiences, and lives that long ago were handed to the rock world on platters ... you have no need to fret. You're not gaining new leaders. You're keeping the Who.'

JUNE PLAYLIST

Plastic Ono Band, 'Power To The People'
Traffic, 'Gimme Some Lovin''
Terry Reid, 'Dean'
John Martyn, 'Glistening Glyndebourne'
Flamin' Groovies, 'Teenage Head'
Genesis, 'The Return Of The Giant Hogweed'
Pink Floyd, 'Echoes'
Alan Stivell, 'Ys'
Bob Marley, 'Acoustic Medley'
Fairport Convention, 'Bridge Over The River Ash'

JULY:
EVERY PICTURE
TELLS A STORY

On Saturday, 3 July 1971 the *New York Times* carried news of the latest hijacking of an airliner. In this incident an armed couple had taken control of a plane operated by the Texan airline Braniff, demanded $100,000 in cash – which the company paid – and forced the flight to divert to Monterrey in Mexico where they released a hundred passengers and then took off again. On the same day Evonne Goolagong, described by the paper as 'the 19-year-old daughter of an Australian aboriginal sheep-shearer', won the women's singles title at Wimbledon. The big new movie reviewed inside the paper that day was *Shaft*. The big new album of the week was Joni Mitchell's *Blue*. Across the Atlantic Grand Funk Railroad had embarked on the latest stage of their campaign to broadcast their apparently great popularity by playing a free concert in Hyde Park in front of many holidaying American visitors and a few curious Londoners.

Given the time differences it's likely Jim Morrison was already dead in Paris by the time that edition of the *Times* went to press. According to those close to the singer, his body had been found in the bath of a rented apartment in the Marais district early that Saturday morning. The first news of his death didn't reach the United States until after the weekend when Clive Selwood, who ran the Doors' label Elektra in London, responded to phone calls from the music weeklies asking if he could confirm the rumour. He called the band's manager Bill Siddons in Los Angeles. Siddons called Morrison's girlfriend Pamela in Paris and was told to get on a plane and 'take care of arrangements'. Morrison had already been dead for forty-eight hours but no announcement had been made. The *Melody Maker* passed on the rumours to their readers in their issue of 8 July but weren't able to confirm the news until a week later.

When Siddons arrived in Paris he was met with a closed coffin, which subsequently encouraged those who preferred to believe that Morrison wasn't actually dead and had somehow slipped away. There was no inquest because the French authorities believed he'd died of a heart attack. Nobody in his circle pressed for one because they knew from his usual behaviour and the company he was keeping that drugs were involved. Forty years later Marianne Faithfull claimed that Morrison had been given heroin that was too pure by her former boyfriend Jean De Breteuil, who had been one of the guests at Mick Jagger's wedding six weeks earlier. Other, more outlandish stories claimed that the singer had actually died in a nightclub and his body had been spirited away so that the club could retain its licence. Morrison was twenty-seven, the same age at which Jimi Hendrix and Janis Joplin had died in circumstances of similar carelessness only a few months earlier.

The cult of Jim Morrison turned out to be even more powerful than those of the other two. As Bill Siddons later reflected, Morrison was an alcoholic but he nevertheless had the kind of public personality that made people wish to project their own hopes and aspirations on to him. They couldn't believe his death could be quite as tawdry as it appeared. He was coming off a well-received album, *L.A. Woman*, and his image had been preserved for all time in a series of powerful photographs in which he looked like Don Draper's idea of a rock god (ten years after his death one of those pictures made a memorable cover of *Rolling Stone* with the line 'He's hot. He's sexy. He's dead.'). Morrison's elevation into a cult hinted at a new truth about the music business which was becoming ever more apparent as it turned into an industry. It was no longer strictly necessary for its performers to be alive. In a handful of cases it was probably better if they weren't. 'Live fast, die young and leave a good-looking corpse' was the traditional advice. In Morrison's case the doctor who examined his body rather than his publicity photographs deduced that he was nearer fifty-seven than twenty-seven. Thankfully those publicity pictures told a different story.

The official statements about Morrison's death seemed calculated to mislead. When Morrison's girlfriend registered his death with the US Embassy, she said he had no known relatives. This was not the case. She knew it was not the case. Some members of Morrison's family were too prominent to be easily overlooked: his father was still serving as a Rear Admiral in the United States Navy. *Rolling Stone*'s headline stated 'James Douglas Morrison, Poet: Dead at 27', and added that he had passed peacefully, which suggested they had a liberal definition of the term. Bill Siddons' statement said 'he died in peace and dignity' without explaining how he could possibly know. By the time Siddons had arrived he had to take the word of Morrison's friends for that. Still, the manager could have been forgiven his naiveté. He was only twenty-three.

Three days after Jim Morrison's death Louis Armstrong died at the age of sixty-nine. He was still living in his modest home in Corona, Queens, NY. Here in his later days the king of jazz could be found out on the street playing with the neighbourhood kids. When asked why he never moved to somewhere more grand he replied, 'We didn't think we could have any better neighbours any place else so we stayed put' – a policy no rock star has ever seen fit to pursue. Armstrong's obituary made the front page of the *New York Times* and appeared three days before the announcement of Morrison's death. The latter was a small story on an inside page that pointed out to its middle-aged readers that the Doors were a rock group who played loud, amplified music, still a minority taste.

There were even signs that the era of the rock group, which had been the totemic performing unit of the previous decade, was passing. In the UK chart for the week ending 18 July 1971

202

solo albums began to outnumber albums by bands. This was the week Carole King's *Tapestry* made its first appearance, at number thirty-two, and Joni Mitchell's *Blue* went in at forty-two. Leonard Cohen's new record *Songs Of Love And Hate* stalled at thirty-one but his debut album had re-entered the chart on the back of the use of its songs in the recently released Robert Altman movie *McCabe & Mrs. Miller*, which starred Warren Beatty and Julie Christie. James Taylor had two albums in the top twenty. Neil Young's *After The Gold Rush* was climbing the charts again in its thirty-second week. Graham Nash's *Songs For Beginners* was at number fifteen.

The break-up of the Beatles, which was still only slowly being accepted as a reality, seemed to be echoed in every area of the music business. In 1971 name musicians increasingly expected to be able to behave like jazz players, turning up in different line-ups as mood and personal ambition dictated. While this provided the music papers with the excuse for endless speculation about who was about to join whom, it couldn't entirely compensate for the fans' resulting loss of belief in a group as the teenage gang of their dreams. Into this post-Beatles vacuum came a new breed of individuals, either single performers in their own right or people so charismatic they were clearly going to burst the bounds of any band that sought to contain them. Three of these individuals, all of whom put their mark on the summer of 1971 in their different ways, were Londoners born and bred and each carried within him some of the worldliness and humour which is the birthright of all Londoners. None of them came from cockney stock. They were all, in one way or another, the children of immigrants, all were indulged youngest children, all had left school as soon as the law allowed, and all had entered the music business in order to avoid being condemned to a normal job. In July 1971 they all still lived in the city.

One of them lived right at its heart. If the theatregoers who were flooding out of the Saturday evening performances of *Hair* at the Shaftesbury Theatre that month had looked up as they crossed the road, they might have seen a light burning in one of the rooms on the third storey of a building housing a popular tourist restaurant called the Moulin Rouge. This was run by the Greek immigrant Stavros Georgiou and his Swedish wife Ingrid. The couple had divorced but remained together to run the business. Their three grown-up children were all involved in keeping the place going. The most reluctant of the three was their youngest, Steven.

Steven always thought he could be a pop star and had grown up close enough to London's Tin Pan Alley to have some idea how to go about it. Because at the time there was no precedent for anyone with a foreign-sounding name ever turning up among the homegrown pop stars on *Ready Steady Go!* or *Thank Your Lucky Stars*, Steven had changed his name to Steve Adams and then, in a further, curious jump, to Cat Stevens, in which guise he'd had his first hit 'I Love My Dog' in 1966.

Cat had a flair for writing pop songs that seemed more substantial than the standard fare. He had a good, romantic voice and the looks of a leading man. The sixties had been mainly about groups; at the time even the best-looking male solo artists still seemed like spare parts, mincing around for the TV cameras, shooting their lace cuffs, dandling microphones at the end of leads, simpering at the camera and finally railroaded into awkward, stool-perching duets with the variety stars who inevitably topped the bill on the TV shows on which they guested. Cat had further hits, 'Matthew And Son' and 'I'm Gonna Get Me A Gun' among them, and joined the last of the great ill-matched package tours where he appeared with Jimi Hendrix, Engelbert Humperdinck and the Walker Brothers before, weakened by overwork, he collapsed with TB and was hospitalized, thus bringing his first career to an end.

When Cat re-emerged in 1970 he was a regular James Taylor, newly legitimized via an actorish moustache. Now he played a guitar, sat on a stool, used his deep, dark eyes to project sincerity and sang older but wiser songs with names like 'Pop Star' about his past experience in the star-maker machine, and 'Lady D'Arbanville', inspired by his girlfriend, the nineteen-year-old American model Patti D'Arbanville, who had appeared in Warhol's film *Flesh* when she was just sixteen. Cat wrote the first of these songs when she left him to go back to the USA for a few weeks. In a world moving as fast as his was in 1970, such separations seemed endless. It wasn't until 1971 that you could place an overseas telephone call without the help of an operator. Even for a jet-setting rock star who was selling records in millions, the other side of the Atlantic was as remote as the moon.

For Cat there wasn't even time to find the luxurious pop star pad his earnings would no doubt have bought him. Thus he remained living above his parents' restaurant on the edge of Soho as he moved to follow up his success with *Tea For*

The Tillerman, his second album of original material in 1970, with *Teaser And The Firecat* without pausing for breath. He was twenty-two. Between the spring of 1970 and the summer of 1971, an interval of barely fourteen months, Cat Stevens recorded and released 'Where Do The Children Play?', 'Wild World', 'Father And Son', 'Tuesday's Dead', 'Morning Has Broken', 'Moonshadow' and 'Peace Train'. These are the songs that formed the core of his repertoire. These are the songs that people still turn out to hear him sing almost fifty years later.

Cat Stevens became enormously popular in 1971 for a number of reasons: he had a lovely voice, the kind of voice which was easy to live with, and an angelic face, the kind that seemed to match the sensitivity of his material. Many of these songs, such as 'Remember The Days Of The Old Schoolyard', 'Oh Very Young' and 'Father And Son', had a rueful tone to them which made them appealing to people in their mid-twenties who were suddenly discovering the hitherto unknown sensation of nostalgia. Songs like 'On My Way To Find Out' and 'Miles From Nowhere' hinted at an interest in matters of the spirit which would eventually become more explicit. Cat's position as the harbinger of consciousness-raising was further underlined in 1971 when he provided the songs for Hal Ashby's much-applauded *Harold and Maude*, in which young Bud Cort had a romance with seventy-nine-year-old Ruth Gordon, Cat's song 'Trouble' carrying the weight of a memorable and wordless final scene. (Interestingly, this was one of a number of films released in 1971 which played upon the subject of May–December love affairs. Others were *The Last Picture Show*, in which high school senior Timothy Bottoms made love to Cloris Leachman, the neglected wife of his teacher, and *Sunday Bloody Sunday*, in which Peter Finch and his wife Glenda Jackson were both having affairs with young artist Murray Head. Even more interestingly, this second film featured the first kiss between two gay characters in a mainstream movie. It was directed by John Schlesinger, who nonetheless felt it best not to declare his own sexuality. Minutes before they were due to shoot the scene, the crew had approached the director and asked in a pained manner, 'Is this really necessary?')

For all his interest in spirituality Stevens was no more above the pleasures of the flesh than his more obviously libidinous peers. Lots of beautiful women wanted to sleep with him and being a gentleman he didn't like to let them down. Carly Simon's big break came when she got the job of supporting Stevens at the Troubadour in Los Angeles in April 1971. On the same night, Stevens introduced her to her future husband James Taylor. But before that Stevens and Simon were briefly an item, at least in London, where she had come to record her second album with Stevens' producer Paul Samwell Smith. She wrote its title song 'Anticipation' about the experience of waiting for Stevens on their first date and subsequently also penned 'Legend In Your Own Time' about him. Within weeks she was sitting in a suite at the Gramercy Park Hotel in New York while a drunk Kris Kristofferson, whose songs 'Help Me Make It Through The Night' and 'Me And Bobby McGee' lorded it over every other singer-songwriter on the airwaves in 1971, sang a song he had composed just for her. It was called, for the avoidance of doubt, 'I've Got To Have You'.

The 1971 generation of singer-songwriters, finding themselves the biggest show in town, were increasingly infatuated
with each other and with the idea of figuring in each other's
songs. They measured their success in terms of pulling power,
in the bedroom as well as the concert hall, and didn't hold
back from writing about it. This was powerful medicine for
those doing the writing as well as those being written about.
In Sheila Weller's book *Girls Like Us*, Carly Simon describes
the experience of seeing herself through Stevens' eyes. 'He
would look at me and it would be dazzling, the reflection of
all things miraculous.'

In the same year Leonard Cohen penned 'Chelsea Hotel
#2' about his experience of sleeping with Janis Joplin. Many
years later, in a more modest time, he would apologize for the
indiscretion. According to the song, in Cohen's case Joplin
was prepared to break her rule about only sleeping with
handsome men. Janis used her celebrity to sleep with men
who ordinarily would have been out of her league. According
to Peter Ames Carlin's book about Bruce Springsteen Joplin
wasn't choosy about how famous her lovers were. She went
looking for the then unknown musician after spotting him
backstage at a show in Asbury Park and she clearly wasn't
after a long-term relationship. In the higher echelons of the
music business there had always been predatory alpha males.
Now they were joined by a handful of females no less keen
to leave their mark. As Joni Mitchell sang on the title track
of her new album, 'songs are like tattoos'. In Cohen's song he
further comforts Joplin with the disingenuous 'we are ugly
but we have the music'. Most of these performers were far
from ugly and they had the music as well. The looks of artists

like James Taylor, Cat Stevens and Carly Simon may not have been as laboured over as they might be nowadays but they were as much a part of their appeal for the fans – who would have been horrified to be characterized as such – as for the teeny-bop stars they were all so happy to condescend to.

TV was important to finding Cat Stevens a place in the hearts and homes of his audience. In July 1971, three months before the release of *Teaser And The Firecat*, he recorded a BBC TV special with producer Stanley Dorfman. Dorfman, who had come up through *Top of the Pops*, had carved out a niche at the corporation with half-hour TV specials that used the new colour technology on the new wave of solo artists. In 1970 he had recorded similar specials with James Taylor, Elton John and Joni Mitchell. In 1971 he recorded Neil Young when he was in the middle of touring the UK with the songs that turned up the following year on *Harvest*.

Cat Stevens Sings Cat Stevens was a classic of the genre. Its title was classic Dorfman, underlining the small miracle that these talented, charismatic people were also self-sufficient. Stevens was accompanied by Alun Davies, the guitarist who worked closely with him through this period, and bass player/percussionist Larry Steele. Nothing proclaimed Stevens' membership of the new generation of singer-songwriters as powerfully as the fact that he performed sitting down, something few had done in the hectic decade in which he had first made his name. Like Carole King doing *Tapestry*, this seemed to be less a performance than a session on which the audience were invited to eavesdrop. In Dorfman's programmes the audience were often seated behind the performers so that they could only be seen occasionally. The girls nodded sympathetically behind their shiny curtains of hair. The men with their horn-rimmed spectacles, wispy moustaches and heavy corduroys composed themselves into postures indicative of sage appreciation. This was not *Ready Steady Go!* but it was no less *au courant*. Some of the songs he played on that show were, in his words, 'really old'. That meant they had been recorded as long as four years before. His songs still had the simple hooks and sentimental appeal that they had when Stevens had no pretence to anything other than hit singles, but this time they seemed to have more weight.

Dorfman's was a format that framed the singer-songwriters of the time perfectly by allowing that they were interesting enough to be able to carry half an hour of TV time – inclusive of tuning-up, unrehearsed patter and mumbled asides, which were all part of the package – and flattering the audience by suggesting this music was worthy of the serious attention of adults like them. The deliberate modesty of the visual presentation was as important to the appeal of the music as the time-honoured razzle-dazzle of Ike and Tina Turner had been to theirs. Artistes appearing to reverse away from the limelight can be just as magnetic as those seeming to rush to embrace it. The new Cat Stevens albums all had cover paintings done by the artist rather than photographs of him. This achieved the double miracle of putting his artistry front and centre while appearing to withdraw his personality from the equation.

In late 1971 Penny Valentine interviewed Stevens for *Sounds* at the place in Fulham he'd finally moved into and asked him how he felt about the shift from groups to solo performers. 'The barriers have been broken down now, there aren't so many false idols,' he said, sounding all his twenty-three years. 'Musicians are now like friends of the people they play for. It's now like the complete expression of an artist that is becoming the medium, a period where Carole King emerges because she's beautiful but very plain and simple lyrically, where James Taylor becomes huge even though his voice isn't anything ultra-extraordinary, where Joni Mitchell and all these people can simply express themselves. So instead of the music holding them up, they hold the music up.'

Cat was describing the stardom that didn't appear to be stardom at all, which is what made it the most powerful form of stardom of all. It's the kind of stardom that keeps him in the public eye almost fifty years after he made the records on which that stardom was initially based. In his case the audience's sense of connection with that music has survived retirements, more than one religious conversion, a further change of name and repeated attempts on his part to deny the music and put it behind him. What Steven Georgiou did in the frantic eighteen months between spring 1970 and autumn 1971, now regularly used on the soundtracks of smart post-modern films and TV programmes beloved of Generation X & Y, has come to define him in a way he will never grow out of or get away from. Nothing Cat Stevens has done since July 1971 has counted half as much as what he did then.

Like Cat, the second of the triumvirate of London boys who wrote their name across 1971 was of immigrant descent. Mark Feld's father was of Polish/Jewish extraction and his mother was a market trader. Mark was cut from different cloth. He embraced the soft science of salesmanship as much as Steven Georgiou searched for an answer within himself. At the same time as Cat Stevens made the change from prancing pop idol to sedentary troubadour, Marc Bolan, as Feld had called himself since he made the mental move from Stoke Newington to Soho in the mid-sixties, was making a journey in the opposite direction.

In the winter of 1970 he was twenty-three and had been in and around the music business for seven years, trying to find a vehicle for a talent as much for chutzpah as for music. A genius when it came to matters of presentation, Bolan had devised Tyrannosaurus Rex back in the hippy days as an act that played sitting down. He got this idea from seeing a Ravi Shankar concert. Sitting down lent them the air of supplicants, and their music, acoustic strums and sub-Tolkien doggerel delivered in a simpering tone, was a sound for which the terms 'airy' and 'fairy' could usefully be employed. There was something in their album titles, *Prophets, Seers And Sages: The Angels Of The Ages* and *My People Were Fair And Had Sky In Their Hair . . . But Now They're Content To Wear Stars On Their Brows*, which seemed to defy the market to accept them. For over a year Tyrannosaurus Rex were an appendage of the DJ John Peel, following him as he spun records in the lower common rooms of colleges and universities the length of the land, sitting cross-legged on their rug with their bongos and acoustic guitars, looking for all the world like people who were simply too fine and pure to be bothered by the prospect of worldly success. The events of the year 1971 would render that idea hilarious.

Regardless of how long a pop career may be spun out for or how inflated the reputation that is constructed on its back, it is still owed to a period of inspiration which is relatively brief. The music business is one in which it is so hard to catch a break that all performers, no matter how elevated the claims they make for themselves and their art, have to be opportunists at heart. Once that opportunity is spotted they tend to pursue it with the single-minded determination of sharks, often in direct defiance of every claim they have made for being above such considerations. One of the key lines in John Lennon's interview with *Rolling Stone* in February had been 'you've got to be a bastard to make it and we were the biggest bastards of all'. This rule applies to all performers, no matter how charismatic or deficient in charm, but none more so than Marc Bolan in the year 1971.

They had one other thing which they could trade on. Even at their daffiest and most effete, Tyrannosaurus Rex always had hooks. Beginning in 1971, the newly abbreviated version of the group, now trading as T. Rex, placed those hooks in the shop window. *T. Rex*, the first album to appear under the more consumer-friendly brand name, was released a week before Christmas 1970. The cover showed Bolan and new percussionist Mickey Finn as pin-ups rather than hippy idols. For the first time he was carrying an electric guitar, a signifier like a Kalashnikov propped against the cave wall behind a contemporary holy warrior. The record did well, despite the fact that 'Ride A White Swan', which eventually rose to number two in the UK charts, wasn't on it. Bolan continued playing for the longhairs with his new partner and a bass player, but he was beginning to attract a different audience, one that was younger, more female and not overly bothered about the music he had made in the past.

In mid-January 1971, just three weeks after the release of the last album as a duo, the three of them plus drummer Bill Fifield went into Advision studios and recorded two songs. One of them, 'Hot Love', a title which had previously seemed about as likely to be applied to a Tyrannosaurus Rex song as to a Virginia Woolf novel, came out as their next single just two weeks later. One week after that it went into the chart at number thirty-one, rising to seventeen, then seven, and then climbing to number one where it remained for no fewer than six weeks, selling over a million copies in the UK alone. From this position it lorded it over the tawdry chaos of the British singles chart, over Ray Stevens' 'Bridget The Midget', Judy Collins' 'Amazing Grace', Neil Diamond's 'Sweet Caroline', Perry Como's 'It's Impossible' and the inevitable singles by John Lennon, Paul McCartney and George Harrison. For a younger generation who felt the sixties had never quite belonged to them, T. Rex at number one felt like the harbinger of a new age.

With the pressing prospect of an American tour to undertake in April, Bolan decided to make the drummer permanent. While 'Hot Love' was riding high and Bolan was doing his victory lap of press interviews the band were frantically rehearsing in the basement of an estate agent's in Pimlico. The make-do-and-mend, seat-of-the-pants reality of the way Bolan operated was always at odds with the grand pronouncements he would make in interviews. He decided to make a virtue out of improvisation. 'I love putting singles out,' he told *NME*. 'Lennon's into that and "Hot Love" is so right because it's so new.'

The American tour, which was made up of support slots way below the likes of Mountain, Johnny Winter and Humble Pie, could not have been further removed from the world of TV shows like *Top of the Pops* and magazines like *Fabulous 208* that were already banking on the emergence of Bolan to boost their ratings and circulations. This wasn't a struggle he was built for. Bolan was not one for digging out a valuable away point. Nothing sticks in the craw of a rising musician quite like the hopelessness of trying to convince people in one territory just how popular they are in another territory. The Atlantic seabed is littered with the whitened bones of those acts who thought their celebrity in the UK entitled them to a free pass in the USA. All too many have retreated as soon as it didn't work out, disguising their hurt pride behind a veil of Old World condescension. T. Rex were like that. They were altogether too thin a prospect to make their name on the concert stage. They needed a single market, preferably an overcrowded island over-served with media and with a fatal taste for triviality; they needed the unclouded focus of an entire family looking at the same flickering box on a Thursday night, ideally with father arriving in time to snort, 'Is that a boy or a girl?' And it needed to happen quickly. Marc's pop appeal was fading almost from the moment he realized he had it. Youth's a stuff will not endure, and no pop star seemed more built for youth than Marc Bolan.

Nonetheless he used his brief time well. Things were so busy for T. Rex in 1971 that there were no proper recording sessions for their breakthrough album *Electric Warrior*. Bolan's producer Tony Visconti simply pursued him as he toured America, slotting in sessions as and when the schedule allowed, very much as Ahmet Ertegun had done with Ray Charles fifteen years earlier. The songs were worked up in hotel rooms and on buses, arranged in the studio and put on tape while they were still hot.

They recorded 'Jeepster' and 'Monolith' at Media Sound in New York, with Robert Margouleff engineering, as he was doing with Stevie Wonder at the same time. In Los Angeles they hooked up with backing singers Flo and Eddie, the former Turtles Howard Kaylan and Mark Volman, who got them into Wally Heider's studio, there to add the swooning harmonies that made sure the finished records soared from jukebox speakers. This latter session produced 'Get It On', which went to number one in the UK in late July and remained there for four weeks. Renamed 'Bang A Gong', it also became a top ten record in the United States.

Although the records were full of smart touches such as Rick Wakeman's piano glissando at the beginning of 'Get It On', T. Rex were underpowered as a live proposition and without the double-tracking the singer's voice was clearly inadequate. But in the studio Visconti turned the weaknesses into strengths. Bolan's head may have been full of Tolkien but his heart was in the 1950s and he had a gift for re-tooling old riffs. 'Beltane Walk' was a straight pinch from Jimmy McCracklin's 1958 hit 'The Walk'. 'Get It On' quoted the line 'meanwhile . . . I was thinking' from Chuck Berry's 'Little Queenie'. When Visconti asked him for the title of the tune they were about to cut during a session at Media Sound in April, Bolan said 'Monolith', which seemed consistent with the self-importance of the time, but then couldn't stop himself adding 'or the Duke of Earl' with a snigger that gave away his teddy boy self.

Bolan's attitude to the fruits of success was similarly old-fashioned. That spring he and his wife June Child moved from west London to a chic address in London's Little Venice. He bought a white Rolls-Royce which he couldn't drive. At the same time he betrayed most of the people who considered themselves his patrons and all the things that people had assumed were his principles. John Peel, who had previously been his meal ticket, was dismissive about 'Get It On' in public and the two never spoke again. David Platz, the man whose Fly label had introduced him to the pop charts, was another he turned his back on. Bolan reneged on his contracts and in a few months that summer his new manager Tony Secunda scored huge advances for his artist from overseas territories on the back of the major success he was having in the UK. Everyone who worked with him that summer has memories of the charm wearing thin as success piled on success. He stopped talking about the power of meditation and openly espoused the joys of having lots of money. He began drinking and drugging, which had an immediate effect on his looks, his key currency. He began speaking in quotes. When he was trying to be serious he talked the most frightful balls. When he was talking about the glory of pop he sometimes seemed like the only sane man in town.

What particularly disturbed the conservatives of the hippy press was the way he cavorted for the cameras and the fans as if it was no longer enough just to play the music. 'I've always been a wriggler,' he told the journalist Keith Altham. 'I just dig dancing. It was just a bit difficult to wriggle when

I was sitting cross-legged on the stage.' Most of those who had been Marc's patrons during his hippy days recoiled at his new Becoming. Peel was foremost among them. He confessed himself puzzled as to why Marc had chosen to take this amplified route to stardom and said that he simply didn't think he was as good at the pop stuff as he had been at the material of his students union days. It's tempting to wonder whether Peel, like many members of a generation suddenly experiencing the disagreeable sensation of being made to feel old by the emergence of new youth, actually found himself liking the stuff and just couldn't bring himself to admit it. Like the students who had been interviewed storming out of Bob Dylan's concerts five years earlier they had turned that feeling into an elaborate moral fable where their beloved had been led astray by the money changers in the temple and the inevitable outcome had been betrayal. The truth, as vouchsafed to the young fans who went and bought *Electric Warrior* in droves when it came out in the autumn, was that T. Rex, insubstantial though they might be, sounded just fine, and 'Get It On', 'Hot Love' and 'Jeepster' soundtracked the youth club dances of the kids who were born in 1958 every bit as well as 'Satisfaction' had done for the people who'd been born in 1950.

1971 was the beginning of the era when you started to read about music before hearing it, particularly in Britain where the radio outlets were so limited. This meant that a whole generation of music buyers grew up forming opinions about music and the people who played it that were based on how those people set out to justify that music in print. In print it was easy to build an argument that Bolan's music was infantile because it saved you having to respond to it as pop music was surely intended to be responded to: in the moment, over the air, into the ears, via the pleasure centres and up from the floor through the feet. It wasn't music you could take seriously unless you considered the business of having a good time a serious business, which of course is one of those divides between rock fans and real people. The argument that raged over the corkscrew curls and be-glittered visage of Marc Bolan in 1971 is the same one that kept the British music press going for the rest of the century – the struggle between the instincts and the intellect, between pop and rock, between roundheads and cavaliers, if you must, the fight between what we think we ought to like and what we actually do like and the refusal to recognize the fact that this is music and in music the right sound will ace the correct thought every single time.

Those two ways of looking at the world collided over the head of Marc Bolan in a field in Essex on the weekend of the August Bank Holiday of 1971. The Weeley Rock Festival began as the initiative of local councillors who wanted to put their small town on the map and raise some money to relieve suffering in the newly independent Bangladesh. They staked out ground, identified the weekend of the bank holiday and put out some feelers for talent. The next thing they knew they seemed to have signed up most of the longhair bands in the UK. They booked far more than the running order could ever accommodate. Band followed band remorselessly all the way round the clock with literally no respite. Status Quo played at six o'clock on Friday morning. At three on Saturday morning some poor souls were voluntarily submitting themselves to the Groundhogs' recital of their new album *Split*. Rory Gallagher played his amplified blues at five in the morning, an hour no blues was ever intended to see. Tens of thousands of people turned up with home-forged tickets, thus saving themselves the £2 entrance fee. The Hell's Angels, who had been charged with security, clashed with the market traders, who had paid money for the concession to sell burgers. The stage was inadequate, the performers invisible to anyone further back than fifty metres. The bill was packed with proven crowd-pleasers like Mungo Jerry, Arthur Brown and Edgar Broughton. The audience were, like all festival audiences, sick with exhaustion. Only a sucker for hubris like Marc Bolan would have wanted to be top of this particular bill.

When he took the stage late on Saturday night he knew that the crowd was a disgruntled animal, made up of people inclined to regard him as a sell-out or somebody who appealed to their younger sister. They were tired and had used their last reserves of enthusiasm on the band that'd come on before him. 'Hello,' he said, introducing himself. 'You may have seen us on *Top of the Pops*.' This passive-aggressive stance was not the way to get the audience on side and his band weren't powerful enough to win them over either. At Weeley he was eventually forced into the humiliation of asking those in the crowd who clearly didn't like him to 'make love somewhere else', a choice of words which perfectly captures his combination of hippiness and conceit. Had he ever thought that he could be the new Beatles in the sense of being able to unite a disparate audience, his nine songs at Weeley disabused him of it. As he tried to push his performance uphill in the face of the indifference of what was not his crowd he must have known that he had made the cardinal error of thinking he could go on after the third of our trio of London boys, someone who burst out in the summer of 1971, came as close as anyone to filling the shoes of the Beatles and, had the expression existed, went viral.

Our third London boy had also been born above the business premises of a small tradesman of immigrant stock, in his case Scottish; he was also the youngest and most indulged of the family, but he was slightly older. He had come along three years earlier, during the Battle of the Bulge when the outcome of World War Two was not yet certain. He was a very different sort of personality. Any bohemian tendencies were kept well in check. Any spiritual yearnings were on tight rein. His choice of a new home said a lot about him. While Steven Georgiou wished to remain where he had grown up, at the centre of the known world, and Mark Feld was keen to live in a part of London which seemed appropriate for one of his grooviness, the London-based musician who lit up the summer of 1971 had moved that year to a half-timbered detached executive home in Winchmore Hill, a north London enclave noted for its air of bourgeois respectability and freshly made millionaires. His neighbours were footballers and car salesmen, not fashion designers and poets. This suited Rod Stewart just fine.

At the age of twenty-six he could afford the property thanks to his earnings as lead singer of the Faces, a strong live attraction in both Europe and the USA, and to the fact that he'd released two solo records which had been popular in the United States. These records showcased him as a great interpreter of other people's songs, particularly the folkie ones.

These he was steered towards by Paul Nelson, the rock journalist who looked after him at Mercury Records, and who had previously had a great effect on the young Bob Dylan. *Every Picture Tells A Story*, Rod Stewart's third solo album which came out on 9 July 1971, was about to propel him into a different orbit as a solo artist.

When success occurs in the music business it makes the person to whom it has happened feel as if they've woken up on a runaway train with no choice but to keep looking forward and hope that the impact when it comes isn't fatal. At a time when musical taste seemed on the point of splintering along tribal lines, *Every Picture Tells A Story* was the record everybody seemed to buy that year. *Rolling Stone* magazine named it their album of the year, which was one of the last cases where the critics' favourite was also the market's. By the end of 1971 Rod was making so much money that his accountant urged him to get rid of some of it by buying a house fit for the multi-millionaire he had now become. The workload of that year had been so intense that he had scarcely had time to see the inside of the Winchmore Hill property.

1971 was Rod Stewart's shining moment. It was not unpredicted. It was clear to everyone who had heard him since the mid-sixties that Stewart wasn't just an exceptional singer. He also had a genuinely distinctive, real voice, the kind that didn't need an instrument to justify itself, the kind that was capable of carrying a record on its own. There was something in the rasp at the back of his throat, the vibrancy of his middle range and his uncanny ability to put over a song instead of merely singing it that meant he would probably outgrow any group that would have him, whether that was the Shotgun Express, the Jeff Beck Group or, latterly, the Faces. Rod had that gift he shared with people like Sinatra and his own hero Sam Cooke: his singing voice sounded like the perpetuation of his speaking voice by other means, which meant that through music he was able to express the personality he had and build another one that people could grow to love. He modelled his singing style on Cooke, who used to sing above his natural register. It could have been this that made him sound as if he was reaching for something, gave him the yearning, little-boy-lost quality that struck such a chord, and made people overlook the fact that a little boy lost was clearly the very last thing he was.

Everything Rod sang sounded like an old song, and everybody prefers a song they already know. Even the new ones, like 'Mandolin Wind', sounded as though they'd been found rather than composed, which seemed to suit his artisan's attitude to his work. Possibly because he saw himself as a singer who could turn his hand to writing if need be, the standard of his songs was higher than those of his contemporaries who were contractually obliged to believe themselves capable of coming up with a dozen good new songs every time they went into the studio. Rod had the gifted hack's quality of being able to lend instant authenticity to songs. 'Gasoline Alley' was an expression he'd never heard until a girlfriend threw it into conversation but by the time he put it in a song it sounded as if he was singing the story of his life. Everything he did seemed human-scaled. There was nothing macho or aggressive about his voice. He sang songs for people rather than critics. He made everything sound like a campfire singalong. His delivery was an open invitation to join in.

At the time lots of other musicians seemed to be making things darker and more complicated than they needed to be, so when *Every Picture Tells A Story* with its cosy art deco cover appeared in the summer of 1971 it bridged the worlds of Tony Blackburn and John Peel, of AM and FM, of the *Record Mirror* and *Rolling Stone*, of the hippy record shops and the Woolworths singles counter, of Cat Stevens and Marc Bolan, in a way few things had done since the Beatles. At a time when pop songs seemed increasingly opaque, dealing in windy abstractions, confected memories of frontier America or described worlds and feelings which most people couldn't recognize, Rod's songs all made perfect sense to people. In the world of Rod Stewart your dad handed down his old suit and gave you some good advice about how you shouldn't let the ladies get to your money. The alternative society had clearly never penetrated the world around Rod Stewart's parents' sweet-shop in Archway.

As John Mendelsohn said when reviewing the record in *Rolling Stone*, 'he has it in him, has Rod Stewart, to save a lot of souls, to rescue those of us who are too old for Grand Funk but not old enough for those adorable McCartneys from being nearly consummately bored with the current rock and roll scene. It's not inconceivable that he could do it without even opening his mouth. He's physically sensational, the idol of perhaps three continents' heavy trendies, the most profound influence on rock and roll fashion since the Stones tour. He's the single most glamorous rock figure rolling.'

Every Picture Tells A Story distilled the promise of its two predecessor records. Its title song was a picaresque account of the sexual adventures of his late teens, the breakout hit recollected the delighted joy of being used as a plaything by a fleshy older woman, the story of 'Mandolin Wind' was less easy to discern but nobody ever went bankrupt singing about a man's debt to a woman, and the rest came from the same songwriting mills that supplied Motown, Elvis Presley and the public domain. You could have played that record to anyone and they would have found something to like in it and been pulled along in its genial wake. Rod knew that pop shouldn't seem like work. *Every Picture Tells A Story* was the creation of a man of the world. In its tunefulness and easy universality it was the nearest 1971 would get to the way 1969 had felt about *Abbey Road*.

Rolling Stone calling it their album of the year must have triggered widespread rejoicing in the ranks of the Faces. All groups contain within them the seeds of their own demise, and Rod's voice was a classic case. By 1971 his stature in the USA made it inevitable that the Faces would turn up in a city to find that the local promoter had billed them as Rod Stewart and the Faces, a red rag to any bull. All bands have within them, too, a burning issue, usually involving credit and attention, and the way they invariably deal with this is by doing anything but talk about it, instead conducting their negotiations behind their hands, via barbed lyrics or messages sent through managers, producers or girlfriends. The Faces were no exception.

Rod's position within the group was made even more parlous by the fact that he didn't play an instrument but did compose. When he went into the studio he relied heavily on the musicians' ability to vamp something which he could add words to. That's how 'Maggie May' was written, if 'written' is the expression. He used members of the Faces, with whom he was spending most of the time on the road and with whom he had developed a clumsy, appealing but characteristically British style. It would have been surprising if the repertoire of one didn't leach into the other.

Every Picture Tells A Story changed the lives of most of the people who contributed to it but it was only a net gain for Rod Stewart. Martin Quittenton, a former member of Steamhammer who was responsible for the acoustic stylings which showcased Rod best, ended up co-writing two of Stewart's biggest hits and then effectively retired from the music business. The man whom the artist credited ungraciously on the sleeve as 'the mandolin player out of Lindisfarne whose name I can't remember' was Ray Jackson, and he got a £12 session fee for playing the intro without which 'Mandolin Wind' is inconceivable. Before he finished the session they asked him to add some decoration to another song they had recorded but didn't feel would make the cut for the album. 'Maggie May' was only included on the record because it was running short. The feeling of the musicians and the record company was that it didn't have enough tune and it was pushed out as the B side of the first single from the album, Tim Hardin's 'Reason To Believe', where it remained until a radio station in Milwaukee flipped it and so started playing 'Maggie May'.

'Maggie May' started Rod Stewart's career. It became a pillar of his live act. It defined the beginning of his career as a mainstream superstar (and 'superstar' was a term that was just coming in to use) and the end of his career as the kind of rock star who found favour with the people who like to feel they decide on these things. It was responsible for Ronnie

Lane leaving the Faces, which made their eventual break-up inevitable. It defined the Rod Stewart persona, the lairy lad on the lam, with the roving eye, the heart of gold and an almost total lack of introspection.

Rod Stewart's 1971 workload beggars belief. The Faces toured the UK in January and then the USA for February and March, by which time their second album *Long Player* was released. In April they were back in the UK playing universities and recording TV appearances. In May, Warner Brothers released *It Ain't Easy*, an album by Rod Stewart and Elton John's old boss Long John Baldry; the two former juniors-made-good produced a side each. It had been somehow recorded during a week's break in their February tour. *Every Picture Tells A Story* came out on 9 July, at which point they went back to the USA to play, returning when 'Maggie May' was number one to play the Weeley Festival in Essex at the end of August where they so comprehensively upstaged the headliner Marc Bolan. Two weeks later they played alongside the Who at the UK's answer to the Concert for Bangladesh at the Oval cricket ground. In his autobiography Rod Stewart remembers driving home after the show to Winchmore Hill with his posh girlfriend at his side, realizing that he was now truly the rock star. In mid-November the Faces released *A Nod's As Good As A Wink To A Blind Horse*, their second album of original material in a year. Nobody could recall precisely how it came to be recorded. Rod's next solo album, which appeared a year after *Every Picture Tells A Story*, was called, with heavy sarcasm, *Never A Dull Moment*.

Apart from the music, Rod Stewart projected back to the music-buying public two great British passions which had never really been significant in pop music before: football and drinking. The football was a big part of Rod Stewart. Despite coming from the most football-crazed city in England the Beatles never advertised any interest in the game, nor were they expected to. By the time, many years later, that Rod Stewart had installed a full-sized football pitch at one of his homes in Epping Forest, British rock stars were expected to make a fuss about their attachment to the national game, even if they had to have a team suggested for them by a PR. It was one of those interests which was supposed to root them in everyday life, even if their everyday life had been spent in the back of a Transit. Elton John and Robert Plant both had history with football but Rod Stewart was the first rock star to use it as a way to define what he was and what he wanted from life. He had been good enough as a schoolboy to have a trial with Brentford, which was certainly enough to establish his bona fides in the sport. He would turn out for charity matches, boot plastic footballs from the stage during Faces gigs and have his photograph taken in his Scotland strip. His love of football was sincere but it also helped seal him in the affections of a mass audience in Britain, one that was inclined to find the pronouncements and pretensions of the big bands increasingly baffling.

There was no clear decision to render unto the Faces the things that were the Faces' and unto Rod the things that were Rod's. The Faces played Rod's songs as part of their stage act. They even backed him up when he appeared on *Top of the Pops* promoting his own singles. In later years Ronnie Lane said that Rod stole 'Mandolin Wind' from him. It would be impossible to prove that there wasn't some truth in this.

He had a look as well. The younger Rod Stewart had followed the dress codes of first the beatniks and then the mods, but in the Faces he slowly adopted a style of his own which was more than merely a set of clothes. It was a look that was widely followed. He dressed like a disreputable clerk out of Dickens, with his coxcomb of hair, his Fair Isle sweaters slightly too short and his shoes unsuitable for heavy work. On stage he planted the microphone stand like the spike on a pair of compasses and looked out at the crowd with the impudent air of a pitch invader the authorities have been unable to eject. He seemed to be perpetually in the process of falling over, and the quality he seemed to value most in the Faces was they stopped him doing just that. In their pictures they were always tumbling, leaning on each other like Edwardian bucks who had over-indulged in strong waters, as they clearly had. Blue Nun, Guinness, Green Chartreuse . . . they liked their drinks like they liked most other aspects of their life: lush and highly coloured. Now that the Rolling Stones had left the UK the Faces were the only gang in town, and they were enjoying the role big style.

At the end of July 1971 the Faces were playing in Long Beach, California and their record company threw the inevitable party for them. Dee Harrington was twenty-one and she was the kind of girl that only wealth and celebrity could have provided Rod Stewart with the chance to meet. The daughter of an RAF officer, she was well-bred totty, the sort that does something to boys like Rod Stewart. She claimed she was not familiar with his music, though girls like this, hanging around the film business and picking up a little modelling work, are old enough souls to understand the power of not letting on that they have. She must have known that he had the means to show her a good time because he produced a model of the yellow Lamborghini Miura that he had at home, a move which was both gauche and worldly. She left the party with him and within a month was installed in the house in Winchmore Hill. Not long after, he proposed marriage, and she accepted. They never got round to it. She was Rod's starter blonde. There would be many others.

By the summer of 1971 Cat Stevens, Marc Bolan and Rod Stewart had been in the music business for five years and in that short time had banked a lifetime of false starts, setbacks and hard lessons. They all had ambitions to make albums while being astute enough to know their career depended on hit singles. Because they rose to fame in the densely populated hothouse of the UK where the entire population was learning to sit down every Thursday evening to watch *Top of the Pops*, they knew the importance of being able to put themselves over on the small screen. A year before David Bowie appeared on the programme singing 'Starman', Bolan, Stewart and Stevens were already learning that it paid to flirt with the camera. They were the first generation of TV-savvy rock stars.

When the Beatles first arrived in New York in 1964 an American journalist had remarked that they were a 'new kind of people'. Bolan, Stewart and Stevens, the London Boys of 1971, were further varieties of new kinds of people: Bolan, the little guy whose talent could never measure up to his ambition; Stewart, the gifted cynic who knew the arts of survival and played his public image to the hilt; and Stevens, the genuine seeker trying to conceal the fact that behind his good looks he could be a little dull. Britain has produced many other pop stars in their image – fabulous nine-day wonders who deliver less than meets the eye, twinkling old-fashioned entertainers who the audience is convinced are singing for them, and patently sincere while painfully vague singer-songwriters. Before they came along there was nobody to compare them with. These three established new archetypes.

Marc Bolan never did make it internationally and he was not the kind of person to settle for reduced circumstances. When he died in a car crash in 1977 he was a disappointed man. Cat Stevens' spiritual quest climaxed on a beach in California in 1978 when a near-death experience led him to a religious conversion which twenty years later was to make him one of the few Muslims people in the West would know by name. At the time of writing he's making a comeback, still performing the songs he unveiled in 1971. The third of the trio of Londoners doesn't find a comeback necessary because he has never been away. Every year since 1971 has been a further victory lap celebrating his unsinkable popularity. Rod Stewart has had the life his school friends at William Grimshaw Secondary Modern could only have dreamed of. It's to his credit that he always looks as if he can't quite believe it. He's been a household name for over forty years, longer than Louis Armstrong. Like Armstrong, his move into the role of all-round entertainer tended to make people underestimate the unique talent that had earned him the right. At the time of writing he's still on tour. 'Maggie May' is still the song he plays more than any other. Not far behind it is 'The First Cut Is The Deepest', a tune written by Cat Stevens. To his great surprise, and ours, the job he took on to avoid having to take a proper job, the job that was supposed to offer the life expectation of a mayfly, has turned out to be the most enduring occupation of all.

JULY PLAYLIST

Rod Stewart, 'Every Picture Tells A Story'
T. Rex, 'Jeepster'
Cat Stevens, 'Tuesday's Dead'
Leonard Cohen, 'Dress Rehearsal Rag'
Graham Nash, 'Wounded Bird'
The Doors, 'Riders On The Storm'
Shuggie Otis, 'Strawberry Letter 23'
Alice Cooper, 'I'm Eighteen'
Dave and Ansell Collins, 'Double Barrel'
Harry Nilsson, 'Without You'

AUGUST:
WILD NIGHT

I n years to come the Concert for Bangladesh, the benefit concert that took place at Madison Square Garden, New York on the first day of August in 1971, would come to be viewed as one of the defining events of the era. It marked the emergence of a new senior league of rock stardom, as illustrated by pictures of George Harrison, Bob Dylan, Ringo Starr, Eric Clapton and Leon Russell performing together in a new ecumenical spirit. The event also provided the blueprint for every subsequent effort to harness the popularity of rock music and the perceived moral stature of the people who play it to benefit some deserving cause. This was the kind of thing folkies had always done. They were always ready to gather to protest against this or propose that and had a long tradition of linking arms at the end to belt out songs of unity and brotherhood. However, they were just folkies and it was unlikely that anything they did would move the dial of public attention in the wider world or end up on the front pages that landed on America's porches and Britain's doormats. But once a Beatle was involved and the show was at Madison Square Garden, all that changed. This was rock turning respectable for the first time.

The Concert for Bangladesh was as hastily improvised and as ill-considered as every other decision made in the accelerated atmosphere of 1971. The conflict between Pakistan and its reluctant citizens in faraway East Bengal had been simmering ever since the Indian subcontinent was partitioned at the end of British rule after World War Two. The independent state of Bangladesh had been declared in March 1971 and the declaration had been followed by a combination of massacre and natural disasters that left thousands dead and millions displaced or threatened with starvation. It's likely this would have had no more impact on George Harrison than any of the other convulsions the wider world was going through in 1971 if he hadn't noted the effect it had on his friend and teacher Ravi Shankar, with whom he was collaborating on the soundtrack of a documentary called *Raga*. The Indian maestro's father had been born in Bengal and he felt the events keenly. Harrison's engagement with the subject was initially as a result of this. 'Bangla Desh', his song about the catastrophe and the need to draw the West's attention to it, began 'my friend came to me with sadness in his eyes'. Over ten years later, when Bob Geldof felt similarly moved to do something to alleviate the suffering in Ethiopia, the only musician he could go to for advice was George Harrison. 'Do your homework,' Harrison told him, knowing that's what he had failed to do.

In the summer of 1971 the twenty-eight-year-old Harrison was uniquely well placed to make a big gesture on behalf of rock. He was well on his way to selling three million copies of an album which was entirely without precedent. *All Things Must Pass* wrapped its message of the mutability of the material world in swooning pop anthems which were multi-layered to such a degree that the entire universe seemed to be humming in accord. All summer you could walk under ladders at the top of which decorators would be distractedly singing the 'Hare Krishna' refrain from 'My Sweet Lord', try on clothes in boutiques to the accompaniment of 'The Art Of Dying' or pay ten new pence to hear 'What Is Life' from the pub jukebox. The message may have been profound by pop standards but at its core was the same kind of elementary pop tune that had inspired the Beatles ten years earlier, this time arrayed in acoustic finery and presented as a serious work of art. The other thing that made *All Things Must Pass* unique was that it was three records in a cardboard box. Never mind that the third record comprised studio jams which were shabby even by the complacent standards of the form, the sheer bulk of the package seemed to match the heft of Harrison's ambitions. John Lennon may have been the one shouting his message from the rooftops but if anybody could be said to have been carrying the weight of the Beatles into 1971 it was the group's youngest member.

It was Shankar who first had the idea of doing a fund-raising concert. As soon as Harrison said he would like to join in this became a rock concert, and because he was a Beatle this could only be a big one. As soon as the papers found out Harrison was going to appear there was always the chance of a partial or complete reunion of the band that the world seemed to be missing like a phantom limb. In 1971 the mainstream media, as represented by the newspapers and television, didn't care about pop music. The serious papers didn't cover it and even the popular press rarely went near. What the media did care about was the Beatles. The prospect of their reunion was a story they could run endlessly and the upcoming concert, which was announced in mid-July, only a couple of weeks before it was due to happen, gave them fresh licence.

The first person who agreed to play was Ringo, who was in the middle of shooting the spaghetti western *Blindman* in Spain. The second was Klaus Voorman, the Beatles' old Hamburg friend, widely tipped to replace Paul McCartney in the event of the group re-forming. The third was an Oklahoma-born pianist and band leader who had spent the last few years labouring in the mills of the Hollywood session scene and was finally emerging as one of the key figures of the year. In his book *The Tipping Point* Malcolm Gladwell theorizes that to start a cultural epidemic you need three types: mavens, who know a lot of things, connectors, who know a lot of people, and communicators, who know how to frame a message. In that sense Leon Russell was a one-man epidemic.

Russell had been the opportunist behind Joe Cocker's *Mad Dogs & Englishmen* tour, the hottest ticket of 1970. He was the sloe-eyed figure with the Old Testament hair and ringmaster's top hat who looked as if he ought to be wrestling snakes in a revival tent. He was the musician whose signature rolling piano, fervent tambourine and chorus line of wailing hot mamas seemed to bridge the divide between the barrelhouse and the Pentecostal church and satisfy what was a contemporary taste for a sound that seemed both comforting and social. He also made the sound that the young Elton John was, by his own admission, emulating on records like *Tumbleweed Connection* and *Madman Across The Water*. Russell wasn't bothered about that as long as his telephone kept ringing.

One of the people who rang him was Bob Dylan. Heralded by Columbia's marketing department as a release from 'new singles artist Bob Dylan', as if it hadn't been 45s that first brought him to the attention of a mass audience less than ten years earlier, 'Watching The River Flow', the Russell-produced and -accompanied single which was Bob Dylan's only fresh release of 1971, was a rollicking repudiation of those people who gathered round his door insisting that he had a duty to be the spokesman for a generation. It began with the line 'What's the matter with me? I don't have much to say', which made his position very clear.

Having secured the services of a safe pair of hands like Leon Russell, Harrison decided that he wanted Eric Clapton to play guitar, a comparatively high-risk decision. Nobody knew better than Harrison that Clapton was holed up in his country house at Hurtwood Edge, devoting most of his energy to killing himself with heroin. He knew this because Clapton was laying siege to Harrison's own wife Pattie Boyd and had taken to snorting heroin when she declined to leave her husband and join him. While this was going on Clapton was also conducting affairs with Boyd's older sister Paula and Alice Ormsby-Gore, the teenage daughter of Lord Harlech. Alice was drinking two bottles of vodka a day because there was not enough junk to feed both his habit and hers. Clapton's depression, which was rarely far away, had come in like a storm front following the unaccustomed experience of being rejected by both Pattie and the public who had failed to buy his 1970 album *Layla*, possibly because they weren't altogether clear who Derek and the Dominos were. Since it was Harrison who had suggested they should give themselves a tongue-in-cheek name it's possible he felt some guilt about that. Emissaries were despatched from Beatles offices to go round to Clapton's house and convey this massive can of worms across the Atlantic.

Those applauding this noble fundraising endeavour might have narrowed their eyes had they known that Clapton would only come to New York if it could be guaranteed that he would have access to a supply of his favourite junk, known as White Elephant. Hence while Harrison was appearing in front of the world's press and talking about peace and brotherhood he had minions running round the less salubrious parts of New York City trying to make sure that the aristocratic teenage girlfriend of this over-privileged English guitar player would be able to secure his supply of drugs. They would have been shocked if they had known how closely the underground had come to depend on the underworld. The public at large associated heroin with the parts of New York in which it would never dream of setting foot, districts such as those visited by the young Al Pacino in 1971's *Panic in Needle Park*. Movie theatres were simultaneously showing the trailer for *The French Connection*, a new Gene Hackman–Roy Scheider film in which they played two disgruntled New York City cops condemned to spend hours drinking bad coffee in nasty cars on garbage-strewn streets as they stake out a gang of French criminals who plan to bring a shipment of drugs into the city. New York has never seemed a less glamorous, more threatening, more charmless place than it did that summer thanks to movies like *The French Connection* and *Klute*.

Harrison took out insurance against Clapton's non-appearance by getting Peter Frampton along to rehearsals. He didn't tell Frampton, who had just left Humble Pie, that he was being used as first reserve. That's something Frampton only figured out later. The beauty of having a Beatle at the top of the operation was that everybody else fell into their place in the hierarchy. Other spear carriers included members of Badfinger, one of the acts Harrison was supposed to be piloting through the uncertain waters of Apple Records, where they were invariably the victims of well-intentioned interference. They were called upon to play some of those banks of acoustic guitars which made up the *All Things Must Pass* sound and to provide backing vocals. Jim Keltner was brought in as second drummer to provide a backstop for Ringo, and Billy Preston to play the organ, the rest of the holes being filled by members of Leon Russell's big band. Nothing apart from the hiring of Clapton was being left to chance.

This commitment to bringing in as many musicians as it would take to reproduce the sound of a highly processed studio album like *All Things Must Pass* was without precedent. By the time the Beatles had got round to building up their records layer by layer they were no longer intending to play them live so the need never arose. The Concert for Bangladesh set the template for what became the rock recital, a presentational approach that was to grow in direct proportion to rock's sense of self-importance, the audience's demands that performances sound like the record they heard at home and the extent to which it was felt that the occasion demanded some sort of grand gesture.

In 1971 there was no template for doing this kind of show but necessity dictated that decisions had to be reached quickly. Once it was decided to put on a concert to raise money for disaster relief the story was that 1 August had been chosen because a mystic had decided it was a propitious date. In fact it was the only date that was available, 'Disney on Parade' being due to open in the Garden the following day. It was decided there would be two shows, which had been a standard way of presenting concerts in the sixties. The first would be at 2.30 on the Sunday afternoon. The following one would begin at eight o'clock in the evening. There were no plans to broadcast the show live on radio or to record it for TV. None of the US or British networks were set up to do such a thing, nor would they have had the technical capability. The show was eventually captured with a view to a cinema release by three movie cameras. The master shot from the back of the Garden was largely unusable, as was the angle from the side. The footage that survives was mostly shot by the camera in the pits.

The anticipation around the show was in the main generated by the fact that two Beatles were going to be on stage together for the first time since 1966. Harrison did talk to Lennon about his playing but as soon as John said there had to be a role for Yoko, Harrison wisely stopped raising the subject. He knew that people would be less kindly disposed to the charitable intentions of the show if Yoko Ono was ululating in the vicinity. Having instigated the painful and protracted business of dissolving the Beatles it was clear that Paul McCartney could never have been involved.

The appeal of the Beatles getting back together, or at least not splitting up, didn't have much to do with nostalgia, which was yet to be seen as something applicable to pop music. (In 1971 the only compilation of the Beatles' greatest hits was *A Collection of Beatles Oldies*, a record put out in 1967, only about a year after the newest of the so-called 'oldies' had been recorded. Catalogue marketing was undeveloped.) Pop music lived in the present and it was expected that if the Beatles did ever perform again, something they hadn't done for more than five years, it would be to play new tunes, not to re-play their old favourites.

The ghost of their old group hovered over all four individuals that summer. It didn't matter how much they protested, they were locked together from the point of view of business whether they liked it or not. In the light of this, the success of 'My Sweet Lord' wasn't merely of interest to Harrison. Their deal with Apple and Allen Klein meant that the former Beatles' solo records were, to all intents and purposes, Beatles records. John Lennon might not like the idea of Harrison selling more copies of *All Things Must Pass* than he'd managed to sell of his *Plastic Ono Band* but he knew that he profited from those sales, just as he was credited as the co-writer of such McCartney tunes as 'Yesterday' and others he would have been mortified to be associated with.

Sitting athwart their joint fortunes was Allen Klein. He was the only source of advice and counsel for John, George and Ringo. McCartney had failed in his attempt to get his brother-in-law John Eastman put into Klein's position and had therefore taken steps to dissolve the partnership. While the lawyers were arguing the rights and wrongs all that joint money was frozen. Meanwhile the record business was becoming bigger and more profitable than it had been at any stage in the previous decade. The big money was in advances against future royalties, based upon the promise of what might happen rather than the reality of what had already happened. Klein knew that the one product he would always be able to get a huge advance for was a new Beatles album. Therefore he was concentrating on performing the key duty required of the manager of any group, which is to prevent a group doing what all groups are always on the point of doing – splitting up.

Everybody within the Beatles orbit would at some point in 1971 have imagined that an album containing 'My Sweet Lord', 'Isn't It A Pity', 'Jealous Guy', 'Imagine', 'Another Day', 'Back Seat Of My Car', 'Uncle Albert/Admiral Halsey' and Ringo's 'It Don't Come Easy' would be, if anything, better than *Abbey Road*. During the spring of 1971 the press had filled the news vacuum with speculation that the three of them might re-form with (on the names-out-of-a-hat principle) Klaus Voorman as bass player, which meant the blameless German had to temporarily go into hiding. In the era of Blind Faith, Crosby, Stills, Nash & Young and Ginger Baker's Airforce, where star names could be traded from one band to another as simply as pro athletes might be shipped from one team to another, this helped pass many a long winter evening in many a student hall of residence. This idea that groups could be reduced to separate atoms was brilliantly expressed in the English rock magazine *ZigZag* where editor Pete Frame put his draughtsman's skills to good use constructing sprawling family trees that traced the constantly changing line-ups of such restless aggregations as John Mayall's Bluesbreakers or Jefferson Airplane.

Some people saw this as a healthy symptom of the over-due jazzification of rock in which a group was merely a temporary alliance. The members of the Beatles had never looked at life like that and from the moment they broke up George Harrison was uncomfortable with life on his own. The Beatles' performing experience had been as narrow as it was deep. When Lennon played the rock and roll festival in Toronto with his thrown-together Plastic Ono Band in 1969 he had thrown up before going on stage because of his nerves. He'd spent thousands of hours on stage but he'd never spent any time with anyone but the Beatles. He'd always looked to his right and seen the same faces. George felt much the same. Although all of them took every opportunity to describe what they had created as 'just a band', at the same time they had great faith in the power of that band's brand and worried that people would not accept them as readily if they were out on their own.

Harrison's junior position in the Beatles' second-line had given him the opportunity to shine without needing to be a load-bearing wall. As soon as he was free from the Beatles he'd rushed to join Delaney and Bonnie's Friends where his contributions were largely unheard as he merged among the teeming multitudes at the back. In the Beatles his comparative youth had allowed him to play the mulish adolescent when it suited him. The fact that he was in a group with the two most talented and productive songwriters of the age meant that only his best songs got on their records, which shielded him from criticism. Unlike Lennon and McCartney in their very different ways, George Harrison was not a leader. All groups pretend to be democracies while depending on one member being prepared to endure the derision of the others by leading. Harrison was never comfortable being that person.

As the prime mover behind the Concert for Bangladesh he was in an even more exposed position. Had he been a few years older he might have been sufficiently cautious not to take the risk. In this situation he had to advocate for something which had never been tried before, a high-profile charity concert featuring rock superstars, while keeping those stars on side when many of them, like Clapton, were wrestling with terrors of their own and all of them were entertaining the single thought that goes through the mind of a performer once outside a familiar zone of operation: how will this make me look? Whatever anxiety they felt could only be a fraction of what Harrison was feeling. When Bob Dylan said he was nervous about going out in front of the twenty thousand people in Madison Square Garden, Harrison had to remind him that he had never been out front in the Beatles, had not yet toured with his solo material, and that the few steps towards the microphone at centre stage were going to be a very, very difficult journey for *him* to make.

Dylan's appearance at Madison Square Garden on 1 August was to prove a pivotal moment in his career. He had just moved back to New York City after spending five years living in Woodstock in upstate New York. In these sylvan surroundings people sometimes broke into his house in the middle of the night, hence his wife and children lived in fear of nutcases, drug casualties and random truth seekers. He wasn't alone. Rock legends didn't yet have security. On 22 May the staff at John Lennon's house Tittenhurst Park, where he was recording his new album, had found one such wide-eyed apostle sleeping in the grounds. The meeting between Lennon – by his own admission 'just a bloke who wrote some songs' – and this desperate man who believed that all those songs were addressed specifically to him was filmed. In this man's beseeching eyes, where the childish hopes of the revolution jostle with years of drug use and probably mental illness, it's possible to see what made people like Lennon and Dylan determine that in future they would build higher walls and remain behind them.

Dylan tried to reassert control over his life by moving back to New York, taking a town house at 94 Macdougal Street close to the folk haunts of his early Greenwich Village days. The real-estate decisions of rock's superstars frequently betray how far removed they can be from normal life, and this was one such. This attractive, commodious, double town house had the notable disadvantages of sitting tenants in the basement and a front door which opened directly on to the street. This alone would have made life difficult enough, even without the attentions of A. J. Weberman. He was the man who came into Dylan's life in the year 1971 and became a byword for the vampiric tendencies of those people who think their affection for songs grants them ownership of the person who writes them.

No accounting of the wages of fame has ever dared invent a pest like A. J. Weberman. Nowhere in the history of film or sport do you find people like these vampires who began to attach themselves to rock. Weberman was a ghoul, a bore and probably a clinically ill person, who felt the imminent arrival of the Alternative Jerusalem licensed him to suspend the laws of human decency. In early 1971 he felt entitled to lead demonstrations outside Dylan's Macdougal Street house with other members of his self-styled Dylan Liberation Front and on occasions to actually enter his house without an invitation, then to go through his bins in an attempt to decode where Dylan was 'at', as if that could be done and as if the location of Bob Dylan and his mental disposition was something that could be said to have an urgent bearing on the lives of people in their twenties all over the world.

People like Dylan and George Harrison were used to attention but this was a new dimension of torment. Most of their lives as public property had been spent in the back of large cars or in hotel suites where they suffered along with comrades in arms who had signed up for the same life. Now that they were married and were attempting to spend more time at home building a family life they saw these threats through the horrified eyes of their wives and children and wanted nothing more of them. Weberman's demonstrations didn't simply disturb Dylan's peace and frighten his children; they also made him a pariah among his neighbours. He tried to build a wall at the back to protect his children's privacy. He had no

248

permission to do so, and when he came back one weekend he found his neighbours had knocked it down.

Having been largely out of sight for five years and having made regular adjustments to his appearance with beards and spectacles and having never in the first place been a big TV star, Bob Dylan's name was more famous than his image. He hired John Cohen, the photographer who had taken pictures of him when he first came to New York, to take pictures of him back in the city. He made sure Cohen brought a long-lens camera with him so that he could be photographed from across the road, apparently merging with the crowd. Throughout his life this has been his dearest wish, to escape observation in order to be able to observe. To an extent he had succeeded. In its report on the Bangladesh concert the *New York Times* stated that one of the security guards looked at this man in his late twenties who was walking on stage to such tumultuous applause and asked if this was a member of the Beatles he didn't recognize. At the end of May Dylan had gone to Israel for a few days and was photographed at the Wailing Wall in a skullcap, which fuelled speculation that his next 'thing' might be religion. On the beach at Tel Aviv he was buttonholed by the *Jerusalem Post*. Even the Israeli licensee of his recordings invaded his privacy by taking an ad in the paper congratulating him on his thirtieth and welcoming him to the country. There seemed to be no escape from attention. If that was the case he concluded he might as well go back to work.

Dylan was one of the first of the famous names of the sixties to reach this watershed age. His father had recently died, which gave him something further in common with Harrison, whose beloved mother had passed away the previous year. Dylan didn't release a new album in 1971, though he did put out *Bob Dylan's Greatest Hits Vol. 2*, which was to become the best-selling record of his career. One of the reasons it sold so well, apart from providing the new generation of rock LP buyers with an LP of rock by Bob Dylan that they could buy, was that it was packaged in colour pictures of Dylan taken at the Concert for Bangladesh in which he'd appeared with his trademark corkscrew curls, denim jacket and harmonica holder, like an older but wiser version of the man they had once regarded as the spokesman for a generation. He wasn't singing country. He wasn't doing anything odd with his arrangements. On 1 August 1971 he sang 'Hard Rain', 'Blowin' In The Wind', 'It Takes A Lot To Laugh, It Takes A Train To Cry', 'Love Minus Zero/No Limit' and 'Just Like A Woman' and could not possibly have been more 'on brand'. When Harrison had turned to the wings to introduce 'a friend', which was soon adopted as the folksy way to refer to a superstar, he hadn't been at all confident that Dylan would be there. When he went off half an hour later, the Concert for Bangladesh could officially be declared a success and Dylan could suddenly see a way to present himself in the new world of enormous halls and crowds which stretched to the horizon.

The Concert for Bangladesh did more for the careers of the people who appeared on the stage and for the profile of the nation it was named after than it did for the people it was intended to benefit. Even the most successful benefits don't come close to equalling what governments and relief agencies can mobilize. Money went missing, either into the pockets of security guards who let fans in without tickets, into the accounts of agents and middlemen, or, most notably, into the coffers of the tax collectors of the United States and the United Kingdom. Harrison had assumed that his sincere desire to raise money to benefit the people of Bangladesh would overcome all obstacles. The record companies didn't see why they should be compelled to release the music packaged in the way that Harrison wanted, particularly with an emaciated child on the cover. The IRS took the view that since the charity wasn't specified until after the concert, the revenue from the concert was income and as such had to be taxed. The British Treasury didn't see how they could waive the purchase tax on the live album just because a Beatle asked them to. Accustomed to being able to command and make it so, Harrison was suddenly discovering a world of adults where his writ didn't run.

This confirmed a lot of his suspicions about the way the world worked. He was already watching the extraordinary worldwide success of his hit 'My Sweet Lord' turn into a legal and financial quagmire. He had started composing the song while on tour with Delaney and Bonnie in 1970. It was initially worked up with Delaney Bramlett, who expected to have some share of the songwriting credit. Bramlett was the first one to point out that it sounded like the Chiffons' 1962 hit 'He's So Fine'. This was drawn to Harrison's attention more than once but he kept going, probably hoping that wiser counsels would intervene to keep him from himself. After all, Phil Spector, the expert on girl group hits of the early 60s, was overseeing the Harrison session. Early reviews also pointed out the resemblance but nothing was done to avert the problem that was more certain to loom the more successful the record became.

The old music business saw 'where there's a hit, there's a writ' stresses the importance of timing and captures the time-honoured wisdom that the lawsuits only arrive once there's a large pile of cash on the table. On 12 February 1971, when 'My Sweet Lord' had been number one in the US, UK, Spain, Sweden, France, Germany, Ireland, Norway, New Zealand, Australia, Austria and the Netherlands, lawyers representing Bright Tunes Music began an action for plagiarism of their property, which had apparently been written by Ronald Mack, the manager of the Chiffons in 1962. At what point in the process the grace note upon which the eventual court case subsequently hinged had been introduced and by whom nobody would ever know, but by then the case was pop music's equivalent of the Jarndyce v. Jarndyce case in Dickens' *Bleak House*, a remorseless engine of profit for the lawyers and a source of unending pain for the participants; it was a machine with a pitiless will all of its own.

Accusations of plagiarism are occupational hazards for successful songwriters, particularly prominent ones. There are only a limited number of combinations of chords, only a certain number of ways you can push around one-syllable verbs and personal pronouns to form them into a twist on a well-known phrase or saying and then mould it into three verses, a chorus and a bridge before somebody somewhere thinks or pretends to think you have deliberately sat down and copied their previous composition and tried to pass it off as your own. If that had been his intention Harrison would probably have chosen one of the thousands of great girl group records that had never troubled the charts and languished in undeserved obscurity. If that were the case Harrison would not have begun 'Something', his most successful song, with a line straight out of 'Something In The Way She Moves' by James Taylor, an artist who happened to be signed to a label of which he was a director. If that were the case he would have taken steps to cover his tracks. He didn't.

The argument with Bright Tunes was purely about dollars. Allen Klein tried to set up a deal whereby Harrison could buy Bright Tunes but the owners had no incentive to sell, and certainly not quickly. The case didn't come to court until 1975 and was not concluded until 1998, by which time Harrison had severed his relationship with Klein and Klein had secretly bought Bright Tunes for himself; he was the only person in the whole deal who knew how much 'My Sweet Lord' had earned and therefore knew how much his former client, who had been forced to admit to 'unconscious plagiarism', would eventually have to hand over to the company he now owned. Whether this was duplicitous or not it was presumably not what George Harrison had had in mind when he went along with John Lennon's wish and handed over the direction of his career to Klein.

All Things Must Pass was the biggest success any former member of the Beatles would ever put his name to. It was critically acclaimed and commercially successful. It was one of the few rock albums that can claim to have combined a certain amount of wisdom with old-fashioned pop catchiness. It was the high-water mark of a sound which married the euphoric drive of early sixties jukebox music with the dense, thick rock sound of 1970. When George Harrison stood there at the end of the Concert for Bangladesh at 10.55 on 1 August 1971, he was the biggest solo star in music. Had he been a politician his approval ratings would have been off the chart. People had always loved his music but now they felt that he had elevated pop above its tawdry history into something altogether finer and more noble. He had done something that nobody had ever done before, and he had apparently done it on his own. He had eclipsed the Beatles.

But whereas for Bob Dylan the experience of going on stage at Madison Square Garden provided a glimpse of a future for him, a future in which his legend grew in direct proportion to the size of the audience, for George Harrison it was more like an ending. The amazing thing is that he would never do anything quite so resounding ever again. He never followed *All Things Must Pass* with anything even remotely comparable. It was difficult to tell whether he was trying. Everything Harrison recorded and wrote after the year 1971, with the possible exception of the first Traveling Wilburys album in the late 1980s, was pale and tentative. It was as if he no longer entirely believed in himself, as if he was no longer capable of playing the confidence trick of writing a fresh song. All songwriters like to ask 'Where did that come from?' when a new song strikes them. They joke that if the song is any good it must have been written already. For George Harrison, thanks to his bittersweet experiences with the 'My Sweet Lord' case, that could never be a joke again.

*

George Harrison wasn't the only one for whom 1 August 1971 was an ending masquerading as a beginning. For the week of the Bangladesh concert Badfinger appeared to have it made, rubbing shoulders with superstars, going to the after party at Ungano's and getting mentioned in all the press coverage. The tragic thing was that none of this star power ever actually transformed their fortunes, and the comedown was cruel. Badfinger's first gig following Madison Square Garden was at Huddersfield Polytechnic. Their whole subsequent career was to be dogged by the worst kind of luck.

They had been the first group signed to the Apple label and were widely regarded as having some of the DNA of the Beatles with two strong songwriters. Paul McCartney had written their first hit 'Come And Get It', but they really didn't require star patronage. Then Harrison had taken a particular interest in them. When in 1971 he offered to re-record some of the tracks from their new album *Day After Day* with him as producer, they cancelled an Australian tour so that they could fit around his schedule. In the end he didn't have time and so the album, which had been started with Beatles engineer Geoff Emerick, was completed with the new whizz-kid Todd Rundgren and was released just ten days before Christmas, which is as good a guarantee of oblivion as anything.

Badfinger's biggest score of 1971 came with Harry Nilsson's version of leading songwriter Pete Ham's 'Without You', which was number one in the UK at the end of the year. The Concert for Bangladesh made them well known but they never recovered their momentum and what money they did make was salted away by their new manager Stan Polley. In 1975 Pete

255

Ham killed himself, accusing Polley in his suicide note of being a 'soulless bastard'.

The shadow of 1971 didn't stop there. Eight years after Ham's death Tom Evans also committed suicide following a bitter argument with the other two members of the group about the money from 'Without You'. The song was a huge hit all over again two decades later in a version by Mariah Carey. The legacy which was the cause of such pain and destruction continues to mount remorselessly. 'Baby Blue', which comes from their 1971 album *Straight Up*, was the final song on the final episode of the hit TV series *Breaking Bad* in 2014 and in this form will play for ever on the internet, far too late to benefit any of the people who wrote it.

A great deal of the music recorded in 1971 has had an afterlife that none of the people who played it could have predicted. As the giant hits of that era become dulled by familiarity there's an increasing demand for less well-known songs that nonetheless seem to share some of the same DNA. In the case of Badfinger the years of retrospective success have if anything caused more anguish than the years of obscurity.

The day after the Concert for Bangladesh a report appeared on the front page of the *New York Times* along with a picture of George Harrison, Bob Dylan and Ringo Starr. This was a significant departure for the Grey Lady, which rarely touched on pop music. Even the London *Sunday Times*, which was comparatively breezy, only covered rock via the condescending forceps of its 'popular music' critic Derek Jewell. The *Guardian* had just begun taking reviews written by a student called Robin Denselow who had berated them for their lack of interest in what seemed to him a vital part of the life of young adults. Still, they were more likely to let him review rock bands if he told them they were folk. The adult world regarded mainstream pop music as primarily of interest to teenagers, a tribe who didn't read newspapers.

The *New York Times* report used the word 'Beatle' eleven times – a clear indication of their angle on the story, which was in the nature of an anthropological report on a visit to a strange tribe of erstwhile screamers, all wearing dungarees and T-shirts. 'I'm shaking like a leaf,' confessed seventeen-year-old Debbie from Brooklyn, who had gained entrance to the concert by paying $18 to an official who sneaked her and a friend past the ticket-takers. The paper also got a quote from the policeman in charge, who provided the obligatory reflection on the miracle that so many people should require so little arresting.

The show was well received, as much for the worthiness of its objectives as the power of its performances. Given the seriousness of the cause that had brought them there, this seemed only right. Given the fact that the main players were, by the standards of the time, staring at the prospect of middle age, it also felt right for them. What nobody noted was what was going on beneath the surface, which was the introduction into pop of a number of values that hadn't been evident before. Instead of screams and hysteria there was reverence, continuity, respect, formality, even worthiness. For the first time some of the songs of the Beatles were being performed outside the context of the Beatles. At the same time Bob Dylan was taking some of his songs that were most associated with the ferment of the sixties and performing them as if they were classics. Leon Russell was doing the same with the Coasters' 'Young Blood', a song about under-age sex. The whole show had the feeling of a ceremony with both performers and audience getting used to adapting to changed roles and the establishment of a canonical view of rock.

Not all the people running the American music business that week adopted the same selfless note, nor did the people packing the record shops have their thoughts on higher things. James Brown had the number one soul single with 'Hot Pants (She Got To Use What She Got To Get What She Wants)', which encapsulated his trademark marriage of carnal and mercantile. 'Switched On Bach' was at the top of the classical listings, although it was expected to make way for the newly released soundtrack of Luchino Visconti's *Death in Venice*, the popularity of which owed less to the ethereal nature of the music than the vision of Björn Andrésen, who played Dirk Bogarde's teenage love object in the film. The Bee Gees were at the top of the US singles chart with their soupy 'How Can You Mend A Broken Heart'. T. Rex were at number one in the UK with their bouncy 'Get It On'.

A world away from all this in Los Angeles, Joe Smith was building a record company which seemed removed from the razzle-dazzle of the record business as it was known in New York. His Warner Brothers Records operation carried itself more like a prestigious publisher of books for the discriminating reader or a boutique advertising agency than a mere vulgar peddler of pop tunes. Under the guidance of Smith and Mo Ostin, both of whom were Sinatra-generation ring-a-ding-dingers by upbringing, the company was signing up maverick talent with little regard for its immediate commercial prospects and was marketing that talent via a wry, self-deprecating house style subsequently aped by hundreds of independent labels.

Warners began truffling for that talent within a hurled newspaper of their Burbank headquarters, which is how they came to recruit such an interesting bunch of movie business brats, showbiz kids, beatnik progeny and wilful eccentrics. There was songwriter Randy Newman, whose uncle was a giant of movie theme music; Lowell George of Little Feat, whose dad sold furs to movie stars; Bonnie Raitt, whose dad had been a star of musicals on stage and screen; Ry Cooder, the one-eyed son of a folk music-singing lawyer from bohemian Santa Monica; and, strangest of all, Van Dyke Parks, a child prodigy of classical music who'd come from the South to star opposite Grace Kelly and wound up writing the words to Brian Wilson's rococo 'Heroes And Villains'. They were all absurdly talented and utterly intractable. They made brilliant records of the kind nobody had made before, records that came in striking covers and attracted glowing reviews but sold only a handful of copies. They sold so few of Van Dyke Parks' lushly orchestrated song suite 'Discover America' that one of their adverts boasted about how much it had cost the company. Randy Newman's voice was so difficult to market that Warners' advertising genius Stan Cornyn took an ad saying 'his voice is quite something – when you get used to it'. They were introducing into the marketing of pop records a quality that had never previously been thought relevant – good taste. Their marketing challenged you to share it.

The first Little Feat album, which had come out in January 1971, was gloriously all over the place, from a raging medley of two Howlin' Wolf tunes featuring George and Ry Cooder locking antlers on the glass finger guitar, through 'Brides Of Jesus', which proposed a previously unmapped connection between Procol Harum and the Band, to the almost Brechtian knockabout of their own 'Crazy Captain Gunboat Willie'. According to Ben Fong-Torres' book about Little Feat, that first album sold only twelve thousand copies. Nevertheless in 1971 the world of rock was small enough, the fact that their bass player Roy Estrada was a former member of the Mothers of Invention counted for enough, and the cover, which saw them in front of a Santa Monica mural, was cool enough for it to seem that everyone who cared about that kind of thing had heard it. Warners were even prepared to have a go with avant-garde blues shouter Captain Beefheart, who had already tested the courage of even the most forgiving longhairs with 'Trout Mask Replica' and 'Lick My Decals Off, Baby'. For a short while in the early seventies it didn't seem entirely beyond the bounds of possibility that they might be able to get him on to the radio and into the charts.

It's unlikely that Steve Ross ever heard Captain Beefheart or Van Dyke Parks or Ry Cooder. Ross was the person responsible for underwriting this unprecedented flowering of creativity within the record business. No hipster he. Forty-four at the time, he had been born Steven Rechnitz in Brooklyn, had married into a funeral home business and then diversified into limousine hire and car parking. By 1969 his company Kinney was big enough to be able to buy Warner Brothers-Seven Arts, which encompassed an ailing movie studio and a directionless record operation. Noting that the growth was all in music – even Warner Brothers' biggest movie hit when he took over was *Woodstock* – he put all the emphasis on that side of the business. Most of Ross's background was in businesses with small margins. He loved the idea that entertainment was all about sudden windfalls and therefore he paid his record company executives handsomely and encouraged them to bet big.

The person who probably saw the future most clearly was actually working on the company's lowest rung at the time. Ted Templeman had been the drummer in Harper's Bizarre, a preppy close-harmony group that had hits with cotton-candy revivals of 'Anything Goes' and '59th Street Bridge Song'. When the group broke up he got a job as a 'tape auditioner' for Warner Bros for $75 a week. Nobody really knew what Templeman was up to but every chance he got he would slip into sessions for people like Frank Sinatra and Elvis Presley to learn different ways of doing things.

Templeman had a feeling he knew how to produce records and could help bands sound better. He eventually heard a biker band called Pud from the Bay Area that he thought had potential. He produced their first record which flopped in April 1971 but it was cheap enough for Warners to give them another go. At the same time Templeman had been brought in to handle the already impossible Van Morrison. Van had done his album *His Band And The Street Choir*, which contained the airplay favourite 'Domino', in New York and Warners had released it in November 1970. Like Bob Dylan, Morrison had decided there were now too many tourists in Woodstock and under the spell of his new wife

Janet Rigsbee, who had changed her name to Janet Planet to signify her oneness with the universe, he moved against his will to the other side of the country and settled in Marin County north of San Francisco. Here the couple briefly lived in a sylvan fantasy with a horse called Moondance, a fantasy rather awkwardly celebrated on the cover of his 1971 album *Tupelo Honey*.

Like its predecessor, *Tupelo Honey* showed the tuneful, relaxed side of Morrison. Templeman had a combination of skills rare in a producer: the ears to recognize good tunes and the diplomacy to be able to handle the people who came up with them, even if they were people most would be tempted to punch. He was smart enough to know he had to record the vocals during the brief window before Van lost his patience and then deal with everything else when he had gone home. It was the sound of first 'Street Choir' and then 'Tupelo Honey', and the blithe spirit of 'Domino' and 'Wild Night' plus that Irish show band line-up with horns, which caught the imagination of lots of other musicians that year, most notably young Bruce Springsteen back in New Jersey.

Looking back in later years, the equable Templeman vowed 'I would never work with Van Morrison again as long as I live. He's a marvellous talent but he's fired everyone who's ever worked with him and he understands nothing about the recording process.' He remembered that when *Tupelo Honey* was finished he spent two days working on what he considered a perfect mix of the album, only to have Morrison put out an earlier, rougher version. Two days after the record came out Morrison rang him in the middle of the night to say that he'd been wrong. 'I could have wept.'

The lessons Templeman learned in 1971 paid back when he worked with more pliable talents as the record business continued to turn into an industry and began to understand how to turn inspiration into formula. One of the guitarists on Morrison's album was a young San Franciscan player called Ronnie Montrose. In 1973 Templeman recorded his band Montrose, developing a signature pop metal sound which he later took to the bank with Van Halen. The second album he made with the biker band, now called the Doobie Brothers, started off with a song called 'Listen To The Music', the first of a string of Templeman productions that would go on to enjoy a seemingly eternal commercial life. It was formula music but done in the best possible taste.

Warner Brothers wasn't allowed to enjoy its position as the sole artist-friendly record company for long. In August 1971 David Geffen was preparing to launch his own Asylum label. Geffen was twenty-eight and had already made the first of many fortunes as the manager of Laura Nyro and Crosby, Stills, Nash & Young. In a milieu where most people prided themselves on a laid-back approach, Geffen was a bulldog. Attempting to get a deal for his new client the twenty-three-year-old songwriter-performer Jackson Browne, he took him to play for Columbia boss Clive Davis in his New York office. Halfway through the meeting Davis's secretary came in to say that his boss was on the phone. Geffen turned to his client and said, 'Pack up your guitar.'

Geffen was a grandstander. That's why acts like Joni Mitchell and Crosby, Stills, Nash & Young were eager to work with him. He might have been a jackal but he was their jackal. They would go into his office just to hear him shout at people on the phone on their behalf. Geffen spent months shopping Browne around to the majors and got nowhere; finally, he did as Ahmet Ertegun suggested, which was start his own label. The 11 September *Billboard* announced the establishment of Asylum Records. Joni Mitchell would be moving there from Warners but Geffen's protégée Laura Nyro wouldn't. The item said Joni would be joined by Jackson Browne, John David Souther and an 'as-yet unnamed group featuring Bernie Leadon, Randy Meisner, Glenn Frey and Don Henley'.

Asylum was so named because it was supposed to represent a shelter away from the depredations of the majors. Since in each case Geffen was the manager, the music publisher and record company, which is rarely in the best interests of the artists, the wheels were bound to come off at some point in the future; but as 1971 drew to a close the David Geffen–Eliot Roberts management firm and their accompanying Asylum label was the pinnacle of the new funky glamour.

Jackson Browne was sent into Crystal Sound Studios with the engineer who had recorded James Taylor, who at the time had the top male solo album, and the rhythm section that had played on Carole King's *Tapestry*, the top female solo record. Browne took a break in the middle of recording to take his jeep round Utah and Arizona and came back with the basic idea of a new song which began 'I'm running down the road, trying to loosen my load'. When he played it for his neighbour and fellow struggler Glenn Frey the latter was desperate to have it for his new group, which by now had fresh dentistry thanks to Geffen and were called the Eagles, and so with Browne's permission he finished it.

He took it to London in February 1972 where they recorded it for their first album.

The window of opportunity that opened in 1971 for anyone who could be described as a singer-songwriter allowed entry for musicians from every point of the compass. One of the breakthrough albums released that month was *Just As I Am*, the debut of the gifted, diffident, entirely gimmick-free Bill Withers. The thirty-three-year-old was still working on the payroll of an aircraft construction firm in 1971 when his song 'Ain't No Sunshine' began climbing the charts. The whole first album, which also included 'Grandma's Hands' and 'Harlem', was recorded in just three sessions of three hours each. They thought it would take four sessions but so apparent was the perfection of what they had achieved that producer Booker T. Jones was able to cancel the last one.

Bill had wise eyes, wore a grandad vest and carried an acoustic guitar which he hadn't actually owned for a year before he was at number one. His songs about economically disadvantaged, honest people in the ghetto, people who were sometimes weak and sometimes strong, people who sometimes drank too much, went off the rails and in one extreme case killed themselves, weren't aimed at a pre-existing category. This new market for long-playing albums was still too new to have become criss-crossed with familiar tracks for future marketeers to follow. Record companies, management firms, producers and artists themselves hadn't yet set themselves up to base the new thing on the old thing. Most of what was being done was being done for the first time. In the case of Bill Withers it was also being done for the last time.

Warner Brothers even decided to take a risk on a solo album from Gram Parsons, who was best known at the time for his drinking and drugging and had been asked to leave Keith Richards' rented home at Nellcôte because he was preventing the guitarist from concentrating. In October in New Orleans he got a call from Chris Hillman, in the midst of a tour with the Flying Burrito Brothers, during which they recorded the ragged but appealing 'Last Of The Red Hot Burritos'. Hillman suggested Parsons come out and join them for a couple of shows in Maryland. Hillman also suggested Parsons investigate the lissom, long-haired folk singer he had seen a week earlier in a club in Washington. The folk singer, who had a child to look after, wouldn't take the train to Baltimore so Parsons, accompanied by his model wife Gretchen whom he'd recently married, was compelled to go to Washington. It was there he met the woman on whom his legend eventually came to depend, Emmylou Harris.

1971 was full of such accidental meetings between troubadours. Kris Kristofferson was on a flight to Chicago when he met the sixties balladeer Paul Anka who told him he had recorded one of his songs. Once in Chicago, Kristofferson went to see Anka's show in the lounge of an expensive hotel. In return, Anka came to see Kristofferson in a club where he was being supported by a local songwriter called Steve Goodman. Anka was impressed by Goodman's own 'City Of New Orleans' and a song about a returning Vietnam veteran called 'Sam Stone', which was written by Goodman's friend. Goodman took Anka and Kristofferson to another club where the friend, a mailman called John Prine, was having a nap between sets. As a result of that encounter both men got record deals. When Atlantic released Prine's first record in the autumn of 1971 critics were caught between applauding him for his compassionate portrayal of real American lives and adding him to their list of new Bob Dylans, where he took his place alongside Loudon Wainwright III whose second album, featuring such songs as 'Saw Your Name In The Papers' and 'Motel Blues', was satisfying the market's need for sardonic story songs in the style of Dylan.

Wainwright was married to Kate McGarrigle, the Canadian folk singer whose sister Anna had written a song called 'Heart Like A Wheel' which she played at the Philadelphia Folk Festival of 1970. The Texan singer Jerry Jeff Walker was in the audience and he subsequently played it for Linda Ronstadt who instantly recognized it, even in his truncated, imperfectly memorized version, as being something she needed to sing. In 1974 it became the title track of her biggest album. Those days of double-platinum and 'adult-oriented rock' were far away in the future. This was the last summer of the folk club, when you could still find extraordinary talent, talent apparently without precedent, growing wild at the side of the road.

These folkies and roots music kids were different stock. Unlike the Bangladesh stars George Harrison, Eric Clapton and Leon Russell, they were often middle-class kids whose parents had encouraged them in buying a guitar and learning folk songs on the grounds that these songs had to be better than 'Twist And Shout'. They had different hinterlands, and in their efforts to map a place for themselves in this new post-Beatles world they went searching in the heritage. Hence American music in 1971 suddenly had room for all sorts of arcane styles, for Taj Mahal's country blues, the antic cowboy jazz of Dan Hicks and his Hot Licks, Bette Midler's campy torch songs, the art songs of David Ackles and the acapella of the Persuasions, Laura Nyro and Labelle. Promoters and press were prepared to give anything a go and the audience would apparently try anything once. It was the best of times because in many respects it seemed to be the first of times.

The 1971 level of productivity was never going to be matched in the future. It took another five years for the silky soul of Boz Scaggs to break into the charts but a lot of the elements were in place in 1971 when he put out one album, *Moments*, and recorded another, *Boz Scaggs And Band*, at Olympic in London. Bands like Scaggs', even more than Van Morrison's, were introducing elements of all kinds of American vernacular music from the big band stylings of Bobby Bland to the country of George Jones, and seemed to have polish which bands hadn't previously had. Members of Jefferson Airplane, who only two years earlier had been putting America up against the wall at Woodstock, were now members of Hot Tuna playing 'Candy Man' and 'Keep Your Lamps Trimmed And Burning' in a style that owed a lot to traditional fiddle music and at the same time didn't sound the same at all. Similarly the Flying Burrito Brothers supercharged their honky tonky music with the steel guitar of Al Perkins and were touring with a set that combined bluegrass protest songs with bar-room versions of Wilson Pickett. The new darling of the stoner set was the first album by Commander Cody and His Lost Planet Airmen who sang in praise of the life of the working man and his hot rod Lincoln. In August Gene Clark released *White Light*, a solo album that was finally worthy of his uniquely moving sing-ing style. Commercially it didn't amount to much but it was well received, as was the first album by Judee Sill, which came out with the first tranche of Asylum releases in September. The world of rock was still small enough for a song like Sill's 'Jesus Was A Crossmaker' to become familiar to most people who read the music press and listened to the right radio programmes.

The world of rock musicians was small enough to ensure that a prodigiously talented player and singer like Nils Lofgren was constantly in demand. In 1971, having just come from working with Neil Young on *After The Gold Rush*, he released *1 Plus 1*, the second record by his band Grin, while also becoming a temporary member of Crazy Horse whose first album had been released in February. This featured the first version of Danny Whitten's song 'I Don't Wanna Talk About It'. Almost ten years later this would be an enormous hit for Rod Stewart; at the time it went largely unnoticed. Like 'Heart Like A Wheel', 'City Of New Orleans', 'Life On Mars?', 'Doctor My Eyes', 'Tiny Dancer' and scores of others it was one more letter posted in 1971 that didn't arrive until years later. It would take the world a long while to catch up with the number of great songs with which 1971 was so generously endowed.

AUGUST PLAYLIST

George Harrison, 'What Is Life'
Bob Dylan, 'Watching The River Flow'
Leon Russell, 'Stranger In A Strange Land'
Crazy Horse, 'I Don't Wanna Talk About It'
Little Feat, 'Willin''
Judee Sill, 'Jesus Was A Crossmaker'
John Prine, 'Hello In There'
Gene Clark, 'For A Spanish Guitar'
America, 'Ventura Highway'
Neil Diamond, 'I Am I Said'

SEPTEMBER: FAMILY AFFAIR

E arly in September 1971, a young man called Stuart Love, who worked for Warner Brothers in the New England area as a promotion man and talent spotter, booked a day in Intermedia Studios at 331 Newbury Street in Boston. The studio had only opened the year before, bringing sixteen-track recording to the Boston area for the first time. One of the albums that had been recorded there earlier in the year was the second one by Loudon Wainwright III, which featured 'Motel Blues', 'Saw Your Name In The Papers' and 'Nice Jewish Girls' and led, via the inclusion of one song on a budget sampler album in the UK, to his first UK tour, during which he supported Status Quo – presumably a surprise to both acts.

There were four young men in the band Love planned to make a demo with that day in September. They were Jerry

Harrison, a twenty-one-year-old keyboard player studying architecture at Harvard; his friend and fellow student Ernie Brooks, who played bass; David Robinson, who had grown up locally and played drums; and the band's leader, a rangy, clean-living nineteen-year-old called Jonathan Richman, a guitarist and singer and, like Robinson, a local boy.

Collectively they were known as the Modern Lovers, a name that hit an unusual note. At a time when new bands tended to pick names like Gentle Giant, Supertramp, Little Feat, America and Atomic Rooster, any name that began with the definite article seemed attractively retro and intriguingly arch. Formed the previous year, the Modern Lovers' performances at local colleges and clubs had left audiences more puzzled than excited. The group's lean, driving sound, which owed something to one-off hits of the sixties like 'She's About A Mover' and '96 Tears', was placed at the service of Richman's unique vision, which had been shaped under the spell of the Velvet Underground.

The Velvet Underground had been formed in 1965 by Lou Reed and John Cale. Reed had worked as a jobbing songwriter in New York's Tin Pan Alley while Cale studied the music of the avant-garde. Via this unique combination of limitations and inclinations they arrived at a droning sound which appealed strongly to a very small group of people, one of whom was Richman. Jonathan had been so smitten by the unvarnished realism of the Velvet Underground's songs that at the age of eighteen he had moved to New York in order to be near them. But whereas most people who moved in the Velvet Underground's orbit had tastes, inclinations and sometimes vices that placed them beyond the pale of so-called 'straight' society, Jonathan Richman had first become known in the Boston area for taking his guitar to Boston Commons and singing in a style halfway between skiffle and Tiny Tim, a style that defied people to decide whether he should be taken seriously or not. Speaking to Joe Harvard of the Boston Rock Storybook website in 1997, Jonathan talked about how he developed his unique style, which was the pop music equivalent of the naive school of painting. 'You feel kinda naked and everything. So you just sing. But actually it isn't that you just sing. You just SING. Because it's life and death. You just SING like you're in a bullring. You don't care if you're on-key or off.'

The songs Jonathan sang were similarly out of step. Many repudiated the alternative society that had grown up since Woodstock. In fact if Jonathan was rebelling against anything, it appeared to be rebellion. One of his songs, 'I'm Straight', was a direct plea to a girl, beseeching her to ditch her hopeless hippy boyfriend and accept Jonathan's suit for the good reason that he didn't do drugs. Another was about still loving his parents and the old world – a genuinely revolutionary sentiment in the age of Aquarius. Another was such an artless hymn to the delights of driving around Boston and calling at his favourite shops that even the people who liked the song, having grown so used to a life of ease that they no longer ascribed it any value, could only assume that he was being ironic. He wasn't. Jonathan looked at seventies America with the hungry eyes of a Third World asylum-seeker. The big song was called 'Roadrunner'.

The Modern Lovers recorded three tunes that day in September 1971, 'Roadrunner', 'Someone I Care About' and 'Hospital', and the tape impressed Love's bosses at Warner

Brothers sufficiently that the following year they invited them to California to record with the Velvet Underground's John Cale, by then working for the company as an A&R man and making his own record, *Paris 1919*. By the time Warner Brothers made up their mind to take up the option in 1973, two years after Love had first flagged them up, Richman had lost interest in the sound of the original Modern Lovers and preferred to make quieter, more consoling music.

When Jonathan got to California in 1972 he was introduced to Gram Parsons. The two bonded over their admiration of the simple sentimental songs of the Louvin Brothers. The friendship between the two is more of a surprise to latter-day scholars of American music than it was to the two musicians. In 1972 this pair had no idea that the open terrain over which they ranged so freely would one day be criss-crossed by barbed-wire fences between categories, and every shade of musical style would become a 'format'. At the time Gram wasn't aware he was singing something that would come to be called 'alt-country'. For his part Jonathan had no idea that what he was doing would one day be called 'punk rock'.

Richman wasn't the only category pioneer trying to get noticed that summer of 1971. One evening the *Melody Maker* journalist Richard Williams came home to his London flat to find that somebody had called and left a tape with his girl-friend. The reel of tape was in a small box labelled 'Roxy' and bore the name 'Bryan' and a phone number. Bryan Ferry, the would-be rock star who had dropped the tape off, had chosen Williams because he was a journalist who had a reputation for appreciating musical experimentation. Ferry, who was working as a ceramics teacher at Holland Park

Comprehensive and living in a rented flat near Kensington High Street, suspected that the music on the tape was the kind that might benefit from being explained. What Williams heard seemed promising enough for him to phone Bryan and arrange a meeting at the Golden Egg in Fleet Street. This led to a short feature in the *Melody Maker* at the beginning of August, which focused on the fact that the members of Ferry's group, Roxy, were the kind of people who wouldn't normally be found in rock bands. For a start their average age was twenty-seven and at least two of them had a background in the art world.

Rock musicians had spent time at art college before but they had usually dropped out when presented with the option of life on the road. The members of Roxy hadn't simply come to pop following art school. They had deliberately chosen pop as a way to pursue their career in art, which had certain implications. They were threatening to bring art school to pop. 1971 seemed like a propitious time to make that switch. The palaces of high culture were finding room for the products of cheap media – the exhibition 'Aargh! A Celebration of Comics' was running at the Institute of Contemporary Arts in London at the beginning of 1971 – and it seemed only right that pop should open its glittery portals to many of the ideas being promoted in the art schools, particularly since those schools seemed less concerned with teaching students how to produce something than with teaching them how to think.

The members of Roxy (it would be changed to Roxy Music to avoid problems with an American act called Roxy) had not come together in the usual way. They hadn't spent much time in the back of vans. The leaders were Ferry, who had studied Fine Art under Richard Hamilton at Newcastle University, and Brian Eno, who had studied Art at Ipswich and Winchester and had an interest in music despite not being able to actually play an instrument. Eno could operate a rudimentary synthesizer and he made tapes, which were as important as anything else to a group wishing to apply the montage approach to music. They were joined by Andy Mackay, who was classically trained and also taught at Holland Park, and later on by accomplished guitarist Phil Manzanera. The last member to join the group was drummer Paul Thompson, who was labouring on a building site at the time. Thompson had a very different background. In the end it was his driving drumming on songs like 'Virginia Plain' and 'Do The Strand' that made Roxy Music popular, every bit as much as any of the clever cultural steals or kinetic presentation.

However, as they developed in late 1971 they were careful not to position themselves as just another rock band, notable for a particular soloist or the qualities of its vocalist. They wanted to be appreciated as an art project might be appreciated. Roxy Music were producing music by people who had spent a lot of time listening, reading, watching and thinking; therefore the appropriate selection from their library of influences mattered as much as anything. The right thought aced the right performance and the right gesture aced everything. Ferry was not really a musician. He had not played any kind of musical instrument until a few months before the band began gigging. All the conversations about Roxy Music which took place in 1971 as they found management in the shape of old Harrovian Mark Enthoven and a record company in the shape of Island were conducted against a background of references: not just the obvious ones like Motown but also the avant-garde ones like the Velvet Underground, the non-musical ones like Richard Hamilton and the pre-rock ones like Ethel Merman. It was an inclination that was to become even more explicit as they became more visible. It was clear that Roxy Music's hairstyles and clothes had been thought about every bit as much as the sound. This was pop as a branch of the gestural arts.

This was a new aesthetic at work, in which qualities like authenticity and sincerity were no longer self-evident virtues. Indeed it was possible for things that were plastic and fake to be every bit as admirable. They had been talking like this in the art schools for some years but in the world of pop, which liked to think of itself as having graduated from an obsession with surfaces to a more mature understanding of what was important, this was all new. And art graduates weren't the only people from the so-called legitimate world of the arts to start trying the doors of pop. At the same time that Bryan Ferry was selling his vision of a new kind of pop music in London and David Byrne was meeting up with Chris Frantz at the Rhode Island School of Design and thinking about a band called the Artistics, other people were moving into the direction of pop, this time from the world of classical and avant-garde music.

In 1971 Ralf Hutter and Florian Schneider, who had studied classical music at the Schumann Conservatory in Düsseldorf, moved into a workshop space in Cologne to start making the second record by their group Kraftwerk. The process of making this music had more in common with

279

the workshopping approach of improvised theatre than the performance-oriented approach of traditional rock. As was the case with Roxy Music, it was difficult to know whether the name applied to the group or the project. As was the case with Roxy Music, rhythm was eventually the key element with Kraftwerk. At the time they didn't have a drummer so they started to experiment with a cheap drum machine.

At the same time the two principals of Can, Holger Czukay and Irwin Schmidt, who had studied under Stockhausen and had already made two albums, were given free use of a castle in Westphalia by a wealthy patron. They moved in and, free of noise restrictions, played all day and all night. What came out of it was a double album called *Tago Mago*. Like the Rolling Stones, who were doing roughly the same thing a few hundred miles nearer the Mediterranean sun, this music was more about the groove than songs. This music, which was increasingly known as 'krautrock' and even marketed as such by the people who made it, was taken up by John Peel and others. What nobody for a moment suspected was that within this music being made by these balding beatniks with their rehearsal-room pallor would be the spoor which would lead to the dance music of the twenty-first century and a revolution quite as big as the one that had brought along rock and roll.

These new directions didn't have much in common with the romantic flourishes of what passed for 'progressive' music in Britain or the shifting rhythmic underpinnings and baffling time signatures of the jazz-rock which was still popular in the United States. Just as big band jazz had reflected the bustling optimism of the railway age and rock and roll celebrated the erotic individualism of the motor car, this new music, with its emphasis on surrendering to the joy of anonymity, was anticipating a computer age which few people saw coming in 1971.

Between completing the recordings for the Velvet Underground's fourth album, Loaded, and its US release in September 1970, Lou Reed left the group. His last performance with them was at Max's Kansas City in late August. It was recorded by the socialite and Warhol sidekick Brigid Polk, who was in the habit of committing her entire day to tape. Polk's recording captures other scene makers like Jim Carroll calling for a double Pernod and also the half-hearted applause of the small number of people who were there. Even at Max's Kansas City, even among their own people, the Velvet Underground were rarely more than coolly received.

Also in the audience that night, keeping a low profile in case any of the scene makers should wonder if he was that guy they had seen on some TV pop show, was nineteen-year-old Alex Chilton from Memphis, Tennessee. He had just come out of a two-year switch-back ride as the voice and face of a hit singles band called the Box Tops. The experience had left Chilton exhausted, old before his time and looking for a way back in to the music business on something like his own terms. It wasn't surprising that he should be another one attracted by the music of Lou Reed, which seemed simultaneously nostalgic, tender, bitter and just too disturbingly simple for most people.

In February 1971 Chilton returned to Memphis to sort out his divorce. While there he renewed his acquaintance with an old friend Chris Bell who had been developing his own music locally and played in the band Icewater. Chilton saw Icewater play at the Veterans of Foreign Wars in downtown Memphis and was persuaded to throw in his lot with them. As a base of operations Memphis had much to recommend it. Bell and Chilton were both from comfortably-off Memphis families who didn't mind subsidizing them to spend their days playing music and smoking dope as long as they made some concession to shaping up by signing on to a course at a local college. Chilton and Bell were also fortunate in knowing John Fry, another well-established local who had his own recording studio called Ardent and was prepared to let them use downtime at no charge to work out their music. Furthermore Ardent did a lot of work for Stax, and in 1971 Stax were selling so many Isaac Hayes records that they needed to get rid of some of the cash. Stax had to broaden their base and told Fry that they needed a white rock band. Fry said he had one.

In the summer and autumn of 1971 Christopher Bell, Alex Chilton, Andy Hummel and Jody Stephens worked up their material and began to put it on tape. No unknown band had made a record in quite this way before. The autonomy most bands had to earn was this group's from the beginning. Fry taught them the rudiments of engineering, supervised the cutting of the basic tracks and then tossed them the studio keys. In an era when studio time was a precious resource even for established bands, giving a bunch of youths this kind of carte blanche was unheard of.

The band took their name, Big Star, from a local supermarket. Some of their Memphis friends considered this a

Right: The news of Jim Morrison's death in Paris in July takes days to come through. His posthumous *Rolling Stone* cover begins his iconic era.

Below left: The Weeley Festival begins as a local fundraiser for those affected by the war in Bangladesh but is soon swamped by every long-haired band in the land.

Below right: Marc Bolan, the UK's new king of pop, gets a lukewarm reception at Weeley. He is more at home in the *Top of the Pops* studio. Elton John is seemingly at home everywhere.

Below: In a year when attractive singer-songwriters sleep with each other and write songs about it, it's almost inevitable that Carly Simon should stop off at Cat Stevens en route to James Taylor.

Rod Stewart's solo success guarantees that his days as lead singer of the Faces are numbered. Even before 'Maggie May' is a huge international hit, that success had bought him a luxurious home with supercars in the drive. By the end of 1971 his accountant is telling him to move to somewhere bigger.

Above: Taking on the leadership of the Concert for Bangladesh in August places George Harrison between the spiritual world, as represented by his mentor Ravi Shankar, and Mammon, in the shape of his manager Allen Klein.

Left: Bob Dylan's appearance alongside George Harrison and Leon Russell at Madison Square Garden, sporting the denim jacket and harmonica holder of his protest era, makes the Concert for Bangladesh a triumph.

Above: In the autumn of 1971 the newly formed Big Star are thrown the keys of Ardent Studios in Memphis and allowed to make their own record.

Above: In Hollywood, David Geffen (**right**) is gathering a stable of winsome acoustic stars like America to exploit the young adult market opened up by Carole King.

Right: Van Morrison, seen here in the studio in 1971, turns a rare period of domestic contentment into hit singles and also inspires the young Bruce Springsteen.

Below: The unknown Jackson Browne is composing so many great songs he can afford to gift 'Take It Easy' to the equally unknown Eagles.

Left: Neil Young in the barn on his northern California ranch where he completes *Harvest*, the key album of his career, in September.

Below: Rick Wakeman's transfer from the Strawbs to Yes is headline news in progressive-rock circles.

Above: With *Hunky Dory* recorded and plans for *Ziggy Stardust* already hatched, David Bowie plays an acoustic show at Friars in September. Tickets are less than a pound.

Above: Sly and the Family Stone's long-delayed album *There's A Riot Goin' On* is at number one on the Billboard charts as Attica prison in upstate New York is consumed by a disturbance (**left**). Thirty-eight people, both prisoners and guards, lose their lives.

Below: The affluent Loud family of Santa Barbara, California, are the first to submit to 'reality TV'. The cameras track them throughout 1971 and they never once ask for privacy.

Above: *Rolling Stone*'s Beach Boys cover in October accompanies the release of *Surf's Up* and depicts them as wistful elders of the church of fun.

Top: Elton John poses with his mother and stepfather in Pinner for a major *Life* magazine feature, while Frank Zappa entertains his parents, Francis and Rosemarie (**above**). The photographer notes that all his subjects are on their best behaviour in front of their parents.

Left: Richard Perry and Harry Nilsson, the producer-singer team behind *Nilsson Schmilsson*. 'My plan was he would be my Beatles and I would be his George Martin,' says Perry.

Below: The Who at the launch of *Who's Next* in the garden of Tara, Keith Moon's bizarre playhouse in the Surrey suburbs.

Right: When Led Zeppelin mark the release of *Led Zeppelin IV* by playing Wembley Arena, still known as the Empire Pool, it represents a dramatic increase in scale for live rock in Britain. *Melody Maker* (**below**) is wondering if the release of 'George Jackson' means Dylan is getting back to protest.

Above: Elvis Presley's 1971 shows are premium-priced, heavily ritualized celebrations of his own magnificence rather than musical events. They point the way to the future.

Left: The all-conquering Alice Cooper arrives at London airport with his trademark snake. David Bowie models the look of his new band on the just-released film *A Clockwork Orange* (**below**).

hubristic choice. Others thought it a perfect marker for their ambition. Chris Bell certainly thought their first album was a record that would set the world on its ear. Alex Chilton, having been out there in the self-same world, was unlikely to have been so convinced. Both Bell and Chilton adored the Beatles and modelled their partnership on Lennon and McCartney, crediting everything jointly and strictly alternating lead vocals. Like Lennon and McCartney, each acted as a check on the other's excesses, Bell's sweetness playing against Chilton's edge. It seemed to work.

There is 16mm film of Big Star in 1971, the year of their first record's creation. It shows them recording in Ardent, rehearsing in the living room of a comfortable parental home, smoking rather self-consciously, sporting college scarves and neat knitwear, eyeing up passing schoolgirls in their short skirts, doing art student stunts like walking up to the local draft board and then walking away again, the sort of thing which young men have done since time immemorial. Like the music itself, in songs like 'Thirteen' and 'When My Baby's Beside Me', everything about that first incarnation of Big Star seems like an elegy for lost youth.

They called it *#1 Record*, which probably didn't do them any favours. When it came out in 1972 it did nothing. This was not helped by Stax's buying itself out of its distribution deal with Columbia and therefore having to promote a white rock record through a black promotion and distribution network. Big Star had never seriously played live and therefore they had never looked the market in the eye. They were not over-endowed with ambition. They were stranded in the middle of the country and therefore out of the deal flow. In truth, like many of the groups who revere Big Star's name today, they were probably more comfortable with failure than success.

They made music which used the same ringing acoustic guitars as the Beatles but there was always something plangent at its heart. Big Star were muscly and rhythmic but you could never actually dance to them. Their songs seemed inspired by the traditional pop preoccupations – finding a girl, going out on the street, getting high – but they were never quite put together in a way the people who actually did those kind of things could grasp. When they played around Memphis they were never really popular. It wasn't until Bell had left the group, when their label Ardent had the hare-brained idea of staging the first international Rock Writers Convention and flew a sampling of scribblers from all over the United States and Europe to Memphis, that they finally played in front of an audience odd, snobby and ill-coordinated enough to actually like them. Like the Velvet Underground they had all the attributes of a great pop group apart from the popularity. In the years to come there would be thousands of similar bands.

At the same time as Big Star were in Memphis, sitting on a secret that they confidently expected to delight the world, David Bowie was working in Trident Studios in Soho and preparing to unveil his second coming. Putting yourself in a position to succeed in the music business is very often a confidence trick. The business always aligns itself with those it thinks are about to succeed and in reaching this conclusion it's influenced largely by what the rest of the business appears to be thinking.

In September 1971 a number of those people appeared to believe that David Bowie was in that fortunate position. His manager Tony Defries had persuaded RCA Records in the United States that they should sign him. At the same time he was punting him as a songwriter. Peter Noone's version of 'Oh! You Pretty Things' had been a hit and Defries knew that there were other, similarly catchy tunes to come. He even set up a meeting with the horror actor Christopher Lee with a view to providing him with some songs. It may be that Bowie had more confidence in the songs than he had in himself. The first Ziggy Stardust songs had been gifted to Freddie Burretti, his pretty young friend from the gay club, possibly because he thought nobody would accept his playing the rock god himself.

On 25 September Bowie played a show for 250 people at Friar's in Aylesbury. Friar's was a popular place to play, not too far from London but not close enough to be crowded with scene makers. He took to the stage with a guitarist he introduced as Michael Ronson and started by playing two songs by the Californian songwriter Biff Rose. He then said he was going to play 'one of my own we get over as quickly as possible'. This was 'Space Oddity', which he still seemed to regard as an embarrassing reminder of his time as a one-hit wonder. After that he played half a dozen of the songs he had been recording at Trident in Soho with Ken Scott. These included 'Changes', 'Song For Bob Dylan', 'Andy Warhol' and 'Queen Bitch', which he introduced as being about a friend called Lou Reed who was in a group called the Velvet Underground.

Only a few days before this show he had actually spent time with Reed, the person he had thought he was talking to backstage seven months earlier. On this occasion he was in New York to sign his deal with RCA, who held a party to mark the fact, and invited Reed, who had signed a solo deal with the label. Through somebody else he met at the party Bowie got an introduction to Iggy Pop, who had recently left the Stooges and, like Reed, seemed to have hit the wall as a member of a group. For both Reed and Pop the appearance of this interesting guy who was a big admirer and appeared to be poised for success in the UK was a very promising augury indeed. This was the other element of the confidence trick. The Americans thought the Brit was bigger than he was and he thought they were more legendary than they were. The association with these two names, who were on the radar of taste makers like John Peel and Richard Williams, helped further legitimize Bowie's claims to fame.

All three were subsequently yoked together in legend and, what was even more unexpected, in the charts. The following year Bowie co-produced Reed's breakthrough album *Transformer*. In 1977 he performed a similar service for Iggy on *The Passenger*. At the time they were just three guys who had walked away from a succession of failures. All the leathery rock and roll revivalists who had come along in late-sixties America had had their shot and failed. The MC5 had never been able to turn their high profile into a real following. Their 1971 album *High Time* pleased them but it was a commercial stiff. The same producer, the Englishman

Geoffrey Haslam, assembled *Loaded* from the last sessions of the Lou Reed-led version of the Velvet Underground. Iggy Pop had left the Stooges because they didn't seem to be achieving any traction and he had a heroin problem. San Francisco's Flamin' Groovies made *Teenage Head* for the Kama Sutra label in January 1971 and then the singer Roy Loney promptly left. All these American groups formed a new cohort of bands that became best known for being unpopular. They were hailed for being passed over, rated for being underrated. Now that even classic outsiders like Neil Young and James Taylor were comfortably in the mainstream it was a perfect time to position themselves as beautiful losers.

On 7 November 1971 Alice Cooper headlined at the Rainbow in Finsbury Park. Just a couple of days earlier the Who had opened the venue, which was intended to bring a Fillmore-like concert experience to north London. Tony Defries had begged tickets from the promoter to make sure that David Bowie and his band could get to see the show. Although they were just days away from the release of *Killer*, which would be Alice Cooper's second album of 1971, that night they played songs from the earlier *Love It To Death*, including 'I'm Eighteen' and 'Black Juju', which climaxed with Alice in an electric chair. Trevor Bolder, who was worried about Bowie's imminent plans to glamorize his own backing group, was reassured by the band's meat-and-potatoes hard rock. 'They were wearing make-up and were a real heavy band. It was a big jump from being a blues band in T-shirts and jeans, long hair and beards to wearing make-up and flashy clothes,' he remembers. Bolder's defensive 'at least they can play their instruments' reaction to these strangely dressed weirdos is the authentic voice of 1971.

Vincent Furnier, the leader of the group, had been kicking around the music scene since the mid-sixties and having adopted the name of a woman had been co-opted into Frank Zappa's carnival of oddities alongside the likes of Wild Man Fischer and the GTOs (Girls Together Outrageously). Convinced that he and his band would never prosper in front of blasé West Coast audiences he moved them to Detroit, linked up with a new producer Bob Ezrin and manager Shep Gordon, and between them they decided to ape the sound of Detroit bands like the MC5, Stooges and Detroit and showcase it in an act calculated to amuse and enthral a new generation of fans. It was no coincidence that their first hit record was called 'I'm Eighteen'. That age, which had previously been the default age of rock fans, was suddenly the mark of a disaffected younger generation. *Melody Maker* sniffily but tellingly described them as being 'for the punk and pimply crowd', which is not something they would have said about Led Zeppelin or the Who, both of whom were also beginning to attract a younger and more demonstrative demographic. In a supremely condescending opinion piece for *Life* magazine at the end of July, which is some indication of how many living rooms were suddenly aware of Alice, Albert Goldman said, 'People project on him, revile him, ridicule him and some would doubtless like to kill him. At the same time he knocks out the young boys with the daring of his act and the rebelliousness of his image. After all, the ultimate rebellion of our time is the simple refusal to be a man.' Given that at this time reaching the age of majority meant some of the boys Alice Cooper was entertaining in the American heartland could find themselves sent to Vietnam, there's probably some truth in Goldman's analysis.

Shep Gordon, who had done his best to make the band a *succès de scandale* in LA and had to move out when he found that they literally couldn't get arrested, did what Bryan Ferry and Kraftwerk had done and suggested that Alice Cooper was a project as distinct from the band as Ben Hur from Charlton Heston and that for Alice the future lay in thinking vaudeville rather than rock and roll. Gordon knew that you have to get beyond your fan base if you want to get bigger. That meant television. TV was Alice's thing, and he arrived just as small US stations were handing over late-night slots to the house hippy and seeing if they could get an audience of nocturnal dope smokers. Alice Cooper was pushing against an open door. No TV producer was going to pass up the opportunity to give airtime to a man who would pretend to electrocute himself, wielding knives and instruments of torture and filling the stage with flags in a way that hadn't previously been seen in rock. TV producers didn't have to like the music. They just had to prefer the act to a bunch of blokes standing still and operating heavy machinery, which was pretty much what you got out of a live performance by Pink Floyd and Led Zeppelin. (At the same time the film director Adrian Maben was planning to circumvent Pink Floyd's lack of animation by filming them in the amphitheatre at Pompeii, insisting that at least one song had to climax with somebody banging the large gong at the back of the stage, because that way at least there would be one thing worth looking at.)

It mattered little that all TV did was expose the end-of-the-pier production values behind Alice's tricks. For the first time for a while there was the prospect of something that might get genuinely shocking. In Detroit he appeared on *Tube Works*, in Washington DC he did Barry Richards' *Turn On*. When he came to Britain in November it was just in time to be on one of the first editions of *The Old Grey Whistle Test*, which had been launched on BBC2, the most minority of the three channels available in Britain at the time, and was intended to do for the burgeoning album market what *Top of the Pops* did for the singles chart. The band were sequestered in a small presentation studio usually reserved for weather forecasts and mimed to a track because in its early days the programme didn't yet have the technology to allow bands to play live. It didn't matter. It was what they looked like that mattered. The camera lingered on Alice's jumpsuit, which was slit down to his navel, the glittery stars and fringed sleeves of the band's suits and the mascara, which looked as though it had been applied by a drunken sailor. They looked cheap but it simply didn't matter, because where Alice was concerned the thermals of outrage proved so easy to whip up, particularly in Festival of Light Britain, that by the time his next album came out in 1972 he was a bona fide phenomenon.

By the time David Bowie launched Ziggy Stardust in June 1972 and Roxy Music released 'Virginia Plain' a month later and Mercury Records got the nerve to sign up the New York Dolls the following summer, Alice Cooper was already playing stadiums and nobody in the music business was going to bet against the potent combination of glitter and outrage.

*

On 11 September 1971 John Lennon and Yoko Ono appeared on Dick Cavett's TV chat show. The US late-night talk format had only recently reached the UK with the launch of Michael Parkinson's show in June but in the USA it was well enough established to have spawned many different varieties. Cavett's reputation was for being hipper and more big-city-sophisticated than Carson. He regularly hosted music stars such as Jimi Hendrix and Sly Stone, who had a reputation for being difficult to keep on track. (Cavett had recent experience of dealing with difficult situations. In June 1971 he recorded a programme with journalist Peter Hamill and health magazine publisher J. I. Rodale during which the latter actually died in his chair. Late in 1970 the Southern politician Lester Maddox had stalked off Cavett's show, prompting Randy Newman to write the opening couplet of his song 'Rednecks'.)

On the night of 11 September the entire show was devoted to the couple he had been instructed to introduce as 'John Ono Lennon and Yoko Ono'. Lennon entered wearing a military shirt, white bell bottoms and polished black boots. Ono was in hot pants, black tights, a beret and a velour shirt slit to her navel. Lennon carefully placed her between him and the host in order to make sure that he wasn't the main focus of the interview. He did this because, as was clearly evident to all concerned, including himself, he was the main focus of the interview.

Lennon chewed, fidgeted and smoked throughout the next hour, which unfolded apparently without structure, as most interviews did at the time. There was no sense that a researcher had sat down with the couple and elicited a number of stories which the interviewer would then tee up at pre-arranged times. It was anything but a collection of polished anecdotes. By modern standards it was rambling, desultory, even dull. The anxiety all three were clearly feeling – Lennon because he was always nervous, Ono because she was the woman who had broken up the Beatles, Cavett because he wanted to look as if he wasn't impressed by having such a star guest – was partially hidden behind a mask of unconcern. The conversation meandered around various subjects: hair, drugs, politics, Japan, England, other chat shows and the apparent gulf between the alternative world and the straight one. Much of the agenda had been set by the interview Lennon had given to *Rolling Stone* earlier in the year.

While nothing was delivered in terms of new information, this appearance might have set the template for the hundreds of subsequent occasions when rock gods have descended from Olympus and entered a TV studio, attempting to conceal the nervousness they are clearly feeling behind a display of fake casualness. Most answers trail off into shrugs, non sequiturs and funny voices. The studio audience laugh nervously as if they don't quite know how this is supposed to work. The main value is in the opportunity it affords to watch these exotic creatures at close quarters. As the playwright Alan Bennett observed, watching people behave is nothing special; watching them trying to behave is always fascinating.

Yoko had been brought there because she was John's consort and also because she could be employed as a human shield to ensure that Lennon didn't have to talk too much about the things people wanted to know about. This set up a curious dynamic between them. Throughout the interview he set her up to tell stories and then, like so many practised show-offs, couldn't stop himself telling them himself. He'd been socialized in a group in which nobody deferred to the other members, perfecting a form of choral banter which got them through all interview situations. Nobody could ever compete with that, particularly Yoko, who was curiously uncharismatic and certainly not ready for prime time. After an hour, during which they showed clips from two of Yoko's art films, Cavett said what a shame it was that Lennon couldn't perform a song from the album he had come in to promote, *Imagine*, which was released that day. Lennon apologized that he hadn't been able to find the time to rehearse a band and instead introduced an excerpt from a TV film which he promised people would be able to see soon. This began with the couple walking through the garden of the house in Tittenhurst Park and then Lennon playing the white grand piano in the garden room and singing. The audience, who had not heard the song before, paid close attention to the words. They may have been struck by the contrast between the grandeur of the house and some of the lines, particularly the one that went 'imagine no possessions, I wonder if you can'.

At the very same time as Lennon and his wife were on the Dick Cavett show in New York, four men who had little intention of imagining a world without possessions were tunnelling their way into a vault beneath Lloyds Bank in London's Baker Street. They had rented an adjacent shop and then locked themselves in for the weekend, methodically drilling their way into a fortune at the bank next door. One of their number was stationed as a lookout on a nearby roof and kept in communication with the men in the vault via walkie-talkie. It so happened that on the same night a man living in a flat in nearby Wimpole Street retired to his bed with a powerful shortwave radio, intending to pick up the signal from Radio Luxembourg. He found the usual transmissions interrupted by urgent verbal communications between men who were apparently discussing something that was numbered in the hundreds of thousands. Realizing that these transmissions could only be coming from somewhere nearby, the man contacted the local police, who accused him of an over-active imagination. When he kept hearing the voices the man called Scotland Yard who despatched a couple of detectives to spend the night huddled around his set while uniformed men were sent to check every local bank branch for signs of illegal entry. They failed to notice anything was going on at Lloyds, and the following day the robbers escaped with half a million pounds. It was the largest bank haul in British history up to that point.

(The men were subsequently caught and convicted. The Baker Street job remained a favourite source of speculation and myth. In 2007 it was the basis for a film called *The Bank Job* which suggested that the theft of the money had been a cover for an operation to secure some compromising pictures of Margaret, younger sister of the sovereign, which were being kept in a safe deposit box by Michael X, a criminal and self-styled black radical who was prominent at the time in London's alternative society and was an associate of Lennon. During the Cavett interview Lennon talked about how he had cut off his hair and donated it to Michael X to be auctioned to raise money for his headquarters The Black House.)

On the same Saturday night that Lennon was talking to Cavett and the bank job was proceeding in London, Sly and the Family Stone were in the middle of a three-night stand at Madison Square Garden in New York. Sly's record of non-attendance or tardiness at shows had meant that nobody except the Garden's promoter would hire him, and even then his contract was full of the penalties he would incur in the event of his not doing a bang-up job. It didn't appear to make much difference to Sly. On the morning of the concert in New York he woke up in LA. That day he missed six flights, finally arriving in New York at 4.30 in the afternoon and reaching the Garden at eight. At eleven o'clock, the time at which his performance was scheduled to end, he was about ready to go on stage.

His acclaimed album *There's A Riot Goin' On*, which seemed to emanate from a very dark underworld, had just been released but he hadn't had time to teach the band how to play it and so the show was dominated by tired perform-ances of golden oldies. The *New York Times* review pointed out that Sly relied too heavily on his party classics. What's more interesting is the review did not make any connection between the music and the very real riot that was taking place only a couple of hours from Manhattan.

Since Thursday of that week Attica prison in upstate New York had been in the hands of the inmates after one of the most serious riots in American penal history. These riots had been triggered by the worsening conditions in jails, a dramatic shift in the racial balance of the inmates which had seen Attica go from a majority of whites to a majority of African-Americans in less than two years, a rise in black radicalism and the death two weeks earlier in a Californian prison of George Jackson, who had been shot by the authorities reputedly for his left-wing views and all-round uppityness. The rioters were holding thirty-three prison guards as hostages and, in obedience to the recent fashion, were even demanding planes to fly key rioters out of the country.

On the day of the concert the State Corrections Commissioner was pictured negotiating with the rioters on the front page of the *New York Times*. By the following Tuesday the prison had been retaken. The order had been given when the prisoners' leaders, who were mainly Muslim, had allegedly threatened to slit the throats of four guards. There was massive over-use of force in the retaking of the prison and thirty-eight people died, both prisoners and hostages. The release of Sly's album, with its Stars and Stripes cover, somnambulant vibe in its music and sense of anomie hinted at in its lyrics, could not possibly have been more timely. *There's A Riot Goin' On* was the sound of a city falling apart.

It's arguable that Sly's album was the most influential record to come out of 1971. Certainly there's a whole world of moody, hypnotic, rhythm-box-based music which would be inconceivable without its example. In fact the whole category known by the contemporary shorthand 'urban' can be traced back to what Sly did in that house in the decidedly suburban surroundings of Bel Air. Celebrated though lots of those records might be, few of them get to lord it over the competition from the top of the album charts the way Sly's did in 1971.

John Lennon's *Imagine* went to number one in both the UK and the USA but its true moment didn't come until 1981 when in the wake of Lennon's death it was embraced as a hymn, as Phil Spector always said it would be. In fact, many of the beginnings made in 1971 didn't reach their public until many years later. 'Hospital' from the Intermedia Studios recordings was not released until the first Modern Lovers album came out in 1976, at which point it was hailed as part of the future of rock and roll rather than the antique it was. The same could be said of the Velvet Underground's *Loaded*, which was their idea of an album full of potential hit singles. That didn't happen, but many years later songs like 'Sweet Jane' and 'Rock N Roll' became the 'Twist And Shout' and 'La Bamba' of the alternative set, their initial unpopularity worn as a badge of honour.

Jerry Harrison, the keyboard player of the Modern Lovers, went on to join Talking Heads who had actual hit records ten years later. Around the same time the drummer David Robinson was playing with the Cars, a band from Boston who were eventually so big that they bought the studio where they'd done that demo in 1971. At the time of writing Loudon Wainwright is approaching his fiftieth year as a performer, still spinning variations on the same comic character – himself. In 2008 he re-recorded many of the songs he first made at Intermedia for an album called *Recovery*, a recognition that these are still the songs that define him. 'Motel Blues', which describes the empty but nonetheless quite exciting prospect of anonymous sex with a fan encountered on tour, continues to resound. Bombay Bicycle Club, who weren't born in 1971, did their own version. They were belatedly following in the footsteps of Big Star, who had latched on to it in the seventies. As Bob Dylan wrote, 'there's no success like failure'. This particular song, with its shrugging acceptance of the tawdriness of the game, was also perfect for Big Star whose entire legend has, like Nick Drake's, been steadily built up by successive generations of believers on the basis of the fact that, by any earthly measure, they failed. In some respects indie rock is much like the early Church. The whole world of indie, with its bone-deep belief that indie music is too fine, too soulful, too pure ever to appeal to the masses, has been built up around groups like the Velvet Underground, Big Star and the Modern Lovers, who signally failed to make it. Alice Cooper and Roxy Music may have had the hits. They have never had quite the same mystique. The mystique ended up being worth almost as much as the hits.

Because the music business hadn't yet become an industry and the music media was relatively underdeveloped, companies hadn't yet got round to copying what appeared to be working for other companies. Bands like the Velvet Underground and Big Star were one-offs, not part of any particular wave. They were interesting and different and they were all signed by major record companies. They didn't have any problem being drawn to public attention. The problem they had was winning any public approval. Their records, like those of the Stooges, MC5 and Nick Drake, were widely available and widely un-bought. The cliché goes that very few people bought the first Velvet Underground but every one of them went and formed a band. That may be so, but it took them another five years to do it. When these bands were eventually embraced and had their moment of reverent acclaim, during punk rock, it was as heritage acts. The punk rock moment had flickered in 1971. It didn't catch light. When it eventually did so, it was as much nostalgia as anything else.

SEPTEMBER PLAYLIST

Sandy Denny, 'Blackwaterside'
Bob Dylan, 'George Jackson'
Loudon Wainwright III, 'Motel Blues'
The Modern Lovers, 'Hospital'
Black Sabbath, 'Sweet Leaf'
David Bowie, 'Andy Warhol'
Can, 'Halleluwah'
John Lennon, 'Imagine'
The Band, 'Life Is A Carnival'
Area Code 615, 'Stone Fox Chase'

OCTOBER: WILL THE CIRCLE BE UNBROKEN

I n the autumn of 1971 *Life* magazine, the photo weekly that had celebrated post-war America and the values of the generation responsible for its baby boom, was beginning to feel its age. Facing competition from scores of specialist magazines and finding it difficult to attract young readers, it planned to cut its claimed circulation from seven million a week to five and a half. It's a measure of the power of print media in the early 1970s that this seemed a precipitous decline. In the same September issue that carried *Life*'s sober coverage of the aftermath of the Attica riots the Jackson Five were on the cover. They posed amid their many trophies and gold discs with their parents Joe and Katherine, spearheading a major photo feature called 'Rock Stars and their Parents'.

To put together this story war photographer John Olson had travelled all over the world. His brief was to capture these supposed tearaways and reprobates with their proud mothers and fathers. It was clear from the copy where *Life*'s sympathies lay. 'What do parents do when a much-loved son or daughter stops listening to rock records and leaves home to start making rock records of his own?' said the text, with the sort of pained concern that would later be reserved for speculating about their sexuality.

Frank Zappa was pictured against the violent purple of his living room with his parents Francis and Rosemarie. Elton John was seen in the Pinner home of his mother Sheila, a government clerical worker. Eric Clapton was pictured with his grandmother Rose Clapp, who had raised him on behalf of her sixteen-year-old daughter. There was no mention of his actual birth mother: the public wasn't yet ready for the degree of complexity that might be involved in a non-nuclear family. Ginger Baker's mother was running a hairdresser's. Marjorie Cocker was working as a waitress in a local café. Grace Slick held her new baby China upside down while her blue-blood mother Virginia Wing looked on. Slick was not the only one with a background more privileged than she traditionally let on. Floyd Crosby risked embarrassing his son David by admitting he and his wife were both in the New York Social Register.

Olson reported that all his subjects were uniformly well behaved when their parents were present. It was rare to see rock stars in the context of a family. They preferred to encourage the idea that they had been raised by wolves and had created themselves through the sheer force of their own will. Yet here they were, tamed for once, looking slightly

302

preposterous in their hippy finery amid their parents' lovingly tended ornaments and family photos, wondering if this was still the place they ought to think of as home. The rock stars in these pictures, and scores of others who had risen on the sixties tide and then been beached in the new decade, were having to direct their thoughts to setting up their own versions of home.

By 1971 many had accumulated enough funds to establish their newly acquired partners and children in the grand style befitting their nouveau-riche status. The problem was that as a rule they didn't have much talent for domesticity. Years on the road had left them temperamentally unsuited to laying their heads down in the same place they woke up; it made them at best fidgety nest builders and easily bored. Their situation was made worse by the fact that they were pursued by another family, this one made up of fans. In 1971 Pete Townshend was experiencing the same problems as had driven Dylan out of Woodstock, with fans feeling entitled to turn up at the door of his home in Twickenham as if he were their old mod mate rather than a man with a family. This wasn't conducive to the peace of mind of his pregnant wife. Half the time Townshend was away at work anyway. In 1971 nobody expected men of any kind, particularly high achievers like these, to break their stride to spend time attending the births or getting too involved in the upbringing of their children. In the famous world, just as in the workaday world, nobody contested the idea that work, fame and status took priority every time.

Paul McCartney was an exception to this rule, raising his children with Linda in what amounted to a fantasy of rural domesticity on a farm in Scotland, though making sure he was in London close to the best medical care when their daughter Stella was born in September. Anyone who had been a Beatle could be forgiven for not wishing to have any unannounced callers for the rest of their life. In 1970 George Harrison moved into Friar Park, his 120-room Xanadu near Henley-on-Thames. The house was so badly in need of restoration that he and Pattie spent the first few months in sleeping bags. His main requirement was that it should be big enough to accommodate a recording studio, which was indicative of the fact that the priorities were still professional.

Harrison wasn't alone in this. In 1971, at the height of his fame, James Taylor was effectively homeless. The homestead pictured on the back cover of *Mud Slide Slim And The Blue Horizon* was not yet built. When his new girlfriend Carly Simon was first taken to see the property on Martha's Vineyard, she found it had been designed with more thought for recording than food preparation, and was horrified that it was used as a crash pad by James's hippy friends. This was a new style of living for those who could afford it. For the first time it was possible to indulge teenage-style whims with a millionaire's bank book. Thus when Taylor returned from his period in London he could pay to have his Ford Cortina GT shipped back to the United States. When he finally returned from tour he had been away so long his own dog failed to recognize him.

Graham Nash moved into a house in San Francisco's Haight-Ashbury that had been done up by some hippy friends. His only requirements were a sixteen-track studio, a billiard room in the basement and a room on the second floor for David Crosby to crash in. Nash's memoir is a good guide to the world as seen by these millionaire princes. He remembers that at Stephen Stills' house there were generally two sisters who were always naked. 'These girls were incredible playthings. They were available to whoever they fancied fucking,' he mused many years later.

These patchouli plutocrats seemed a new type of human being. They were immensely wealthy but required by their profession to conduct themselves like vagabonds. They had to pretend that they spent most of their time lying on their backs watching the clouds scud across the sky when the reality was that they were consumed by a combination of burning ambition and frantic productivity to which most things around them tended to be sacrificed. The heightened sensitivity which everyone applauded in their songs was often achieved at the expense of their own personal relationships, where they moved decisively to dispense with any romantic tie that was in danger of subtracting more than it was adding.

The work was so all-consuming and the act of creation came so easily that they hardly thought of it as work at all. For Neil Young, 1971 was the year he composed and recorded *Harvest*, the album that made him a superstar, and he did it in an almost permanent state of domestic upheaval. At the end of 1970 he had sold the Topanga Canyon home he had shared with Susan Acevedo, his wife of two years, and bought a 140-acre ranch in northern California. Some say that Susan was expecting to move with him, along with her young daughter. It was made clear to her that this would not happen. Instead she was compensated with enough to invest in her own restaurant.

Soon after this Carrie Snodgress caught Young's eye in the acclaimed film *Diary of a Mad Housewife*. He made contact with her. One of the first intimations of his dawning celebrity status came in the realization that it would not be taken amiss if a rich and famous rock star contacted just about any attractive, prominent young woman merely on the basis of having seen her on a screen or in the pages of a magazine. The actress was amused that Young presented himself as 'the man with the single suitcase and two pairs of jeans'. She knew he'd been able to pay over three hundred thousand dollars cash for his new home, so he was clearly no vagabond. Within a very short time Snodgress's career, which had previously appeared so promising, had been subsumed into the halo of Young's apparent magnificence. She was nominated for an Oscar for Best Actress. When the awards ceremony came that April they weren't there. Whether this was her decision or his is not clear. What's known is that Young complained about having to wear a tuxedo. At the time Hollywood was way below rock and roll in the prestige stakes and hadn't yet got round to worrying about baubles. Glenda Jackson took the award for *Women in Love*.

Snodgress moved into Young's ranch in mid-1971, bringing members of her extended family with her. Like the court of a rising baron in medieval times, those who were served at their master's pleasure could be fearsome in-fighters. In his own book *Waging Heavy Peace*, Young admits that Acevedo, who was credited for patching his famous jeans on the back cover of *After The Gold Rush*, had also made him a waistcoat which she had sewn using some of her own hair as thread.

On achieving incumbency, Carrie Snodgress made sure she unpicked every last stitch.

Harvest had to be made on the fly throughout 1971 because Young spent most of the year on the road as a solo. The songs were pouring out of him in such a stream that they couldn't help but reflect the lives of the characters who found themselves in his orbit. 'Old Man' was inspired by a middle-aged man who worked as a caretaker on his ranch. 'The Needle And The Damage Done' was about his erstwhile bandmate Danny Whitten who would kill himself with heroin a year later. Young began recording in Nashville in February. He had gone there to tape his appearance on a TV show in which Johnny Cash sought to restore his rebel values by performing alongside the new-generation singer-songwriters. Young took advantage of the presence of James Taylor and Linda Ronstadt to get them into the studios to sing high harmonies on 'Heart Of Gold'.

When he passed through London in February he went to Barking Town Hall to record a song with the London Symphony Orchestra. (According to the producer Glyn Johns, who was there as an observer, Young's hipster buddy Jack Nietzsche was relieved of the baton by a member of the orchestra when it became clear that he didn't know how to direct the musicians.) The song was 'A Man Needs A Maid'. It begins 'my life is changing in so many ways', which was certainly true. The singer doesn't know who to trust any more. He's thinking that maybe he'll get a maid, just someone to keep his house clean, to cook his meals and go away. In the years since its composition it's the song that has most often come in for criticism for its apparent sexist condescension.

Neil Young once told me that songs were 'just thoughts'. In the sense that a lot of the best ones are thoughts that arise from the tumultuous subconscious 'A Man Needs A Maid' is a good deal more honest about his needs and his situation than most rock songs written in that hectic year.

Generation Rock attempted to put down roots in some rum locations. Estate agents on both sides of the Atlantic were beginning to see these long-haired millionaires as the solution to that difficult property which had been sitting on their books too long. In 1971 the impulsive Keith Moon and his wife Kim moved into the house in Chertsey that they called Tara in honour of the house in *Gone with the Wind*. It was a futuristic fantasy house consisting of five pyramids built by an eccentric film producer. In 1970 Jimmy Page bought Boleskine House, Aleister Crowley's old mansion alongside Loch Ness, installing an old school friend to live in it with his family. A university friend of Nick Drake's performed the same role in John Lennon's house at Tittenhurst Park in 1971. One of the apocryphal tales told about Drake has him spending time in the house in the summer of 1971 when the occupants were away, gazing wistfully at Lennon's collection of Rickenbackers.

Around the same time Elton John finally moved out of his mother's house in Pinner and used his new-found money to buy an apartment in a development called the Water Garden off Edgware Road. Within a year his friend John Reid had moved in. Nobody suspected that they might be sleeping as well as cooking together, neither the journalists who turned up there to interview him nor the various members of the Dwight family who very much enjoyed the company of the presentable young Scot. As Philip Norman said in his biography of Elton, 'there was as yet no general notion of a closet and consequent need or pressure to come out of it. London in 1971 was full of paired young men, unexceptionally living in flats together.'

A lot of these new spreads, plucked from the property pages of *Country Life*, weren't particularly happy. At the time of life when most of their school contemporaries would have been settling down with a mortgage and watching their children grow up, these apparently lucky people whose knack for hit records had taken them to the stars and distant planets were coming back to earth to find that fitting in wasn't easy. In 1971 the Kinks released *Muswell Hillbillies*. This was a record ostensibly about the dislocation felt by inner London working-class families upon being rehoused in comparative comfort in the suburbs. It could just as well have been about Ray Davies, who had moved from Muswell Hill to a stockbroker house in Borehamwood and was quite unable to relax. For him, like so many others who found themselves discontented in the mansion on the hill, there was only one thing to do. Go back to work.

In show business family was a commodity that could always be sold. Family acts were popular in the music business in 1971. The *Billboard* chart for the first week of October has Donny Osmond at number one with 'Go Away Little Girl' and his family group at number nine with 'Yo Yo'. The Osmonds' breakthrough success earlier in the year with 'One Bad Apple' had been a fairly shameless pastiche of the leading family act of the year, the Jackson Five. Richard and

Karen Carpenter were not far behind at number four with 'Superstar'. All three of James Taylor's singing siblings made albums in 1971. *Rolling Stone* hailed them as 'the first family of the new rock'.

On 28 October 1971 *Rolling Stone*'s cover story was all about an outwardly successful but deeply dysfunctional family band from California. The picture featured a group of men in their late twenties, some wearing eccentric headgear, most sporting biblical beards. The cover line read 'The Beach Boys: A California Saga'.

The story within was destined to become a classic piece from that brief interlude when pop writing collided with the New Journalism, in the golden moment before the PRs took control and press became primarily a matter of disaster avoidance. The style of Tom Nolan's story has since been imitated by scores of writers seeking to get inside those bands who had grown into national institutions. It combined admiration for the group's achievements with distaste for whole areas of their strange inner world in a way that hadn't been done before, certainly not in the music press. (At the same time *Rolling Stone* was having a look round Ike and Tina Turner's home for a cover feature. The story quoted a record company executive recoiling from the guitar-shaped coffee table in the living room and musing that he never knew it was possible to spend so much money at Woolworths.)

Very little of the story was about music, which was a significant development. *Rolling Stone* was still the black and white double-folded underground magazine with adverts for smoking paraphernalia and *Easy Rider* posters in the back. It was yet to become the *Life* magazine of the denim bourgeoisie. Nolan's story, which abounded in the kind of prurient detail that music fans pretend not to be interested in but clearly are, was the culmination of a year-long effort by the band's new manager, a former publicist called Jack Rieley, to reposition the group, who seemed to have been left behind by the events of the late sixties and were in danger of being marooned permanently on the wrong side of rock history.

In the first half of the sixties the Beach Boys could do very little wrong. The second half was a protracted nervous breakdown. Brian Wilson, their leader, songwriter and producer, and oldest of the Wilson brothers, withdrew from touring and buried himself in the studio; Mike Love, their singer and most reliable source of embarrassment, led them into a tour with the Maharishi Mahesh Yogi just as his serene stock was beginning to tank; the band's confidence was so dented that they seriously toyed with changing their name to the Beach; they were locked in litigation with their record company over unpaid royalties; and, most disastrously of all, Murry Wilson, the brothers' overbearing and interfering father, had sold Brian Wilson's catalogue of songs, which included the likes of 'Good Vibrations', 'Don't Worry Baby', 'Wouldn't It Be Nice' and 'God Only Knows', to the publishing division of A&M. The price was less than a million dollars. His reasoning at the time was that the value of sixties copyrights was unlikely to hold up in the new decade and therefore this was a good time to sell. He did it in the same year that the Beatles publisher Dick James, looking to retire from the business and realize his assets, sold their even more valuable catalogue to ATV Music for what history proved to be a comparable pittance. On top of all that the drummer Dennis Wilson's unfortunate choice in friends had led to the band being mentioned at the trial of the diabolical family attached to Charles Manson. When the murders committed by Manson's zombies became front-page news the Beach Boys were forced to admit that Manson had written the B-side of their cheery hit 'Bluebirds Over The Mountain'. What's more, they had neglected to credit him.

Most of Jack Rieley's efforts went into turning round the perception of the group rather than its music. In the late 1960s the Beach Boys' records had still been popular but the group itself didn't have a following. They had no aura. They were admired for their singles but had never quite made the shift into the album market, where what mattered most was whether people considered you credible. The Beach Boys didn't feature in any of the big rock festival feature films. They had made a successful attempt to woo the hippies at the Big Sur Festival of 1969 but were too short-sighted to allow themselves to be in the attendant film. Thus their image was marooned somewhere in the lost land of Pendleton shirts and dads who wouldn't let you borrow the car. In the age of patchouli oil the Beach Boys still reeked of Pepsodent. Despite all the plaudits directed at *Pet Sounds* they were primarily regarded as a singles act. They didn't have the remotest scintilla of hip. When the Grateful Dead invited them on stage at the Fillmore in April 1971 it was as much a shock to the hippies as it would have been to Andy Williams' audience had he brought on Captain Beefheart. The one thing the new conservatives who made up the rock audience couldn't tolerate was the thought of anyone who might be conservative.

For his story in *Rolling Stone*, at the time the only publication in the world that would run long, discursive, almost book-length accounts of rock legends, Nolan was given access that nobody has had to a rock act since. He was fortunate enough to catch the Beach Boys at a time when they still somehow thought that a lot of what they said to journalists wouldn't make it to the printed page. The piece, which ran in two parts over two issues, started off with a picture of Brian in his bathrobe in his health food store The Radiant Radish in the middle of the night. It's a picture that eloquently captures the dislocation from everyday life that is available to people who have too much money and not enough work.

The fall-off in the quality and quantity of Brian Wilson's songwriting output following the indifferent reaction to 'Heroes And Villains' in 1967 is often explained as the inevitable result of his depressive state, occasioned by the shelving of *Smile*, his intended magnum opus. Another way of looking at it is Wilson was suddenly brought face to face with his songwriting mortality and suspected that he couldn't do it any longer. Only Ray Davies, who single-handedly wrote and sang lead on fourteen consecutive brilliant top twenty singles for the Kinks between 1964 and 1968, could possibly understand the pressure somebody like Wilson was under, to keep coming up with a new tune that everybody could fall in love with. The signs were that he couldn't do the simple stuff any more. The only way he could follow the ornate 'Good Vibrations' was with the grandiloquent 'Heroes And Villains'. This was a glorious piece of montage, the kind of thing that attracts admiration rather than love. It wasn't 'Don't Worry Baby'.

The Tom Nolan piece depicts a twenty-nine-year-old man alternating between long periods of adolescent idleness and bouts of frantic, compulsive behaviour. He eats Reddi-wip from the can. He disappears into his bedroom and won't come out. He has violent mood swings. He has an impractically gigantic dog. When he tells Nolan about his young daughter Carney playing with the penis of Carl's son there are glimpses of a world in which hippy fecklessness has conspired with money to seemingly bring about a new strain of opulent neglect. What emerged from Nolan's account was an individual who had been broken by the pressure to maintain his success and feed his extended family; the picture it painted was of a broken reed rather than a superman. It ensured that henceforth the Beach Boys' music would always exist in the past, suffused with the sadness of a long-gone summer, fated in time to become as distant but every bit as potent as the wartime tunes favoured by the old men of the TV comedy hits of 1971, Archie Bunker and Alf Garnett. The article finished with a line from Murry Wilson, the father whose funeral the following year neither Dennis nor Brian could find the time to attend. 'Henry Mancini is a God-given talent,' he said, 'and so is Brian Wilson.' We readers of *Rolling Stone* were all meant to snigger at the fatuity of comparing the man who wrote 'Good Vibrations' with the guy in the cardigan who hacked out 'Moon River'. Nobody made the point that they were both just musicians.

The Beach Boys had struck a new record deal with Warner Brothers, a deal predicated largely on the company's affection for what the band had been rather than what they were. The new songs which the other members came up with varied between adequate and lacklustre. This quickly became a problem. If the Beach Boys couldn't come up with at least a couple of Brian Wilson songs Warner Bros would probably pass. This put the band in a predicament that would be faced by many bands in the future. They had to come up with the songs their record company had paid an advance for. The problem was the one person who had a proven record of coming up with such songs either couldn't or wouldn't supply them. The Beach Boys had the additional problem that they were a family as well as a group. There were two brothers, a difficult cousin and two very demanding parents looking to Brian, the older brother, the great white hope, the former genius who was now padding about in a bathrobe, and wondering whether they would ever get their meal ticket back.

Surf's Up, the seventeenth album by the Beach Boys that emerged in the autumn of 1971, started out as a fudge born of desperation and thanks to good fortune and perfect timing went on to attract great acclaim. It was probably the first case of a band making a tribute album to itself. It was a celebration of the band's own aura, an attempt to painstakingly re-create as adults what they had once instinctively done as teenagers, a touching bid to prove that the boys of summer could go on and on, singing about their days of wine and roses in much the same way that Sinatra had done for the Korean War generation. It would not be the last album of its kind. If the title wasn't elegiac enough the cover picture, based on a piece of Western sculpture called 'End of the Trail', supplied what was missing. Everything about the record harked back – to the white-toothed, corn-fed 'Disney Girls' of 1957 and the Coasters' 'Riot In Cell Block Number Nine', reworked as 'Student Demonstration Time'; 'Don't Go Near The Water' hankered for the clean ocean of childhood; and the baroque title track was exhumed from the sessions for *Smile* and restored as agonizingly as a Piero della Francesca fresco.

It was the heritage of the old song, its magical back story, that made the difference. While the album was being readied for release Van Dyke Parks, who had written the words five years earlier, predicted 'if they call it Surf's Up, they can pre-sell another 150,000 copies'. He was right. The album was the Beach Boys' biggest success since the mid-sixties and it resulted in the newly bearded band being embraced by the new rock establishment. As the demographic wheel clicked round and the teenage audience was steadily outnumbered and eclipsed by this burgeoning audience of former teenagers, the artists of the sixties discovered that their real future was in their past. For the Beach Boys, who had declined the opportunity to play at the Monterey Pop Festival in 1967 because they hadn't prepared any new songs, it took a while for this particular penny to drop.

Surf's Up was the beginning of the Beach Boys' second career, one founded entirely on people's desire to summon up the past – a past many of them had never lived through. At first the band were reluctant to include all their old songs about cars and girls, fearing that their new hairy audience wouldn't appreciate them, but eventually, with the success of George Lucas's *American Graffiti* in 1973 and the subsequent release of their multi-platinum greatest hits package *Endless Summer* in the United States, the Beach Boys discovered the great truth: people were far more interested in the past, theirs as well as the audience's, than they were in the present. It was a realization that was yet to dawn on the Rolling Stones. The past was a market the record business hadn't yet woken up to. At the time it was impossible to buy a compilation of the greatest hits of the Beatles. The Who were preparing to exploit the same market with *Meaty Beaty Big And Bouncy*, a collection of their sixties singles featuring four young fifties urchins on the cover which came out in the autumn of 1971. What the Beach Boys eventually keyed into was a deep need to travel back to a simpler, less hip and edgy world, lyrics that dealt with recognizable emotions and situations within the context of tunes you could whistle. In defiance of the sixties wisdom that you're only as good as your last hit, the Beach Boys were the first group to prove that if your last hit was powerful enough it really didn't matter how long ago it was.

F. Scott Fitzgerald famously wrote that there are no second acts in American lives. The Beach Boys are pop music's contradiction of that idea. In fact they are a perfect illustration of the characters at the end of *The Great Gatsby*, 'boats against the current, borne back ceaselessly into the past'. At the time of writing they have marked fifty years of fame and prominence. Most of that half century has been spent tapping into a legacy that was established in a very short period of time, a period arguably as brief as the three years between 1964 and 1967 when they were producing masterpiece after masterpiece. It's important to bands that they feel they are moving forward, that they can keep coming up with new songs. This is vital for their self-respect. But as one unmemorable album pursues another from premature acclaim to the bargain bin of history, as each auspicious beginning is followed by the familiar flatness, as each round of press interviews and TV appearances gives way to faint embarrassment as the new songs are dropped from the set list never to return, we in the audience increasingly identify with the line that makes a popular T-shirt slogan at festivals: play some old. In the forty-five years since *Surf's Up* that elegiac note has been sounded again and again through new albums and untold sun-worshipping compilations. Through deaths, divorces, family fractures, illnesses, breakdowns and court cases, finger-pointing memoirs and spasms of revisionism, the Beach Boys have continued to hang out the old shingle and, sometimes with the aid of hired hands who have learned them by rote and performed them better than they ever did, sing those anthems of their youth. The place those songs came from may never have existed. That doesn't stop us all wishing to go there.

On 12 October, broke, busted, betrayed but still unfailingly polite, the rocker prince of the fifties Gene Vincent died from a perforated ulcer. He had just returned from a discouraging tour of the few English clubs that would still book an act whose main achievements seemed to be so long ago. In his last interview he confessed that the young people no longer had any interest in what he did and nowadays he tended to play for the forty-somethings. He was thirty-six, which seemed unconscionably old for a rock star. Sadly he couldn't stick around long enough to benefit from the revival that would inevitably have come. For artists like Gene Vincent music was something that went forward in a straight line and there was no way those kids would ever be his audience again. But what people like the Beach Boys were beginning to see was that music actually followed the motion of a clock and if you hung around long enough it might eventually be the right time for you all over again.

Vincent may also have worried that his musical style put him firmly in the past. He wouldn't have noticed that there were lots of signs that even the most adventurous musicians were being drawn to the very same past. There were the beginnings of a rapprochement between the most psychedelic bands and the corniest old songs. The Grateful Dead may have wanted to call their 1971 double album *Skullfuck* but that didn't mean they didn't also want to include their versions of Merle Haggard's 'Mama Tried' and Buddy Holly's 'Not Fade Away'. (When in the summer the Dead had invited the Beach Boys to join them on stage at the Fillmore they had played Haggard's 'Okie From Muscogee' together. It may have been anti-hippy but they could all recognize a well-made song when they heard one.)

At the same time the folk-rock act the Nitty Gritty Dirt Band went into a Nashville studio with traditional musicians Doc Watson, Roy Acuff and Mother Maybelle Carter in what was billed as an unprecedented meeting of different generations. There was lots of nervousness about whether you could ever bridge the apparent chasm between the traditionalists and the longhairs, between the world of 'Wreck On The Highway' and the world of 'Both Sides Now', between the old world and the apparently new one. In the event it wasn't a problem. After all, Doc Watson was only forty-eight at the time and John McEuen of the Dirt Band was twenty-six. This is an age difference that would be scarcely worth remarking upon now. At the time it seemed immense. The Nashville sessions brought forth a lavishly packaged triple album of old songs given reverent new treatments. It was the first of three such albums. They all had the same name: *Will The Circle Be Unbroken*.

It was small wonder that the old certainties suddenly seemed an appealing refuge. The modern family appeared to be under great stress. Between 1970 and 1972 the number of divorces in the UK doubled. Germaine Greer's *The Female Eunuch*, which had been published in 1970, asserted that 'the housewife is an unpaid worker in her husband's house in return for the security of being a permanent employee ... but the lowest paid employees can be and are laid off, and so are wives. They have no savings, no skills which they can bargain with elsewhere, and they must bear the stigma of having been sacked.' In the United States the relaunched *Cosmopolitan* was putting its perky can-do spin on the same issues.

The issue of *Cosmo* on the street when *Surf's Up* was released in the USA announced an extract from the book *Any Woman Can* in which 'Doctor Reuben told the divorced, single or sexually marooned girl everything she wants to know'. The doctor's name was David and he was riding high on the success of his *Everything You Always Wanted To Know About Sex*. There was a boom in respectable sex manuals such as this, *The Sensuous Woman* and *The Happy Hooker*, books which could suddenly be openly displayed on the shelves of young married couples. However, nobody of any prominence would have dreamed of telling the media about any aspect of their sex life, either directly or in fictionalized form. 1971 was the year it was finally considered safe to publish E. M. Forster's novel *Maurice*. The novelist had died the year before.

Very little of these shifts in manners and mores that were taking place in the world seemed to seep into the world of pop music. Since the death of Janis Joplin in late 1970 the music business was down one prominent female voice. Joni Mitchell was still stung by having being described by *Rolling Stone* in their round-up of 1970 as 'old lady of the year' because of her affairs with a number of prominent male musicians. Sexual politics were not part of polite conversation, even when popular entertainment seemed to be trying to move them up the agenda. When Sam Peckinpah's film *Straw Dogs*, which featured Dustin Hoffman failing to protect Susan George from a gang intent on rape, was reviewed in the *New York Times*, critic Vincent Canby seemed more bothered about the editing than the content. 'Perhaps the toughest – and most erotic – scene in the film,' he wrote, 'is the one in which she is raped by one of the thugs, an old boyfriend, an encounter that begins with the exercise of force and ends with the woman's complete and willing submission.' His review of Stanley Kubrick's *A Clockwork Orange*, which came out in December 1971, is less concerned with the morality of the gang rape it depicts than the 'tour de force of extraordinary images, music, words and feelings'.

On both sides of the Atlantic the so-called serious press were very serious. In 1971 the *New Yorker* devoted no fewer than seventy pages to an extract from Charles Reich's best-selling ecology book *The Greening of America*. In October *Ebony*'s cover story promised 'Dick Gregory on genocide'. Even the arrival of Darine Stern as the first black model on the cover of October's *Playboy* seemed an occasion more for sober congratulation than licentiousness. On 29 October *Time Out*, the London listings magazine, used a black and white picture of a topless female holding a hammer to illustrate nothing in particular. It had been supplied as a still from the underground movie *Robert Having His Nipple Pierced*. The female was Patti Smith, then twenty-five and hardly known to anyone except the subject of the film, Robert Mapplethorpe.

The popular press were breezy but seemed to know their place. Because there was no celebrity press there weren't any celebrities such as we might recognize today. The constellation of sports stars, TV presenters, fashion models, popular authors, disc jockeys, chat show hosts and pop politicians who keep the bright red ball of public interest in the air today didn't exist; nor, obviously, did social media or anything like it. Readers didn't have any expectation that they could look inside the homes and private lives of the stars. Only on continental Europe were there the kind of colour magazines that followed every step of the lives of Brigitte Bardot or Johnny Hallyday, that trained long lenses on sun-kissed beaches or published a detailed breakdown of the dresses worn by middling TV actresses. The main celebrity spread in *Life* magazine in October was their photographic coverage of the party thrown by the Shah of Iran for the 2,500th anniversary of the Persian monarchy; guests included Prince Philip, Madame Tito, Imelda Marcos and Haile Selassie, who was accompanied by a dog with a diamond collar. Movie stars were glimpsed passing through airports but their parties, social rites and body issues were a mystery to most people. 1971 was the high summer of the priapism of Warren

Beatty yet none of his frantic trouser activity made it into the papers, thanks to the traditional omertà enjoyed by any company town and the parallel feeling that no respectable printer would dare to publish the details. (Ironically, his partner in celebrity fornication, Jack Nicholson, starred in the October release *Carnal Knowledge*. Interestingly, he played a man incapable of forming a proper relationship with a woman.)

Television exploited traditional stereotypes of the family for entertainment purposes. *The Homecoming*, a major TV movie prepared for Christmas, featured the Walton family and was set in the Blue Ridge Mountains during the Depression. Its promotion of pre-war stoicism and family values led to *The Waltons*, one of the biggest franchises in American TV. At the same time Dolly Parton was releasing her album *Coat Of Many Colors*, which celebrated the same kind of poor but honest family she came from in Tennessee. Family stability was celebrated in TV dramas set at both ends of the social scale. On 10 October ITV unveiled *Upstairs Downstairs*, a costume drama set in the Edwardian era featuring the Bellamy family of Eaton Square in the carpeted areas and the stock lower-middle-class types downstairs on the linoleum. It was obvious that the English would like it; what was less easy to predict was the appeal it would have for American audiences. It would run for years and provide the template for numerous hit shows, up to and including *Downton Abbey*.

In early 1971 a television producer called Craig Gilbert went looking for an average American family. Gilbert's marriage was unravelling at the time, as were those of some of his friends, and he was interested in what might be happening to that fundamental American institution at the end of the decade of 'do your own thing'. Between 1964 and 1975 American divorce rates doubled, from 24 per cent to 48 per cent. Popular entertainment was still nervous about reflecting this new reality. In 1969 the producers of *The Brady Bunch* had wanted the mother of the family to be a divorcee but the network vetoed the idea.

Gilbert had persuaded a public interest broadcaster to commission a series of documentaries about the intimate life of an average American family. The expression 'fly on the wall' was not in use in TV at the time; nor was 'reality television', which explains why he found it so hard to cast his show. He was about to give up on his quest when he was introduced to Pat Loud. Pat was forty-five, a smart and clearly telegenic upper-middle-class housewife and mother of five from affluent Santa Barbara, California. She and her husband Bill agreed to take part in his pioneering project.

There was something of the show-off about both parents. Bill, a permanently tanned alpha male, probably thought it would benefit his business, which was supplying shovel teeth to the mining business. Pat surveyed him and her five teenage children through a plume of smoke and Jackie Kennedy shades, radiating the impression that she was a couple of steps ahead of everyone else. Their children were similarly confident attention hogs. To the amazement of the crew, who were with them twelve hours a day for the best part of nine months, the Louds never once asked for the cameras and sound recording to be turned off.

The crew tracked them through the summer, as they enjoyed a life which would have seemed inconceivable to most average Americans and also probably to Pat and Bill when they were growing up in the 1930s. They and their friends drove fancy cars, smoked long cigarettes and drank hard liquor by their pools, congratulating themselves on their good fortune, confident that nobody else in the world was having a better time than they were and tacitly assuming that their children would follow in the footsteps they had so energetically hacked out for them. What the camera actually saw was that their children stumbled around in a miasma of unfocused disaffection, assuming that life somewhere else had to be better than the sumptuous idleness in which they were passing their time.

The first day's filming took place in New York in May. This was the film makers' first meeting with the eldest Loud son, Lance. Lance, who had spent most of a troubled childhood in his bedroom, only venturing out to see a child psychiatrist, had dropped out of school and college and was living in the Chelsea Hotel on his parents' dime while he sorted out what he wanted to do with his life. Pat travelled out to see him over the Labour Day weekend. There was little about the life Lance had embraced that didn't force her to raise an eyebrow. His room-mate at the Chelsea went by the name of Soren Ingenue. On her first night in New York Lance took his mother to see Warhol superstar Jackie Curtis in a transvestite musical. If she realized her son was homosexual she didn't let on to the camera.

In 1971 the word 'gay' was not yet common parlance and the subject of homosexuality was only just beginning to be accepted in polite discourse. In September 1970 Joseph Epstein, a respected man of letters, had written a piece for the cerebral journal *Harper's* called 'The Struggle for Sexual Identity' which concluded by saying 'there is much my four sons could do in their lives that might cause me anguish, that might outrage me, that might make me ashamed of them and of myself as their father. But nothing they could ever do would make me sadder than if one of them were to become homosexual. For then I should know them condemned to a state of permanent niggerdom . . . to be lived out as part of the pain of the earth.' In April Jill Tweedie had introduced the subject of Gay Lib in the *Guardian*, pointing out the challenge it represented to the status quo. 'Gay Lib,' she wrote, 'does not plead for the right of homosexuals to marry. Gay Lib questions marriage.'

By the end of filming, on New Year's Eve 1971, the Loud family had undergone their share of trials. The fractures in the family had climaxed during a vodka-laced lunch to celebrate the Santa Barbara fiesta when it became clear that Pat was tired of Bill's catting around. 'You know that Carole King song "It's Too Late"?' she says to a friend. 'Well, it's too late, baby.' She tells her husband, 'I think you're a goddam asshole.' One evening when Bill arrives back from another business trip she tells him, on camera, that she has begun divorce proceedings. Bill takes the news as if it was just another difficult day at work.

The broadcast of *An American Family* in the spring of 1973 was a watershed moment in the history of TV. As Craig Gilbert has said, 'nobody criticised the film; they just criticised the family'. It led to a furious national debate about what the previous five years of prosperity and free love had done to the American family. Viewers dealt with their envy of the Louds' material comfort, the four cars, the foreign trips, the whisky sours, their unsinkable self-confidence, by tutting over their heedless, unexamined lives. One newspaper called them 'affluent zombies'.

In subsequent decades the format would be perfected by people considerably less scrupulous than Craig Gilbert. Scenarios like the one he was unwittingly a party to would be deliberately contrived in pursuit of higher ratings and greater advertising revenue. *An American Family* left a peculiar legacy. Lance Loud went on to become a minor personality on the fringes of punk rock and managed to have a career out of an undefined desire to show off. He was a gay icon before people knew that there were such things. His grandmother, born in a narrower world, described him as 'the first of the spoiled'. Even *Rolling Stone*, which wasn't traditionally in the habit of looking down on young people, complained, 'what Lance knew of life he knew from movies and television shows, from rock records and comic strips'.

If *Rolling Stone* suddenly sounded like the voice of the older generation, that was because it was. By 1973 the sixties generation was starting to settle into the comfortable shoes of domesticity. They couldn't stop themselves disapproving of their younger brothers and sisters, with their tight, glittery T-shirts, their taste for the meretricious temptations of metal and glam, and their apparent lack of interest in the joys of comfort and continuity.

OCTOBER PLAYLIST

The Beach Boys, 'Surf's Up'
The Grateful Dead, 'Me And Bobby McGee'
Dolly Parton, 'Coat Of Many Colors'
Carpenters, 'Superstar'
Neil Young, 'A Man Needs A Maid'
The Kinks, 'Muswell Hillbilly'
Frank Zappa and Mothers of Invention, 'Peaches En Regalia'
Laura Lee, 'Women's Love Rights'
The Nitty Gritty Dirt Band, 'Will The Circle Be Unbroken'
Al Green, 'Tired Of Being Alone'

NOVEMBER: HUNKY DORY

I n the autumn of 1971 I spent most of my spare time in a small north London record shop called Harum. It was a friendly place run by a couple of brothers and it seemed to attract all the would-be cognoscenti in the vicinity. Usually I couldn't afford to buy anything; I was mainly going there to be in the company of records. I would flick through the new releases, hungrily devouring all the details of the personnel listed on the covers. I even got to know the names of the designers and photographers, smirked at the in-jokes in the credits, and noted which musicians' names cropped up most often. Only rarely did I buy anything and when I did it tended to be from the bargain bin, which generally contained white label review copies of new albums that had been sold to the shop by some lucky music paper journalist who happened to live nearby.

I've still got the copy of Ry Cooder's *Boomer's Story* I brought back from one of these trips. I've also hung on to Danny O'Keefe's 'Good Time Charlie's Got The Blues'. I don't believe I've ever got past that one song. It's such a great song I didn't really need to. I've also got a record on the Paramount label by a band called Detroit. Previously they had been known as Mitch Ryder and the Detroit Wheels. Back in May the thrusting of Mitch's hips had disturbed some of the feminist activists who had been marching on Washington over the war in Vietnam. This album was Mitch's bid for hip acceptance. It had the first version of Lou Reed's 'Rock N Roll' I ever heard. Reed liked the way the guitarist Steve Hunter played and subsequently invited him to play in his band. That's how I really pieced together whatever I knew about rock and roll – from reading the credits on record jackets in Harum. That was the order in which you were introduced to music in 1971. You read about it first and heard it second. It meant you created your own star system in your head.

In building this you were beginning to learn that certain labels were more likely to be a guarantee of specific qualities than others. There was Island for folk-rock like Fairport Convention's *Angel Delight*, Charisma for brow-furrowing greatcoat music like Van der Graaf Generator's *Pawn Hearts*, Asylum for harmonious music from the West Coast like Judee Sill's 'Jesus Was A Crossmaker', Atlantic for crunching house party music like the J. Geils Band's *The Morning After*, Shelter for smart blues-rock hybrids like Freddie King's *Getting Ready*, Elektra for lyrical projects of rare refinement like Mickey Newbury's *Frisco Mabel Joy*, and John Peel's Dandelion label for music like Bridget St John's

Songs For The Gentle Man which was seemingly too delicate for this world.

The vinyl shortage was way off in the future, there was lots of talent around and no telling what the public might prefer, so a shop like Harum would buy in at least one copy of all these records. The actual vinyl would be stored behind the counter in a masterbag. The cover was put in a plastic dust wallet and placed out in the racks under Rock A–Z. It was there I got my education in what made a record great.

The people who had traditionally worked as 'producers' rarely got their names on the covers because they were in the employ of the companies that manufactured and marketed the records. Their job had been to represent the interests of the label's stockholders by ensuring artists signed to that label made the kind of records the label thought it could sell. This usually meant the kind of records they had been able to sell most recently.

In the latter half of the sixties this had changed. In the eight years since George Martin, an archetypal example of the producer as company man, had proposed that the Beatles' first single should be Mitch Murray's insufferable 'How Do You Do It', the traditional division of labour over which producers would preside had been shattered by the unique genius of those four men. Just as they had fused the previously discrete disciplines of singing, playing, songwriting and recording into an entirely new discipline called 'making records', so their determination to work both sides of the glass when it came to establishing the sound of those records and even the way they should be packaged had inverted the hierarchy between the executive and the factory floor.

The control room of Studio 2 at Abbey Road, where the Beatles made most of their records, could only be approached by a steep staircase from the studio's parquet floor, which perfectly illustrated where the power had traditionally resided. All that had changed in the summer of 1967 when the Beatles unveiled *Sgt Pepper*, a record which seemed to have been made in defiance of all the sacred tenets of the trade. They hadn't entered the EMI studios that year with songs so much as ideas for records. The first side of *Sgt Pepper* ended with a song whose lyrics came verbatim from a Victorian circus poster. The second side started with a ponderous piece played on the sitar, an instrument that had only previously featured in Western entertainment as a form of comic relief. The album finished with a sustained orchestral chord which left most listeners unsure whether they should take the record off or not. The finished record came packaged in a cover that didn't make it immediately clear who it was by. The album didn't have a traditional love song on it. It didn't have a dance song on it. It didn't have an old favourite. It had none of the sheet anchors which the old wisdom strongly suggested were important to thrive in the marketplace. None of this prevented it selling in quantity and being celebrated all over the world.

In the wake of the Beatles' unprecedented success the record business slackened the reins that had given them complete control of the talent. This wasn't because they had been converted to the virtues of creativity unfettered. It was because they had discovered that it appeared to work. An act left to its own devices, working in its preferred studio with the engineer and producer it had chosen, was more likely to come up with a hit than the same act being forced to go along meekly with the company's way of doing things.

This opened the way for a new generation of producers and engineers capable of mediating between the often petulant demands of the musicians and the requirements of the market. Like David Selznick in F. Scott Fitzgerald's famous phrase, a select few of these producers were the kind of people who could hold the whole equation of making great records in their heads. Because these people worked for themselves and not the record companies they could negotiate their own royalties on sales and were more concerned than anyone with the quality of what they produced. George Martin had left EMI's studio at Abbey Road to start his own studios in the West End of London in order to be able to command the money he never would have earned as the company's salary man. The record companies temporarily abdicated their traditional role of trying to predict public taste and looked to the producers to ensure that the recording was brought in on time and on budget and would sell. With the odd exception, such as Carole King's *Tapestry*, whose producer happened to own his own company, the majority of the big albums of 1971 were made without any involvement from the record company at all.

Sometimes this was a good thing. Sometimes it wasn't. The experience of Pink Floyd in 1971 indicated what happened when nobody was in charge. Pink Floyd had a curious relationship with their record company EMI. As part of their new deal they were given unlimited time in the company's studios. They soon decamped to George Martin's newly established AIR studios because there they could record on sixteen tracks. This expanding new technology afforded them all manner of new ways of indulging their great weakness, which was not being able to make up their mind. Veterans of the sessions for the record that eventually became *Meddle* recall interminable days taken up by experimentation with the capturing of sounds made by household objects, sessions during which each member of the group played without being able to hear the others, which featured Heath Robinson arrangements where the tape led directly from one tape recorder to another, and which eventually resulted in a lot of ideas labelled 'Nothing One', 'Nothing Two' ad infinitum.

Experimentation nonetheless had its place. The 1971 recording which has had most impact on subsequent generations of music makers was Black Sabbath's *Master Of Reality*. Here for the first time guitarist Tony Iommi de-tuned his instrument by three semitones. This was in part to slacken the strings and cope with the pain he felt after having injured his fingers as a teenager in an industrial accident in a Midlands engineering works. On tracks like 'Into The Void' this had the accidental happy effect of creating the slurry signature sound imitated by scores of young bands over the subsequent twenty years from the age of heavy metal to the era of grunge.

The word 'producer', I was learning, could be used to describe a wide range of different skill sets and personalities, from Rodger Bain, the uncelebrated professional who oversaw the genuinely ground-breaking opening trio of Black Sabbath albums that culminated with *Master Of Reality*, through auteurs like Phil Spector who used musicians to produce the sound they heard in their heads, and craftsmen like George Martin who knew how to add the dabs of colour or extra texture that made the Beatles records so vivid, all the way to impresarios like the lanky, charismatic Richard Perry. In 1971 the Brooklyn-born Perry, who had come to notice as the producer of the unexpectedly successful *God Bless Tiny Tim*, produced big albums for Harry Nilsson and Barbra Streisand just as Irving Thalberg produced movies in the golden age of Hollywood. In both cases he took artists worried that they were outside the rock fold and put them in a new frame. In the case of Streisand he nudged her in the direction of songs by writers like Laura Nyro and Randy Newman. Perry was good with people; a cajoler, a ringmaster, a jocular tyrant. His people-handling skills were worthy of Billy Wilder. He knew you had to capture the performance before the artist thought it was perfect, at which point it was actually stale. When the diva was skittish the night before the vocal recording of 'Stoney End' he made sure she heard him mutter, 'I never thought Barbra Streisand would be frightened by a song.'

Harry Nilsson was so keen to get him on board he agreed to Perry's stipulation that the producer should call all the shots. 'The plan was to make a Beatles quality album. My plan was he would be my Beatles and I would be his George Martin,' he recalled. This scenario had been teed up by the band themelves. When the Beatles had been asked to name their favourite group they nominated Nilsson. They weren't being entirely facetious. They recognized that a lot of what the Beatles had offered was contained within this absurdly talented individual. It was a further part of Perry's plan that Nilsson uproot from Los Angeles and make the record at Trident Studios in London. He considered London the recording capital of the world, an inspiration in itself and home to musicians with a combination of accomplishment and Limey playfulness that might fire Nilsson's imagination.

In 1971 the London studio scene was a crossroads where somebody like Perry could easily whistle up a left-over jazzer like Herbie Flowers, a rocker like Chris Spedding, tarrying mid-way between Ian Carr's Nucleus and Andy Fraser's Sharks, former Spooky Tooth man Gary Wright, who was to contribute the opening chords of 'Without You', and not one but two master American drummers, Jim Gordon and Jim Keltner, who were both waiting, like ancient mariners, at the pleasure of various former Beatles. And, because this was Harry, whose reputation for being clubbable went before him and got him into all sorts of trouble, Ringo Starr himself. They all made their way down Wardour Street where there was never anywhere to park, and down St Anne's Court, there to load their gear into the ancient iron lift that was the only way to reach the studio on the top floor. What they played when they got there combined mastery with playfulness in a way that would have been difficult in LA.

You only had to look at the cover of *Nilsson Schmilsson* when it appeared in November 1971 to realize that slickness wasn't part of the plan. Like so many of the albums of 1971 it was the frayed edges that gave it character. The mistakes were left in. The diamond hadn't been polished. The same vulnerability evident in the title and the cover, featuring a blurred picture of the artist stealing downstairs in the middle of the night in his bathrobe to quell a case of the munchies, came through the music.

There's no better example of this than 'Jump Into The Fire', which was largely improvised in the studio by drummer Jim Gordon, guitarist Chris Spedding and bassist Herbie Flowers. As it continued past the five-minute mark with no immediate end in sight Flowers mischievously slackened his strings hoping he could bring it to a conclusion. His joke remains on the finished version. Martin Scorsese loved 'Jump Into The Fire' so much that he tried to fit it into every movie he made, until finally finding a place for it in 1990 in *GoodFellas*. When Ray Liotta leaves his house for what will prove to be his last day of freedom it's to the accompaniment of Herbie Flowers' bass riff. (For his work on this immortal recording Flowers earned a session fee of £12, as he did for his even more distinctive bass line in Lou Reed's 'Walk On The Wild Side'.)

Unsurprisingly, Perry and Nilsson didn't get through the project without butting heads. Perry remembers a summit meeting over tea at the Dorchester where he confronted the artist with his earlier promise that he would let Perry have creative control. 'Well, I lied,' said Nilsson. They got in a cab, went straight back to St Anne's Court, and Nilsson immediately delivered the vocal on 'Without You'.

They spent the month of June making the record. When they were short of material Perry would march Nilsson around the music publishers of the West End in search of suitable songs. When these were not forthcoming he would force Harry to eke out whatever fragments he had into songs like 'Coconut', 'The Moonbeam Song' and 'Driving Along'. Rarely has an artist gone into the studio with so little and come out with so much. 'Without You' was the song that made the difference. Harry had heard Badfinger's comparatively drab version of their song on the radio in LA and instantly identified with the sense of utter desolation in it and intuited how he could use the power in his voice to insert a note which hadn't been there before. In doing so he unwittingly invented the power ballad, a form that has moved a great deal of soda in the years since.

The ad for *Nilsson Schmilsson* in *Billboard* said 'Harry's made a rock album'. It went on to sell five million copies, picking up many sales from fans who had given up hoping that the Beatles would get back together and were attracted by its combination of passion and whimsy, melody and soul. The following year the same team reconvened in Trident ostensibly to do it all again. RCA had little to do with making the first album; when they asked what they could do to help with the follow-up Perry got them to pay for a film to be made of the whole process. By then Harry had tipped too far into drinking and drugging, divorced his wife, abandoned his child in the way his own father had abandoned him and succumbed to the feelings of unworthiness which were rarely far away even during his most sublime melodic transports. On *Son Of Schmilsson*, the refrain of the catchiest song went 'you're breaking my heart so fuck you'. Commercially at least it was mostly downhill for Harry Nilsson after 1971. Rarely has an artist seemed so determined to undermine his own success.

Ken Scott was the engineer in charge of the next album to be made at Trident. Like so many of the young men aspiring to the title 'producer', Scott had started work as a tea boy in a recording studio in 1964, straight out of school. Since the studio was EMI in Abbey Road he graduated through the company's civil service-like structure from working in the tape library to eventually becoming a recording engineer. Despite working closely with the Beatles, Jeff Beck, Pink Floyd and Procol Harum, he was never tempted to dress like the artists. One colleague remembers him turning up for *White Album* sessions wearing a three-piece suit and carrying a Samsonite attaché case. Where Perry was the bon viveur and orchestrator of mood, Scott was pure nerd.

Like many house engineers Scott went freelance in 1970, working at Trident Studios in Soho on recordings for Elton John, the Aynsley Dunbar Retaliation, the New Seekers and everything in between. It was here he met David Bowie, a young man whose direction was sufficiently vague for Scott to be unsure whether he was a session pianist, a producer or a performer in his own right. The first time Ken Scott engineered a Bowie session it was in the spring of 1971 and the song was 'Hang On To Yourself', but the singer was Freddie Burretti, who was, he remembered, small, camp and wore silver hot pants to the studio. By mid-1971 Bowie was signed to the management company Gem which could afford to pay to make an album. He wanted a producer who wouldn't boss him around but at the same time would prevent him from making a fool of himself. Linking up with Scott, an engineer seeking to graduate to producing, was a perfect marriage of convenience.

In Scott's memoirs he remembers the summer of 1971 as a particularly active time. He worked on Van der Graaf Generator's *Pawn Hearts*, Lindisfarne's *Fog On The Tyne* and recordings for Apple featuring everyone from Mary Hopkin to the Radha Krishna Temple. On one occasion he was called out to Tittenhurst Park to engineer a John Lennon session for 'I Don't Wanna Be A Soldier' and was dismayed to see the working-class hero repeatedly snorting cocaine in the hope that he could get his vocal right. The Bowie sessions, on the other hand, he remembers as being achieved without benefit of either alcohol or drugs. Both Scott and Rick Wakeman, who played piano on the album, remember the first time they heard the songs that would make up *Hunky Dory*. Wakeman called them 'the finest selection of songs I have ever heard in one sitting in my life'. Scott was less immediately struck but as soon as they began recording he realized 'this could be a lot bigger than I expected'.

They recorded the new album in two weeks in June 1971 as the astronauts of the Apollo 15 mission used their buggy to go for a drive on the moon, the nineteen-year-old native Australian Evonne Goolagong began her victorious Wimbledon campaign, and the situation in Northern Ireland deteriorated further with the killing of more British soldiers. The recording was followed by two weeks of mixing. Bowie, who didn't care for being in the studio, wasn't there for the latter stage. The basic band, guitarist Mick Ronson, drummer Woody Woodmansey and bassist Trevor Bolder, learned the songs from the demos that Bowie and his publisher Bob Grace had put together in order to get other artists like Peter Noone interested in his songs. They even wrote a letter to Dudley Moore to see if he was available. It's not clear if he ever responded.

Most of the vocals were done first take, even the complicated ones. There was no use of 'punching in', the technique whereby vocal performances could be assembled line by line, word by word, let alone – as is quite common today – syllable by syllable. Imperfections were turned into features. The phone that can be heard ringing at the end of 'Life On Mars?' was from a pay-phone in the bathroom which the musicians could use to make outgoing calls. Nobody knew the number and consequently it never rung. Until that day.

Although not a hit, *Hunky Dory* perfectly captures the zeitgeist of 1971. From the reference to space travel on its signature song 'Life On Mars?' to the 'two new pence to have a go' in 'Andy Warhol'; from the Ovaltine cosiness of the old English saying that provided its title to the nostalgia for the silver screen which suffused its cover picture; from the Denmark Street lilt of 'Kooks', his song for his first child, to the thin-lipped New York snarl of 'Queen Bitch', it is, like so many of the great albums of 1971, neither one thing nor another, and gloriously so. In the summer of 1971 David Bowie enjoyed one perfect, delicious moment when he had nothing to lose, everything to gain and all the right people behind him. He had no record company giving him advice, he had a bunch of musicians hanging on to his coat tails who knew that it was either this or dragging their tails back to Hull to become hairdressers, he had a producer who needed a record to be seen as a success, he had a head full of post-cards from his recent travels in America and nights out in the Sombrero club, and no fan following beyond a bunch of people who asked no more than to be pleasantly surprised. What came out was a unique kaleidoscope of previously sup-pressed feelings, grand gestures, borrowed clothes, gauche versifying and, more important than all these things com-bined, great tunes. *Hunky Dory* may have been composed at the piano in Haddon Hall and recorded in a smokey room in Soho. It seemed to have a heart as big as all outdoors.

RCA in New York, who had seen off the competition to sign Bowie, announced the record's release in *Billboard* in the middle of November. The ad used a quote from *Rock* magazine hailing him as 'the most singularly gifted artist creating music today. He has the genius to be to the 70s what Lennon, McCartney, Jagger and Dylan were to the 60s.' It was the kind of rhetoric that seemed to match the ambition of the record. The *New York Times* called Bowie 'the most intellectually brilliant man yet to choose the long-playing record as his medium of expression'. *Hunky Dory* felt like music that was pushing boldly forward into a brave new world and it was important for the rhetoric to keep pace. The job of a record reviewer, which had previously been to point out that track four was a mid-tempo shuffle in which the lead vocal was shared between John and Paul, suddenly became about finding the words to properly express the new importance of the music.

Hunky Dory didn't come out until the middle of December. By the time it had appeared Bowie had started making the record that would follow it. Again he got Ken Scott involved, although he warned him that he might not like it as much as its predecessor. He took two of the songs he'd been trying with Freddie Burretti earlier in the year, a version of Ron Davies' 'It Ain't Easy' that had been destined for *Hunky Dory*, and then wrote a number of new songs that could fit broadly into the idea of fictional rock in a dystopian future. The record, which was finished by the end of 1971, came to be called *The Rise And Fall Of Ziggy Stardust And The*

Spiders From Mars, though nobody working on it at the time thought of it as being particularly thematic or conceptual. It certainly had a more clenched and teen-friendly sound. There was no Rick Wakeman. The group sounded like the house band of Kubrick's *A Clockwork Orange* (which had just come out) crossed with Marc Bolan's T. Rex. RCA were played the finished album by the end of the year and said they didn't hear a single. Bowie, feeling he had proved his point by delivering the album, was happy to go back into the studio first thing in the New Year to record the radio-friendly 'Starman', the song that propelled him into a whole new kind of pop stardom in the UK when it came out in the spring of 1972.

By then he could look back on twelve months during which he had made his first life-changing visit to America, made contact with Lou Reed and Iggy Pop, fathered his first child, released two albums, recorded a third and come up with 'Changes', 'Oh! You Pretty Things', 'Life On Mars?', 'The Bewlay Brothers', 'Hang On To Yourself', 'Five Years', 'Ziggy Stardust', 'Suffragette City' and 'Starman'. If all we knew of David Bowie was what he did in 1971 it would be more than enough.

Solo artists could be difficult for a producer. They were nothing like as demanding as a band. Every band, no matter how placid they may appear on the surface, is a combination of a family, dissatisfied business unit and warring political party. The producer the bands increasingly asked for by name in 1971 was Glyn Johns. In 1971 Johns was twenty-nine. He came from the same Home Counties background as the Rolling Stones. He also had played in bands but at the age of seventeen he got a job as a junior in an independent recording studio and it was his ability to get a good sound from a rock group that made his name. A good proportion of the great quicksilver 45s of the sixties came from faders manipulated by Glyn Johns: the Who's 'My Generation', the Small Faces' 'Tin Soldier', the Rolling Stones' 'Honky Tonk Women' and the Kinks' 'All Day And All Of The Night' being just four of them. His reputation was equally high when it came to the longer form. He engineered the Rolling Stones' *Beggars Banquet* and the first albums by the Steve Miller Band.

Johns' great quality was his willingness to tell star musicians things they might not have wished to hear. He only took on jobs he felt were right for him. Late in 1971 David Geffen summoned him to the USA twice to see what he thought of an exciting new band signed to Geffen's management and to his label. The members of the band, particularly the handsome, confident lead guitarist, were under the impression that their forte was rocking. Johns didn't agree. He was on the point of passing on them altogether when he heard them amusing themselves at rehearsal one day by singing in close harmony. Then he realized that this group could be a latter-day Everly Brothers rather than just another Rolling Stones. He went on to produce their first two albums. They were called the Eagles.

In February 1971 Johns was called by Kit Lambert, manager of the Who, to ask if he would get involved with their new album. The band were already engaged in a Pete Townshend brainchild called *Lifehouse*, which was supposed to be a film, a multi-media epic, a unique collaboration between performer and audience and, on some level, a 'crowd-sourced' piece of art in which the band would facilitate the audience in reaching a new level of consciousness. The Who's weekly concerts at the Young Vic, which had begun in January, were part of this project, which was so complex and yet so nebulous that none of the band or indeed their management understood the idea sufficiently to get behind it. Johns was very keen to work with the Who again but he was blunt enough to tell Townshend the truth when nobody else would. Pete, he said, nobody understands your film idea. Let's drop that and just make a brilliant record.

Townshend didn't put up a fight. Kit Lambert, whose background was in classical music and who was even more given to grand schemes than Townshend, really wanted another rock opera in the mould of *Tommy*. 1971 was the year *Jesus Christ Superstar* was enjoying a mainstream success most rock bands could only dream about and the common view of the Who was that *Tommy*, which came out in 1969, had been their peak. Just as Elvis had believed that the true pinnacle of his success was in movies, so in the late sixties many believed that the increasing sophistication of rock would inevitably lead it into long-form. Lambert wanted to believe this for reasons of scale and prestige. Townshend wanted to believe it because it seemed the only proper vehicle for his seriousness. By being prepared to say that he didn't understand the idea, Glyn Johns delivered us all from that.

The Who moved the recording to New York. The story goes that Lambert was so excited by the way they were sounding and so at a loss to know what to do about it that he just wrote out a note saying 'Keep going!' and pressed it to the control room glass. When Johns came on board he listened to what they had and suggested they should start again, so they came back to London, working initially with the Rolling Stones mobile truck at Stargroves, Mick Jagger's country home, and then at Olympic studios in Barnes, which was always Johns' location of choice. Like Stax in Memphis, Olympic had started life as a cinema. It was originally intended for use as a soundtrack studio and therefore had a big room which could accommodate an orchestra. When the future proved to be in rock bands the acreage of floor space and high ceilings made it ideal for recording loud rock in a way that preserved its drama and dynamics.

While they were making the album the Who were still setting off to play gigs, sometimes as far north as Dundee. There was nothing they had played and recorded that they couldn't perform on stage. Their set list changed all the time, scribbled out by Roger Daltrey just minutes before shows at the Top Rank Suite in Sunderland, the Mayfair Suite in Birmingham, the Assembly Hall, Worthing or the Pavilion in Bath. They had a full diary. That was how they knew they were a band. 'Between 1965 and 1972,' Daltrey recalled later, 'we lived out of a suitcase.'

The work paid dividends. No rock and roll band before or since have been more accomplished live performers than the Who in the years between 1968 and 1972. They had proved it the year before when they recorded shows at the universities of Leeds and Hull for the album that became *Live At Leeds*. Nik Cohn, the chronicler of fifties and sixties rock, called it 'the best live rock album of all time', a title it still holds. The fact that they managed to reach the kind of cohesion they show on *Live At Leeds* without the usual overdubs with which live albums are usually made ready for public consumption is remarkable enough. The fact that they made such a gigantic sound with just the four of them continues to boggle the mind. When they appear on stage in the twenty-first century they need a handful of extra musicians in order to make the sound they could once make as a four-piece within minutes of tumbling out of the van. It is, as Chris Charlesworth said in *Melody Maker* at the time, as if they grew a fifth musician in the process of playing live.

In 1971 they were as volatile as ever but Keith Moon had not yet entirely succumbed to alcohol. Daltrey said they were 'never nearer to breaking up' at the time, just as the Beatles had done and the Stones had almost done. Townshend's anxiety attacks were made worse by the fact that he was nearing thirty and his wife had just had their first child. In his case the standard songwriter's fear of the next single was compounded by the fact that there was an expectation he would produce another entire opera. Everybody was looking expectantly at him to take them forward into the new decade and his problem at the time was that he had too many ideas rather than not enough.

Although Johns is only listed as 'associate producer' he was the one we have to thank for what may be the best album of 1971. He was the one who persuaded Townshend to salvage some big ambitious songs from the big ambitious project, where they would only be weighted down with tiresome exposition, and put them on one single long-playing record. Although the overarching idea of *Lifehouse* didn't survive, it's in the nature of pop that its essence is best distilled into small, powerful units, that it communicates in glimmers and slivers rather than in the sustained narratives and slowly unfolding themes of the grown-up arts; and in fact *Who's Next* is way better than *Lifehouse* could ever have hoped to be and it continues to be played, enjoyed and pilfered from long after the likes of *Tommy* and *Quadrophenia* have grown tiresome. This is largely because of one tune, which may well be the best recording of the best year in the history of recording, the five-minute opening cut, 'Baba O'Riley'.

One of the things that made Glyn Johns a production genius was his lack of interest in how things were supposed to work and his readiness to understand what actually did work. The opening figure of Townshend's, which was played on a Lowrey organ and then put through a synthesizer which only a handful of musicians at the time could be bothered to try to work, was the first time this new instrument had been used to provide not washes of colour but a propulsive rhythm track. In the case of both 'Baba O'Riley' and 'Won't Get Fooled Again' Keith Moon played in time to a rhythm dictated by a machine. In years to come all records would be made like this. Similar experiments elsewhere in the spring of 1971 may have been leading other bands to the same conclusions – though since a synthesizer was so expensive only people who had made a lot of money could afford one – but when 'Baba O'Riley' hit FM radio in August of that year it was, as far as most people who were listening were concerned, the first time. Because 'Baba O'Riley' is poised perfectly between what had been and what was about to be, it's a unique pop record.

The singer might not have known what was in Townshend's head when he wrote the lines 'out here in the fields I fight for my meals' but nobody in the world was better suited than Roger Daltrey to the act of singing it as though the thought had just entered his head. 'Baba O'Riley' is an intoxicating salmagundi of whims and profundities, of grand schemes and short-cuts, of the future as represented by the apparently unmanned keyboard figure at the beginning, and the past as embodied in the devil's elbow fiddle at the end, of the religious impulse represented in the name of Townshend's guru Meher Baba and the technical nod implicit in the name of Terry Riley, whose *In C* had inspired it, of the earnest desire to elevate the audience competing with the urgent need to give it something to get down to, of the psychedelic colours of the sixties meeting this brown new decade, of the AM sensibilities of the group who gave us 45s like 'Substitute' piercing the Marshall stacks of what was yet to become arena rock. 'Baba O'Riley' sits at the centre of *Who's Next*, providing a tent pole so reliable that they could even afford to reserve their other big gun 'Won't Get Fooled Again' for the very end; *Who's Next* sits at the centre of 1971's claim to be the most perfect moment in the short history of rock and roll, and with each passing year that claim grows stronger.

'Baba O'Riley' enjoys a rich after-life. It's used to ramp up the drama when the Los Angeles Lakers come on the court. It's been covered by countless young bands who dearly wish they could come up with anything with quite the same surge. It had a new lease of life in 2004 when it was used as the theme for *CSI New York*. It closed out the London Olympics of 2012, the two surviving members of the band joined by what seemed like an orchestra of accompanying musicians, the lyrics bowdlerized in deference to the event it was closing so that Daltrey now sang 'there's more than Teenage Wasteland'.

At the beginning of November 1971 the Who headlined three nights at the newly opened Rainbow in Finsbury Park, north London. This had previously been the Finsbury Park Astoria, the starting point for the package tours that used to take live music around the country. An unprecedented nine thousand tickets were sold in nine hours. It didn't appear that live rock could get any bigger.

While the cover of *Who's Next*, which features the members of the group retreating down a slag heap having evidently just urinated on a concrete monolith, did at least feature the performers, the fourth album by Led Zeppelin, which was in the window of Harum just a week after the Who had begun their opening stand at the Rainbow, was a complete departure from all the accepted tenets of product packaging.

On the front was a hand-tinted picture from the Edwardian era of an elderly rustic presumably returning home after a day's collecting branches of wood from the forest owned by his master. He is so bowed down by the weight of this firewood that he has to lean on his stick. The photograph is framed and hangs on the wall of an old house, possibly occupied by his forebears who may have moved to the city to find work in industry. Pull back again and we see the house is presumably an old back-to-back in the city, and as we fold out the full cover we recognize that we are meant to conclude this house in its turn has been knocked down and the occupants rehoused in the charmless high-rise on the back cover.

Designer Aubrey Powell's work has been subject to many interpretations over the years. Some Led Zeppelin scholars even think they recognize the man on the cover and can trace a link from him to Jimmy Page via the work of his favoured occultist Aleister Crowley. What's known is that the picture was found by Robert Plant and its use as one of the two key motifs on the record was an important statement about what Led Zeppelin thought of themselves.

What it said most immediately was, we are not Grand Funk Railroad. Led Zeppelin had seen enough of the new generation of hard rock bands coming up in their slipstream, many of them pandering to the same cheap wine and cheaper drugs crowd as they did, to strongly suspect that there was a danger of the finer points of what they did being lost to sight. The popularity of their music may have taken them into purpose-built amphitheatres in the midst of vast parking lots, but it was still composed in a folksy style by a bunch of heads sitting around the fireplace of one of England's many stately ruins. Its performers may have been sleeping in silken sheets in air-conditioned eyries at the top of luxury hotel blocks and conveyed to performances in their own mono-grammed planes but they had all grown up in the narrow chill of bombsite Britain and knew the thousand indignities and inconveniences which that life was heir to. Their music in performance may have been amplified at a level which burst or beggared any form of measurement placed before it but it was initially composed on acoustic guitars, mandolins and recorders. The fifteen-year-old in the Sam Goody music store who was trying to decide between Led Zeppelin and the latest by Bloodrock or Black Oak Arkansas would never have dreamed that the new one from the Limeys had been composed under the influence of Fairport Convention's

Full House or The Incredible String Band's *The Hangman's Beautiful Daughter*. The choice of that man with his bundle of sticks for the cover rather than an expensive shot of Robert's glistening chest was a way of re-emphasizing the great little band that was getting lost inside a band that increasingly seemed to have been put on this earth to redefine the term 'big'. In 1971 Led Zeppelin made the old maths look silly. It was as though they had discovered an entirely new wing in what had previously been thought to be a compact family house. In Barney Hoskyns' book *Trampled Underfoot*, Chris Dreja, formerly the bass player in the Yardbirds, recalls that when Peter Grant got in touch to say Led Zeppelin were playing Madison Square Garden he assumed that he'd got the name of the venue wrong. He simply didn't believe bands could play venues that big.

The design of the album was also an expression of the band's sheer commercial heft and the extent to which they now held the power in the relationship with the traditional star-making machinery. Not only did the cover not have the traditional picture of the musicians who made the record, it didn't even feature the name of the band or the record. This monument to inscrutability was something not even the Beatles in their pomp had dared to do. Atlantic were provided with the finished artwork and told that was the way it would be. Atlantic argued but without any great force. Led Zeppelin and Peter Grant got their way.

At no stage did Led Zeppelin seem to accommodate the things the market expected. They did few interviews, they didn't appear on television, they didn't go in for much in the way of advertising, and none of it seemed to harm their commercial prospects. What it did mean was that they didn't have many allies and other bands were deeply resentful of their success. Critics who knew there was very little chance of being called upon to interview them felt no compunction in dismissing them, particularly for some of their more excessive flights of fantasy. Their musical peers felt that they were never invited in. Led Zeppelin weren't in the family. They didn't participate in all-star jams, they didn't schmooze the industry and the industry didn't schmooze them, through a combination of arrogance, timidity and fear of Peter Grant and Jimmy Page. Led Zeppelin had a reputation for being unpleasant and getting their way, a reputation which they were quite happy to see grow.

While Keith Richards was being exalted as the good, even the virtuous spirit of rock and roll, Jimmy Page was the one people talked about behind their hands. They muttered about his worrying interest in the occult, the age of his teenage girlfriends, the extent to which he might have leaned on the songs of Willie Dixon or the licks of Randy California. You couldn't argue about the power of the product. What nobody could contest was the buckle-kneed heft of the music Led Zeppelin had made in the early part of 1971. *Led Zeppelin IV* was truly music that sold itself.

The 6 November issue of *Billboard* came with a quarter strip ad across the bottom of its front page. This bore four symbols that would have meant nothing to any of its readers. The only thing it was possible to read was the logo of the record company, Atlantic. *Shaft* was at number one and in Amsterdam Rod Stewart was being presented with five gold discs to recognize the success he had seen since the release of

Every Picture Tells A Story in July. There was a four-page ad for *E Pluribus Funk*, the new album by Grand Funk Railroad, an ad which featured colour portraits of all three members of the band. Next to *Led Zeppelin IV* this looked gauche and needy.

In the second week of release the record went from 36 to 8, the following week to 5, then to 2, where it remained over Christmas looking up at Sly and the Family Stone, holding off Carole King's *Music*, which overtook it after Christmas. But while in time those other records slipped away, *Led Zeppelin IV* never did. Along with Carole King's *Tapestry* it pioneered a new dimension of the music business which could only be expressed via the compound adjective 'multi-platinum'. To sell in these kinds of quantities you have to be no longer reliant on the normal levels of marketing. To sell week in week out for months, even years, you need a product that is its own most powerful advocate.

Making music louder is not difficult. Making music sound louder is a lot harder. 1971 was the age of the Marshall stack, of mutually assured tinnitus, the time when people like Pete Townshend were telling its inventor that he needed 'bigger weapons', when impressionable young men sat on their bony backsides on the cold floors of venues and passed the time waiting for the headliners by calculating the amplification equipment arrayed against them, like cavalry counting the mouths of the cannon they were about to face.

The record starts with the slurring of a tape being run back to a cue point followed by a brief moment of silence. Then the snorting of a wakened beast, the first cough of a semi-truck on a cold morning, a noise which announces that something is about to occur. What matters is the micro-second of silence between it finishing and Robert Plant's echo-soused 'Hey hey mama said the way you move/ gonna make you sweat, gonna make you groove'. Then a drum tattoo that sounds like somebody's pushed a wardrobe full of bricks from the top of a stone staircase announces what seems like a cross between Link Wray's 'Rumble' and Samson pulling down the pillars of the temple. It's the most bravura opening to what may be the most bravura rock and roll album of the era.

Led Zeppelin IV was a glorious grab bag of the polished and the gimcrack, the rootsy and the Brilliantined, of hop-infused Midlands folk and the cheap whiskey of the Delta lands, of ancient and modern, of quiet and loud, of hippy philosophy and apprentice boy aggression, such as had never been done before and probably never was to be done again, of rock and roll and progressive rock, of mock profundity and the odd genuinely bleak insight. It sounds like the actual caverns depicted on its artwork; it feels like the very water coming through the levee; it has the sublime daftitude of the Dave Clark Five married to the sexual threat of Muddy Waters. Some called it 'progressive', which was the word applied to anything longer than five minutes around that time. In fact it was anything but. Whereas some of their contemporaries seemed to be trying to make sounds that belonged in classical music, Led Zeppelin seemed in fact to be trying to tunnel back to the crudest basics.

Andy Johns, younger brother of Glyn, was the twenty-year-old engineer whose idea it was to suspend a microphone from two floors above the entrance hall of Headley Grange and set up John Bonham's drum kit facing the door like a gift for a small boy on Christmas morning. This allowed him to record it so that the groove at the beginning of 'When The Levee Breaks' bounced off the stone walls in such a unique simulacrum of coiled power that nearly fifty years later kids in bedrooms who have never even heard of John Bonham borrow it for their mixes. Johns remembered that even at the time it struck him that this combination of talents and this moment might not come around again. 'I used to get up in the morning thinking, "Today I have another chance to do something that's never been done before."'

To which you could add, and also something that won't be done again. There are reasons why you couldn't do this all again now. A surprising number of them are to do with technology. Since all records came to be made and mixed digitally a certain snap-to-grid slickness arrived at the expense of something with which *Led Zep IV* abounds: a sense of air. Since the world went Pro-Tools people mix as much by sight as by ear, seeking to pack the spectrum with detail and reduce the amount of space in which the imagination can roam. Page's riffs, which had the catchiness which promised further layers of catchiness, were great smudges of sound cutting shapes in an atmosphere which seemed gravid with foreboding. They were like the first footprints in the snow. Today the click track would make sure 'Rock And Roll' didn't speed up in the way it does. The insistence on a single would mean that one track would be dulled by familiarity by the time you got the album home. The increased visibility a video presence would have brought would have meant the people going to see them would have some idea of what to expect. It wouldn't be Sandy Denny duetting on 'The Battle

Of Evermore'. It would be somebody who'd already had a number of hits in their own right whose presence could open the door to another market. Finally, and most importantly, social media, the element within which we all swim today, splashes daylight all over the twilight world of disreputable behaviour, the very world in which Led Zeppelin's mystique took root. Mobile phone technology alone would certainly have cramped the style of their on-tour fornication, with fatal consequences for the unapologetic swagger with which they carried themselves in the autumn of 1971.

Ken Scott is in no doubt that the record contracts of 1971, which in many cases required the acts to come up with two albums a year, made for better records. 'You made decisions quickly because you had to. There was no second guessing yourself.' It is a truth almost universally acknowledged in the record business that the longer somebody takes to make a record the thinner its commercial prospects are likely to be. The first thought is usually the best thought and the more time an artist has the more that thought is likely to be over-ridden by further thoughts that are not quite so good.

Great producers usually have a highly developed sense of when something is finished. Glyn Johns helped make *Who's Next* into a great record by persuading Pete Townshend to row back on some of his ambitions for *Lifehouse*. Like many of the best long-playing records that came out of 1971 it was made immeasurably stronger by the fact that somebody knew when it was finished. In fact some of the biggest records of the year, records such as *Tapestry*, *Every Picture Tells A Story* and *What's Going On*, were by modern standards rushed out before they were apparently ready.

The next record Johns produced after *Who's Next* was the first one by the Eagles and here he came up against a very different way of doing things, a way that indicated how the record business was likely to go in the future.

It was customary in 1971, as it had been in 1968 or 1957, to release an album as soon as humanly possible. That meant the moment the lacquers could be supplied to the pressing plant and the jackets manufactured. There was no machine to prime, no marketing scheme to be perfected, no budget to be hammered out, no accompanying image to be developed, no complex network of media deals to be synchronized, no *Vanity Fair* profile to be timed to make way for the anticipated street date, no complex hullabaloo to be orchestrated.

David Geffen was in a unique position of power with the first Eagles album. Since he managed the band, was their agent and ran their record company, he was able to put his foot on the ball. He was happy with most of what the band had done at Olympic with Glyn Johns but he felt it needed another Don Henley vocal. Johns had moved on to other projects but that didn't prevent Geffen calling him up and asking him to have another go at producing the band's version of the Jackson Browne song 'Nightingale'. They argued about the usefulness of doing such a thing but eventually Johns relented and flew to the States to try again. It didn't make any difference but the significant thing was Geffen thought it was worth trying no matter what the expense in terms of man-hours and studio time and sitting around agonizing.

The first album by the Eagles indicated the way the world was going to go. As the rewards of apparently getting it right became greater throughout the seventies, as it became clear that the big hit albums of 1971 were still hanging about the charts years later, it became even more important to do anything you could to minimize the slightest chance of failure. Once everybody learned how much money you could make by rolling a double six they mistakenly thought that their chances would improve if they spent months blowing on the dice. Time and again the market has told them this isn't true.

It was different looking through the new releases rack in Harum in 1971. The rules of the game hadn't yet been written. There were a handful of opportunities and a handful of remarkably talented people in position to take advantage of them. Terry Manning is a recording engineer from Memphis who worked with Led Zeppelin in the early seventies. He remembers Jimmy Page saying to him back in the days when they were peeling off this music like there was no tomorrow, 'our time is different and I don't think the general public or other musicians will ever get what we do or catch up to it'.

As Manning admits, that sounds egotistical. It also sounds true.

NOVEMBER PLAYLIST

War, 'Slippin' Into Darkness'
Led Zeppelin, 'Stairway To Heaven'
Boz Scaggs and Band, 'Runnin' Blue'
Bridget St John, 'City Crazy'
The Who, 'Baba O'Riley'
Stevie Wonder, 'If You Really Love Me'
Mickey Newbury, 'American Trilogy'
The Staples Singers, 'Respect Yourself'
Tony Christie, '(Is This The Way To) Amarillo?'
Joe Simon, 'Help Me Make It Through The Night'

DECEMBER:
AMERICAN PIE

Looking back on the movies of the year in the *New York Times*, critic Vincent Canby reflected on what he called their 'blank gaze'. In *A Clockwork Orange*, *The French Connection* and *Carnal Knowledge*, he remarked, the audience is not invited to root for or against the main characters. As he was writing this Eddie Egan, the New York cop on whom Gene Hackman's character Popeye Doyle had been based in *The French Connection*, was dismissed from the police department without benefits just before his retirement for acting in real life the way movie audiences had applauded Hackman's character behaving on the screen.

There was even less ambivalence in *Dirty Harry*, the Don Siegel thriller which was released just before Christmas. Clint Eastwood played corner-cutting enforcer Harry Callaghan. 'He doesn't play any favourites,' says a colleague. 'Harry hates everybody.' When Harry strolled through the mayhem in mid-town San Francisco, doggedly chewing the last of his breakfast as he pointed his Magnum at a wounded bank robber and asked him to guess whether he had a bullet left in the chamber, the audience were clearly being asked to identify with Eastwood as the put-upon defender of law and order. While enjoying the film, critic Roger Ebert said its 'moral position is fascist'. That didn't prevent it being such a success that it spawned four sequels, each containing a twist on the same scene.

In his round-up Canby remarked that it seemed possible for a film to perform well on America's coasts and yet die in its heartland, pointing out that most of the stylish alternative pictures made in the wake of *Easy Rider*, such as the James Taylor film *Two Lane Blacktop* and *Drive, He Said*, had actually flopped. The movie industry had looked at the grosses, written off its flirtation with the hippies and gone back to making movies that reflected the concerns of middle-aged Americans. It would be the Christmas of *Fiddler on the Roof*, *Diamonds Are Forever* and *Willy Wonka and the Chocolate Factory*.

In 1971 US cinema attendances were at an all-time low. From seventy-eight million a week in 1946 admissions had slumped to less than sixteen million in 1971. The studios were haemorrhaging cash. A movie like *Dirty Harry* wasn't as big a story as *Music*, the second new album by Carole King released in 1971. The movies seemed to be over. Pictures weren't events. More people would have seen a TV movie that was screened in late November than would have seen Clint Eastwood's tale of fear and loathing. This TV film, *Duel*, was about a man driving through the desert who found himself pursued by a malevolent truck with an invisible driver. *Duel* struck the same chord as *Dirty Harry*. The outside world, whether that meant the potholed streets of Brooklyn or the desert roads of California, was full of monsters and was best kept at bay with a gun. The director making his debut was a young man called Steven Spielberg.

As Christmas 1971 approached Frank Zappa could have been forgiven for looking forward to a rest. He was about to turn thirty-one, he had a young family at home in California and most of the year had been spent on tour at the head of his latest version of the Mothers of Invention. This one featured singer/lampoonists Mark Volman and Howard Kaylan, otherwise known as Flo and Eddie. Zappa's career relied on his ability to stir up outrage. It required a certain amount of energy to deal with the consequences. Back in February the management of London's Royal Albert Hall had cancelled his plans to have the Royal Philharmonic Orchestra perform original compositions such as 'Penis Dimension' for the soundtrack of his film *200 Motels*. This led to a legal case that didn't come to court until 1975. Members of the orchestra, including the distinguished trumpeter John Wilbraham, pronounced themselves disturbed by the idea of being expected to play songs inspired by the sex lives of rock musicians.

Zappa played both sides of the street. While his declared heroes were Stravinsky and Varèse he made sure his act was never too far removed from the lewd humour of the Fabulous Furry Freak Brothers. In June he had recorded a live album at the Fillmore East, the climax of which had been a topical opera inspired by the incident at Seattle's Edgewater Inn where members of Vanilla Fudge, abetted by Led Zeppelin tour manager Richard Cole, were said to have sexually assaulted a groupie with a fish they had reeled in from the balcony adjoining their room. This was widely regarded as hilarious, as was the Dutch documentary made about Zappa in the same year. In this he didn't need much encouragement to turn the conversation to the casual sex available even to a group as superficially ineligible as the Mothers of Invention. The documentary is a reminder of the blasé manners of the time. Partly filmed at the Zappa home, it features members of Zappa protégées the GTOs reminiscing, while looking after the Zappa infants Dweezil and Moon, about their own sexual adventures with rock stars. Smoking a cigarette within inches of the head of a naked baby did not strike anyone as particularly unusual at the time. In the same film Zappa shruggingly outlines his code of the road: 'I like to get laid. How does my wife feel about that? She grumbles every once in a while but she gets used to it. I come home with the clap and she goes and gets us some penicillin.'

In the winter of 1971 Zappa and his band were testing their immunity on a long tour of Europe. The fourth of December found them playing at the Montreux Casino near Geneva in Switzerland. Just as Don Preston embarked on the synthesizer solo in 'King Kong' somebody in the audience thought it would increase the gaiety of the evening if they launched a firework into the rattan covering of the ceiling. Unsurprisingly, the place burst into flames. There were three thousand fans in that room – which was significantly over capacity – and they miraculously managed to escape.

Because there were fans outside who were still trying to get in, the promoters had chained the fire doors shut. The members of Deep Purple, in town to make their new album using the Rolling Stones' mobile, witnessed the conflagration from across the water, a vision which inspired Roger Glover to compose 'Smoke On The Water' about their temporary inconvenience. Montreux could very easily have been one of those tragedies too serious to write an up-tempo rocker about. It was a miracle it wasn't.

Back at their hotel, their equipment destroyed, Zappa's band were all for going directly home. However, their existence at the time was so hand to mouth that this would have meant returning penniless at Christmas. Hence it was decided to borrow some equipment and go to London where they were booked to play four relatively lucrative shows in three days at the Rainbow. This proved to be an unfortunate decision. At the end of the first of those shows, on Friday, 10 December, just six days after they had escaped incineration, Zappa led the band back on stage for an encore and announced that they would play the Beatles' 'I Want To Hold Your Hand'. This was a surprise choice, possibly inspired by the fact that in its previous incarnation the Rainbow had been the venue for the Beatles' Christmas shows. Before the band could begin the song a twenty-one-year-old labourer named Trevor Howell materialized from the side of the stage and launched Zappa off its edge. The iconoclast fell twelve feet on to the concrete floor of the orchestra pit below, his guitar still around his neck. He didn't move. From the angle he landed at, his neck appeared to be broken. The band thought he was dead.

Zappa was in hospital in London for weeks making his recovery. During that time he worked up a grudge about the country which had brought him ill fortune in so many different forms and pondered the unpredictable consequences of fame. The first explanation of the incident offered was that Howell had assaulted Zappa because he was jealous of the effect the guitarist was having on his girlfriend. A later report suggested he was cross because he didn't feel he was getting value for money. Certainly stalls tickets were £1.50, which was a significant increase on prices at the beginning of the year. The courts took the matter seriously. When the case came to trial the following year Howell got twelve months in prison.

The incident, though widely taken as a joke at the time, was the beginning of an emphasis on artist security which was long overdue. Howell's attack, like the stage invasions that had wrecked the Newport Festival in the USA and the Pink Floyd fans who had spoiled the band's planned spectacle at their Crystal Palace show in the summer by wading into the water and letting the air out of the Floyd's inflatable octopus, suggested that as rock got bigger and the venues grew to accommodate the demand the audience was changing in its nature and people could no longer be relied upon to 'be cool'.

On the night of Zappa's misadventure the fledgling Roxy Music played a show at Slough Community Centre. Included in their set were many of the songs that would be on their first album the following year: they began with '2HB' and finished with 'Virginia Plain', which would be their first single. Bryan Ferry's group had had an excellent week. Their plan to make their name without submitting to the rigours of the clubbing circuit appeared to be paying off. That same week they had signed a management deal with the same people who looked after ELP and King Crimson, and Richard Williams had written the first feature about them in the *Melody Maker*, saying they 'had a freshness and flexibility about them which made the majority of their contemporaries sound tired and tawdry' and applauding their 'welcome awareness of the roots and history of pop'. Also on the same night the Who were playing Long Beach Arena in California. They were nearing the end of a year which had seen them play seventy-five shows, appear in movies, cause the standard amount of mayhem, move house, have children and make the best record of their career. In the United States they were moving into bigger and bigger venues to cater for the exploding demand. The dangers of this escalation were more apparent to those on the stage than those looking up at it. At the Long Beach show Roger Daltrey, seriously concerned that people down at the front of the stage were getting crushed, tried to get the crowd to take a step back. When they didn't comply Pete Townshend took over and demonstrated his knack for being quotable and opaque in the same sentence. 'That's how much power rock and roll stars have got. Fuck all. Now either sit down, lay down, but shut up. This is a rock and roll concert, not a fucking tea party!'

As Zappa was being rushed to hospital his ambulance went past London's Inn on the Park where Lou Reed was now living in unaccustomed splendour. RCA were paying the bills for him and his producer, New York scenester Richard Robinson and his wife Lisa, while he made his first solo album at Morgan Studios in Willesden. The musicians playing on the record included two members of Yes: guitarist Steve Howe and keyboard player Rick Wakeman, who had joined the progressive five-piece in time to play on *Fragile*, their second hit album of the year. The majority of the songs on *Lou Reed*, which came out in the middle of 1972, had previously been performed with the Velvet Underground, the group Reed had left in 1970. He appeared to be the beneficiary of that rarest of things in pop music – a second chance.

On the night a year earlier when Reed had left the group his parents had picked him up and taken him home to their big house in the suburbs, for all the world like a college boy who'd found the big wide world too much to cope with. Reed had retired from the music business at that point, apparently abandoning any hope that his songs might ever find a place in the world, and going to work as a typist at his father's accountancy firm. Glenn O'Brien, then editing Andy Warhol's fashion magazine *Interview*, remembers Reed settling down with an attractive former cocktail waitress called Bettye Kronstad. 'Lou, who had no choice about being hip, was fascinated with squaredom. That was part of the appeal of Bettye. She was a nice square chick. They got married. Then I remember seeing her with a black eye that never seemed to heal.' O'Brien detected Reed salving his bitterness at the fact that the songs he thought were great had fallen on stony ground with the belated acclaim he was getting from younger performers like David Bowie and Jonathan Richman. His erstwhile bandmate John Cale mused that his return was the making of Lou because he seemed to find suburbia more inspiring than bohemia. By May 1971 he was recording demos of new songs, including 'Walk On The Wild Side' and 'Berlin', in the Robinsons' apartment. When he got the deal with RCA and the chance to go and record what he liked in London in December 1971 it was both debut and comeback.

While London bohemians like David Bowie were taking inspiration from American acts like the Velvet Underground and the Stooges, New York's bohemians were exalting the English end of the special relationship. When Keith Richards appeared on the cover of *Rolling Stone* in August 1971 – a watershed moment in the establishment of the cult of Keef – two young New Yorkers took particular notice. It wasn't the music that inspired them so much as their desire to emulate the way Keith looked. They liked the way he carried himself, the sweet smell of danger that entered the room before he did. Both started with the hairstyle. One was Patti Smith, who was previously mainly known for her striking appearance and her keenness to glom on to anyone famous. In 1971 Smith was the girlfriend of Todd Rundgren, which didn't stop her giving his new album a glowing review in *Rolling Stone*.

The other disciple of Keith Richards was John Genzale from Queens. John played guitar and had recently joined a band called Actress. In late 1971 Actress found a singer called David Johansen. David wasn't the world's greatest singer but he had more front than Macy's, had done some roles as a child actor and most importantly looked like a younger version of Mick Jagger. On Christmas Eve the new line-up played their first gig under their new name at a welfare hotel on Columbus called the Endicott. There was no money but it was a gig. The only audience were the residents. The band played under-rehearsed versions of songs by Archie Bell and the Drells and Otis Redding. The look was more important than their sound. John Genzale was by now known as Johnny Thunders and he was playing Keith Richards to David Johansen's Mick Jagger. The band were introduced as the New York Dolls. It would be another two years before they got their chance to be the next big thing with the release of their first album and after that another four years before punk rock made them quite well known, by which time they would be no more.

The big hit single of December 1971 was such a big hit that the man who wrote it never needed to work again. Don McLean came from New Rochelle in Westchester County, New York, in the heart of post-war prosperity. Like Lou Reed he had a comfortable background he preferred to play down. He wasn't as rich as some – 'I knew a lot of kids who were born on third base and thought they hit a triple' – but he was very comfortable and knew that he, like his neighbours, could probably look forward to an even more comfortable future.

McLean was keen on the guitar and, like so many successful musicians, thanks to childhood illnesses keeping him away from school he managed to get good at it. At the same time he was also having opera lessons paid for by his sister and swimming underwater to improve his breath control. When he was only fifteen his father died. From that point Don felt able to pursue his dream with the guitar. He was confident enough to venture to the city and seek out the help and advice of established names on the folk circuit such as

Erik Darling and manager Harold Leventhal. He dropped out of college in 1963 and spent six years playing every folk club that would have him. At the same time he was doing a Masters degree in Business Administration at night school.

In 1970 he released his first album, called *Tapestry*. This was on a small label which was subsequently bought by United Artists. On 14 March 1971, while opening for Laura Nyro at a college show in Philadelphia, he unveiled a new song called 'American Pie', which was notable for riddling words, a hooky chorus and taking almost ten minutes to play. Its appeal wasn't immediately obvious to everyone. When he played the songs for his proposed second album to his producer the latter asked why he hadn't got a single. McLean said that not only was 'American Pie' the single, it was also the title track. He was so confident that he'd already taken the cover photographs in which a Stars and Stripes was painted on his outstretched thumb.

The producer, Ed Freeman, put McLean and his band to work on the song in a rehearsal studio for the best part of two weeks. Then, on the day of the session, he introduced Paul Griffin, the piano player who had made distinguished contributions to everything from Dionne Warwick's 'Walk On By' to Bob Dylan's 'Like A Rolling Stone'. It's Griffin's rippling, almost facile piano that prevents 'American Pie' collapsing under the weight of its determination to be the Great American Song and makes it one of the first great pop records which is about great pop records.

There was a gentle ache at the centre of it, like there was in so much music that year. McLean wasn't just a Buddy Holly fan. He felt Holly was the alpha and omega of pop songwriting and when he died the music had died with him. Not everyone tried to decipher all the song's metaphors, to work out who was the jester who sang in a voice he'd borrowed from James Dean or the quartet who practised in the park, but everyone from America's most learned critic to the teenagers dancing along to the chorus recognized that 'American Pie' was about the loss of innocence, in pop music as well as in the grown-up world.

'American Pie' came out as a single in November. It was eight minutes long, which necessitated it being mastered at half-speed and spread over both sides of a seven-inch 45. This didn't prevent it being one of the biggest hits of the year, dominating the airwaves during December and spending five weeks at number one in the early part of 1972. It also played a part in the national conversation, turning it to the time twelve years earlier when the plane carrying Buddy Holly, Richie Valens and the Big Bopper had gone down in Clear Lake, Iowa, back to the vanished world of pink carnations and pick-up trucks, back to Chevys driven to the levee, back to the blithe, dream-like stability of the fifties, back to the distant land of lost content.

Its most ringing phrase, 'the day the music died', became one of the few lines from a pop song to put its brand on not only a date but also a subtle feeling of regret which was the first intimation of a generation reluctantly growing up. Its title was subsequently borrowed for a series of winningly vulgar teenage comedies. Its revival provided Madonna with a new start as her career entered its third decade. It has been called one of the five key American songs of the twentieth century, just below 'Over The Rainbow' and 'White

Christmas'. Like them it's certainly one of those tunes that enjoys almost 100 per cent familiarity even among people who aren't aware of liking it. It taught the young Mike Mills, later of REM, 'this is how you can write a song'. For McLean it's the gift that goes on giving. In April 2015 he auctioned the song's original manuscript for over a million dollars.

'American Pie' was a straw in the wind that December. In the same month the *Village Voice* announced that the mood of nostalgia had 'reached epidemic proportions'. This came in many forms. Laura Nyro teamed up with Labelle, formerly known as Patti Labelle and the Bluebells, to release a record of reverent covers of fifties and sixties soul tunes called *Gonna Take A Miracle*, following which she retired to get married. At the time it was coming out the loose family of musicians around Fairport Convention were enjoying a boozy holiday at the Manor, the Oxfordshire studio recently opened by Richard Branson, to record *Rock On*, their own tribute to the songs of Buddy Holly, the Everly Brothers and Carole King. The first album by Paul McCartney's group Wings contained their version of Mickey and Sylvia's 'Love Is Strange'. Paul held the launch party at the Empire Ballroom. He turned up with his hair moulded into a quiff, as if it was 1959 all over again.

In December Stanley Gortikov, the Capitol Records executive who was head of the American record industry's trade association, gave an interview to *Billboard*. He was asked whether he thought the record business would ever be able to aim its products at adults or whether it would remain, like the toy industry, primarily focused on 'the kids'.

'Adults over 30 have largely been written off as potential record buyers,' he said. 'They don't buy; they're over the hill. Nobody seems to be trying to tap that vast market, despite the basic universality of the music. A marketing breakthrough is needed.'

Gortikov may have been slow to notice what was already occurring. In the same edition a spokesman for an East Coast chain of shops named Schwartz Brothers Harmony Huts said 'this Christmas looks exceedingly good', and added that for the first five days of December they could report sales which were 78 per cent ahead of the previous year. This was clearly not being caused by an exceptionally affluent set of teenagers. The signs were already there that lots of the established bands were selling records to people over the age of twenty-one. Columbia announced they expected to sell more than a million copies of the four-record set recorded by Chicago at Carnegie Hall. Procol Harum had just finished recording their best-known songs with the Edmonton Symphony Orchestra for a live album to be launched early in 1972. Neither of these was aimed at teenagers.

The Rolling Stones' back catalogue was suddenly available on *Hot Rocks*, allowing access to a generation who'd been too young to appreciate 'Satisfaction' first time around. Suddenly rock heritage was marketable. The distant past – the records of five, even six years earlier – was now something to aspire to. The retail industry was waiting with bated breath for the release of the souvenir of George Harrison's Concert for Bangladesh in August. This would eventually come out in the United States in Christmas week, having proved to be far more complicated an endeavour than Harrison ever thought possible. It was almost $13 in the USA and nearly £6 in the UK, in both cases unprecedented prices, and it had a starving child on the cover. Not much teen appeal there.

The reviews were rather better than they deserved to be, tending to focus on the purity of the artists' motives rather than the quality of their performances. 'This is rock reaching for its manhood,' said Jon Landau in *Rolling Stone*, perhaps unconsciously reflecting that the only women credited in the entire undertaking were three of the backing singers.

When the Band had played at the Albert Hall in London in the summer of 1971 Richard Williams, writing in the *Melody Maker*, had described it as the greatest rock show he had ever seen. Sadly the Band's moment as a vital creative force had passed. In September they had released *Cahoots*, their fourth studio album, which indicated that the things which used to come easily now sounded forced. Many of their songs seemed to be trying to measure up to the expectations produced by all that critical adulation. At the same time the fissure between Robbie Robertson, who wrote their big songs, and Levon Helm, who sang them, had widened to a canyon. When they finished the year by playing four nights at New York's Academy of Music they were accompanied by a horn section directed and arranged by the great Allen Toussaint, whose production of Lee Dorsey's brilliant 'Yes We Can' had caused them to call him up, but they only played two songs from the album. The rest were oldies. On the last night of 1971, as the clock struck midnight, they brought on their old employer Bob Dylan. Announcing his last song he said 'we haven't played this in years'. Then, as he would do for the rest of his life, he launched into 'Like A Rolling Stone'. Heritage rock was born.

The twelve months just passed had been an averagely strange one in the life of Elvis Presley. The original rock and roll star had turned thirty-six in January 1971. A few days before Christmas the previous year, stung by a conversation with his father Vernon and wife Priscilla, who had both suggested his spending on gifts for his cronies was getting out of hand, he'd taken a plane to Washington DC accompanied by just two of the dozen courtiers who normally made up his entourage. On the flight he fell into conversation with a Republican Senator and sought to impress upon the legislator his steadfast belief in traditional American values and his growing concern that these were being threatened by the apparently opposing values of the Woodstock generation. Encouraged by the exchange he wrote a long-hand note to President Richard Nixon in which he offered his services as a warrior for stability and abstinence from drugs and an agent working within the music business. What only his intimates knew was that his dependency on prescription drugs was so great that he almost rattled when he walked.

Elvis and his friends dropped this note off at the White House at 6.30 in the morning. Thanks to the security guard having recognized him, later that morning he received an invitation to drop by the Oval Office and say hello to the President. After being told, to his evident disappointment, that it would not be OK for him to take a revolver into the

President's presence and present it to him, he was ushered in, wearing what looked to the puzzled Nixon rather like his performing regalia. His face was swollen by an allergic reaction to the chocolate he had insisted on eating during the flight.

Between the nervous pleasantries, he sought to assure the President that he was determined to resist the erosion of the moral fabric of the young, for which he blamed the Beatles, use his power with them to put them on the right road, and secure for himself a badge advertising him as a deputy of the Bureau of Narcotic and Dangerous Drugs. Nixon got his snap with the King. The King got his badge, which was the thing that really mattered to him. It wasn't the only bauble he picked up in those few weeks. In January 1971 Elvis was presented with an award from America's Junior Chambers of Commerce for being one of the most notable examples of the benefits of free enterprise. This token of his standing in society meant more to Elvis than any gold records. Touchingly, he subsequently took this award with him everywhere he went, much like the orb and sceptre of a medieval sovereign.

In January he began a season at the International Hotel in Las Vegas. His manager Colonel Tom Parker continued to reject the stream of offers which came in for him to tour Europe, citing 'personal security' as the main reason. Others speculated that as someone who had come to the United States as an illegal immigrant Parker had no passport. It wasn't an issue within the Presley court. His client didn't appear to have much interest in abroad, which was one of the most American things about him. The Vegas arrangement suited all concerned. It allowed Parker to indulge his vice, which was gambling, and it brought the audience to the King rather than expecting him to go to them. The many millions the Presley machine turned over that year were spent before they could be banked. Most of it never left Vegas. The artist's share went on guns and toys. The manager's percentage went straight back to the house in the shape of his losses.

In March, Presley went into the studios in Nashville to record an album for the Christmas market and to have a shot at some of the folksy material both he and the contemporary market appeared to favour. He did 'Amazing Grace', the old devotional tune which had been turned into a huge hit by Judy Collins, Gordon Lightfoot's 'Early Morning Rain' and Kris Kristofferson's 'Sunday Morning Coming Down'. He was only intermittently engaged with the material. So many members of the salaried posse who laughed at his jokes and applauded his displays of machismo crowded into the control room to listen to the playbacks that there was no room for the musicians. While his wife Priscilla and their three-year-old daughter Lisa Marie were away supervising the decoration of a new home in California, he was accompanied by one of his rotating cast of mistresses. Joyce Bova was such a regular at the sessions in June that some members of the band assumed she was his wife. Priscilla, meanwhile, realizing that her husband was lost in showbiz and to her as well, was spending her considerable energies in improving her martial arts and seeking her own romantic solace.

The producer Felton Jarvis tried everything to trick Elvis into a mood in which he might deliver. He dressed the studio with a Christmas tree and presents in the middle of summer. He tried to make sure the band was actually playing as he walked in the studio. Nothing worked. The Colonel made sure the dollars kept coming in by securing more advances from RCA for new and repackaged albums. The records slid out piecemeal. They didn't seem to matter to anyone apart from the faithful.

Only on stage could Elvis count for something. In the autumn he undertook a tour of large indoor venues. This time he was in front of his heartland fans rather than the blasé high rollers of Vegas. Sensing the difference, Elvis put more effort into the presentation side of his act. The wife of his musical director Joe Guercio heard the Richard Strauss fanfare 'Also Sprach Zarathustra', newly popularized through its use in Kubrick's *2001: A Space Odyssey*, and suggested, tongue in cheek, that it would work for Elvis. The King was bucked by the idea of beginning the show with a climax and then building from there. 'He didn't want to be a guy just walking out there,' said Guercio. 'He wanted to be a god.'

Although the band contained the finest session players and singers money could buy it was a piece of theatre rather than a musical show. The most memorable moments were visual: the guitar he used as a prop but never played, the daunting displays of karate through which he advertised his maleness, the moment at the end when he held his arms outstretched to reluctantly receive the acclaim of the multitude; some of it was rock and roll, lots of it was show business, all of it was spectacle.

On 30 December 1971, after a Christmas subdued by Presley standards, Elvis confided to his inner circle that Priscilla wasn't coming back. His baby had finally left him. In the last issue of the year of *Rolling Stone* Jon Landau wrote a long review of his experience seeing Elvis on that tour in Boston. It was a full page. At the top was Elvis in his cape, arms outstretched. The headline read 'In Praise of Elvis Presley'. This was a key moment in the reconciliation between the self-styled rock intelligentsia and the person without whom their whole world would not have existed and who was now widely regarded by hip opinion as a busted flush. Landau's entire review was about forgiving Elvis his Hollywood trespasses and at the same time forgiving *Rolling Stone* for having doubted him. It concluded: 'He remains an artist; in fact, an American artist, and one we should be proud to claim as our own.'

This review, written by the magazine's most senior rock journalist, who was all of twenty-four at the time, about a performer who seemed almost biblically ancient at thirty-six, was a glimpse of something entirely new: a performer whose best work was behind him still managing to command vast crowds and the highest ticket prices; an idol inviting people to come unto him to give thanks for his past, their past, and to bask in a precious moment of shared proximity.

At the time Presley was the only one offering this kind of experience. Chuck Berry and Little Richard and the rest were low rent, playing lashed-together oldies shows and not attracting any of the same veneration. Sinatra had slipped away. The Beatles had gone somewhere to fight. The Rolling Stones were preparing to come back. Bob Dylan was putting his toe in the water. Led Zeppelin and Pink Floyd and the rest of the comers weren't yet superstars.

But Elvis was something else. Elvis was the essence of a star. The kind of experience Landau described was clearly an unusual one for him, being accustomed to seeing bands who performed with the urgency of people who had just had their best idea. Presley's complacency was a new thing. 'Elvis wants his people to have fun and he wants to have fun with them. But it's all middle-aged now and he wants them to have a middle-aged kind of fun.' He pointed out that at the end they screamed and shouted and applauded but as soon as the house lights were on they trooped out. 'They never once move to get out of their seats.' At the time this seemed strange. Rock hadn't quite settled into its role as a branch of the entertainment industry.

What Landau saw Elvis Presley do on stage in Boston was what almost all the class of 1971 would end up doing as their careers matured. He was playing the old hits because the audience couldn't summon more than a polite interest in the new ones. He was tapping into the pressing need of an audience of adults to be made to feel young again. He was celebrating his own legend, surrounding himself with a supporting cast whose role was to reflect his own majesty and help justify charging top dollar for admission to his presence. This was a special once-in-a-lifetime night out. It wasn't something you did every day.

What Elvis was doing in what turned out to be quite a short time in Vegas was pioneering the way popular music would be presented and perceived in the twenty-first century. All the acts that have endured from that time and beyond have ended up doing what Elvis was already doing in 1971: taking the stage in front of ranks of musicians, dancers, special effects artists and assorted supernumeraries and fronting a show in which nothing has been left to chance, a show designed above all to reflect the performer's magnitude and make the money required to put on another show. And like Elvis they are relying on the one commodity that endures after the voice is no longer quite the same, the moves have grown rusty and the inspiration no longer flows quite as readily. That is the audience's deep, surprising love for the music they made in the past.

Jon Landau would go on to manage, mould and some would say project himself through Bruce Springsteen, the American artist most closely attached to the mission of Elvis Presley. He would see his charge playing in front of crowds far more numerous than Elvis ever played to, in countries that weren't even countries in 1971, in a world where thirty-six would no longer qualify as even middle-aged – a world, in fact, where middle-aged superstars would become the rule rather than the exception. Like Cortez on his peak in Darien, when he looked at Elvis what he was seeing was a great blue ocean of possibility, a future of unimaginable scale and spectacle, of riches and ritual, of endless repetition of what had gone before for the benefit of those who weren't even born when it all went down; a future of whizz-bangs and worship, of dancers and dazzle, of special effects and souvenirs, of vast crowds comprising all age groups and nationalities paying huge sums of money for the privilege of being able to say they were there, of appearances that weren't so much musical performances as visitations from Planet Fame. When he looked at Presley with his arms outstretched, his super-hero's cape ajar, accepting all the adoration the fans had to give, Landau could have been forgiven for thinking he was seeing rock's past. In fact he was looking at its future.

DECEMBER PLAYLIST

Elvis Presley, 'Funny How Time Slips Away'
Bob Dylan and the Band, 'Like A Rolling Stone'
Don McLean, 'American Pie'
Title music from *A Clockwork Orange*
Roxy Music, 'Virginia Plain'
King Curtis, 'Whiter Shade Of Pale'
James Brown, 'Hot Pants (She Got To Use What She Got To
Get What She Wants)'
Mountain, 'Nantucket Sleighride'
J. J. Cale, 'Call Me The Breeze'
John and Yoko, 'Happy Xmas (War Is Over)'

EPILOGUE

As I said at the beginning of this book, anyone can make a case for the popular music of their youth. It's something we all feel fiercely protective about. Our youth was unique. Our feelings were deeper. Our rebellion was more justified. We lived through such a moment as will never be lived through by anyone in quite the same way again.

There's plenty of that feeling in these pages. A lot of it is rooted in how I remember feeling at the time. But I've also got a certain amount of time on my side and I can base my argument in the number of records and musicians from the year 1971 that have proved to have lasting appeal.

Every year in the UK rock critics gather and hand out the Mercury Music Prize for the most distinguished UK album of the year. Lots of the records on the shortlists and even some of the winners are, within a few years, entirely forgotten.

Had there been a Mercury Music Prize in 1971, the short-list would have included *Hunky Dory*, *Every Picture Tells A Story*, *Who's Next*, *Led Zeppelin IV*, *Imagine*, *Ram*, *Meddle*, *Madman Across The Water*, *Sticky Fingers* and *Aqualung*. There's nothing there that's been forgotten, almost fifty years later.

These days in the United States the records that win Grammy Awards tend to be the ones that have sold the most copies. The ones that win critics' awards tend to be records most people have never heard of. In 1971 America's most acclaimed albums – *Tapestry*, *There's A Riot Goin' On*, *What's Going On*, *Nilsson Schmilsson*, *Blue*, *Pearl*, *American Pie*, *L.A. Woman* and *Mud Slide Slim* – were also its biggest sellers.

But it's not just the big hits of 1971 that seem to have achieved a kind of immortality. The new traditionalists, who weren't born at the time, revere 1971 releases like Nick Drake's *Bryter Layter*, John Martyn's *Bless The Weather*, Sandy Denny's *North Star Grassman And The Ravens*, Gene Clark's *White Light* and the early records by John Prine, Bonnie Raitt, Judee Sill and Loudon Wainwright, none of which meant much at the time.

The spoor of 1971 is transmitted in many ways. Although it was long before the next really big step change in pop music, the hip-hop revolution, there are trace elements in the 1971 records of Sly Stone, Curtis Mayfield, Norman Whitfield and Gil Scott-Heron without which it would have been pretty much inconceivable. Ever since hip hop all records have been made to some extent the magpie's way and some of the most discriminating borrowings have been from textures, rhythms and the musical idiosyncrasies of 1971 recordings by Led

Zeppelin, the Who, Black Sabbath, Can and even Little Feat. By 1971 the basic building blocks had been put in place. Obviously no single year marks the end of anything but it's fair to say, as Churchill said after El Alamein, this was the end of the beginning. The outlines of the rich tapestry were clearly marked.

Pop is as much about technology as it is about music. Any student of recorded sound will tell you that 1971 was the golden moment when technology became a help and wasn't yet a hindrance. There's something about the recordings of 1971 that makes them sound more right almost fifty years later than they sounded at the time. Particularly in their original vinyl forms they have a warmth, crispness, sensuality and presence that generations of recording software engineers have been trying to bottle and market ever since. You can now buy invisible plug-ins for your desktop recording set-up that promise to make your record sound like 'the big room' at Olympic studios, where many of the biggest-sounding rock records of 1971 were made. To all intents and purposes they're selling the very air of 1971.

The sound of 1971 is the sound many acts are still trying to make today. You can hear Rod Stewart and Lindisfarne in Mumford & Sons, Sly and the Family Stone all over hip hop, the spirit of Joni Mitchell's *Blue* in Laura Marling and a thousand other acoustic bluestockings, Pink Floyd's *Meddle* in the tunes to which call-centre workers chill out in Ibiza and Led Zeppelin in numberless generations of young men who take up electric guitars to slay dragons and attract girls. The sound of 1971 is all around us today, in ads for sports shoes, in the soundtracks of movies, at moments when TV producers and similar mood mongerers feel the need to reach for something reliably hip and soulful. When they were looking for a note on which to close out the 2012 Olympic Games they reached not for Muse or Coldplay but for the Who's 'Baba O'Riley'. They knew that no contemporary sound would hit the spot that 1971 album track hit. It crackles in a way records simply don't crackle any more for the simple reason that they're made in a different way.

David Bowie's *Hunky Dory* isn't an archetype of anything. However, only in 1971 could a still unproven artist make such an album while out of contract, starting it with a Tin Pan Alley song like 'Oh! You Pretty Things', which was first put before the public in a recording by the lead singer of Herman's Hermits, finishing it with the Freudian maze which is 'The Bewlay Brothers', wrapping it in a picture of him dragged up as Veronica Lake, then getting a major record company to put it out. In 1971 there wasn't a little indie niche you could insert a record like that into. The middle of the road was the only place to be. Underground was over ground, anything could be a hit. It was into this moment of panic and opportunity that all these 1971 masterpieces were hurled.

There were background factors behind this pop Renaissance. The fact that the Beatles had broken up meant there was a prize to play for. The record business was expanding at such a rate that the companies signed up anyone they thought might have an outside shot. Music was king: TV was nowhere, movies were in retreat, radio was growing, record stores were sprouting up like coffee shops and the only material goods that anyone who counted was remotely interested in were black, vinyl and twelve inches across.

The glories of the sixties had been on seven-inch black vinyl singles. The seventies were all about albums, which in the previous decade had been strictly for middle-aged swingers and fans of Ray Conniff. The numbers that were sold in the sixties would be dwarfed by seventies numbers, which were driven by the mania for stereo, the hi-fi set-ups that could reproduce it and the new mass audience made up of baby boomers for whom a hi-fi would be the first piece of furniture they installed in the damp bedsits they would provisionally call home.

If any of my children were to be cast away in the year 1971 they would be lost. They wouldn't be able to calculate in pounds, shillings and pence and would be frightened by the fact there were no seat belts in cars and you could smoke on the London Underground, surprised that the only people who could afford to travel between continents were millionaires, and taken aback by the fact there were just three channels on the TV, no such thing as a personal computer and no openly gay public figures. However, they would feel entirely at home with the records that were made that year.

If my twenty-one-year-old self could have been transported from 1971 to 2016 he would be struck dumb by the laptops, the phones, the affluence, the foreign tongues on the street, the idea that music could be accessed as if from a tap, the fact that three out of five stories in the news were about the sex lives of famous people and the puzzling realization that he couldn't just go out on Saturday evening and buy a ticket on the door for any show in town.

If my twenty-one-year-old self wasn't paying close attention he might at first think that the alternative society which had been sketched out in the pages of the underground papers of 1971 had actually come to pass. In some respects the sub-culture appears to have conquered the mainstream. A black man in the White House, openly gay people in public life, women reading the news, the latest entertainment stories as the lead stories and rock festivals taking place all over the world. Everything that was once alternative is now mainstream.

The rock and roll sub-culture started with the release of 'Rock Around The Clock' in 1954. That was the first collision between exciting sound and personal charisma that defined the rock and roll age. That's when the hysteria began. If we take the starting point of the rock and roll era as 1954 then 1971 is a mere seventeen years into that era, close enough to the start of the race for people still to remember the noise of the starting pistol. There were direct quotes from that revolution still in some of the big records of 1971, in Elvis's 'That's All Right, Mama', on Rod Stewart's *Every Picture Tells A Story*, in Led Zeppelin's 'Rock And Roll' which was modelled on Little Richard's 'Keep A Knockin'', and even, sentimentally, in Don McLean's 'American Pie'. In 1971 rock and roll was still just seventeen. This feels about right. Maybe rock and roll should always be just seventeen.

Most of the musicians who became superstars in 1971 and are still revered today were war babies. A large proportion of them were between twenty-five and thirty, which may prove to be the most significant age for creativity in musicians. They were slightly older than rock and roll itself and therefore they could remember a world before it existed. This stayed with them as a reminder of a black and white world, a life less congenial, like the weight of Brylcreem on the back of their neck or the discomfort of a girdle. When Lou Reed wrote 'Rock N Roll' he wasn't dialling up a familiar cliché from the lifestyle pages. He was describing the moment when he heard the sound that convinced him for the first time that, as he put it, 'there was life on this planet'.

What these people in their mid-twenties were doing, although none of them were aware of it at the time, was building the rock canon. In this they were more successful than they could have dared hope. Many of the musicians who made those 1971 records are still playing today, in bigger venues than ever, in front of huge multi-generational crowds made up of the children and even the grandchildren of their original fans. The songs those crowds most want them to play are the songs from 1971: 'Stairway To Heaven', 'Brown Sugar', 'Baba O'Riley', 'Tiny Dancer', 'American Pie', 'Heart Of Gold', 'Mandolin Wind' and 'The Last Time I Saw Richard'. Thanks to the radio, the movies, the commercials and the new ubiquity of all manner of music via YouTube and Spotify, these songs are as heavily imprinted on the minds of many twenty-somethings as they are on the people who first heard them forty-five years ago. These records are not just remarkably good and uniquely fresh; they have also enjoyed the benefit of being listened to more times than any recorded music in human history. It's not surprising the music of 1971 is in everyone's bloodstream. It no longer belongs to the people who made it or just to those of us who were lucky enough to be there when they did so. Now it belongs to everybody.

1971 IN 100 ALBUMS

The germ of this book was a column I wrote for *The Word*. The headline was '1971 Was the Annus Mirabilis of the Rock Album'. These are just some of the albums released that year that could be said to support that argument. They're presented here in roughly the order in which they would have first appeared in the UK's more advanced record shops during 1971. In those days international releases were far from simultaneous. Hence, the Velvet Underground's *Loaded* and David Bowie's *The Man Who Sold The World*, for instance, came out in the UK months after they appeared in the USA, and the live album from the Concert for Bangladesh, which was released in the United States in time for the Christmas market, actually came out in the UK in the first week of 1972. I've included it here because it helps round out the picture of a remarkable year.

Janis Joplin: *Pearl*
Carole King: *Tapestry*
Mountain: *Nantucket Sleighride*
Crazy Horse: *Crazy Horse*
Jimi Hendrix: *Cry Of Love*
Lee Dorsey: *Yes We Can*
Velvet Underground: *Loaded*
Nick Drake: *Bryter Layter*
Nilsson: *The Point*
David Bowie: *The Man Who Sold The World*

Miles Davis: *Jack Johnson*
Barbra Streisand: *Stoney End*
Stevie Wonder: *Where I'm Coming From*
Leonard Cohen: *Songs Of Love And Hate*
Yes: *The Yes Album*
Serge Gainsbourg and Jane Birkin: *Histoire De Melody Nelson*
Can: *Tago Mago*
Dory Previn: *Mythical Kings & Iguanas*
Steeleye Span: *Please To See The King*
Donny Hathaway: *Donny Hathaway*
Paul and Linda McCartney: *Ram*
The Rolling Stones: *Sticky Fingers*
Gordon Lightfoot: *Summer Side Of Life*
Graham Nash: *Songs For Beginners*
Leon Russell: *Leon Russell And The Shelter People*
Crosby, Stills, Nash & Young: *Four Way Street*
Jethro Tull: *Aqualung*
James Taylor: *Mud Slide Slim And The Blue Horizon*
The Temptations: *Sky's The Limit*
David Crosby: *If I Could Only Remember My Name*
Pink Floyd: *Relics*
Little Feat: *Little Feat*
The Faces: *A Nod's As Good As A Wink To A Blind Horse*
The Doors: *L.A. Woman*
Rod Stewart: *Every Picture Tells A Story*
Todd Rundgren: *Runt*
Marvin Gaye: *What's Going On*
The Allman Brothers Band: *Live At The Fillmore East*
Emerson, Lake & Palmer: *Tarkus*
Groundhogs: *Split*

Kris Kristofferson: *The Silver Tongued Devil And I*
John Lennon: *Imagine*
Joni Mitchell: *Blue*
The Who: *Who's Next*
Bill Withers: *Just As I Am*
Deep Purple: *Fireball*
Randy Newman: *Live*
Funkadelic: *Maggot Brain*
Gene Clark: *White Light*
Moody Blues: *Every Good Boy Deserves Favour*
T. Rex: *Electric Warrior*
The Carpenters: *Carpenters*
Isaac Hayes: *Shaft*
Black Sabbath: *Master Of Reality*
Genesis: *Nursery Cryme*
Sandy Denny: *North Star Grassman And The Ravens*
Beach Boys: *Surf's Up*
Humble Pie: *Performance: Rockin' The Fillmore*
Gilbert O'Sullivan: *Himself*
Grateful Dead: *Grateful Dead Live Double*
Dolly Parton: *Coat Of Many Colors*
The Band: *Cahoots*
Van Morrison: *Tupelo Honey*
Pink Floyd: *Meddle*
Cat Stevens: *Teaser And The Firecat*
Curtis Mayfield: *Roots*
Lindisfarne: *Fog On The Tyne*
Don McLean: *American Pie*
Sly and The Family Stone: *There's A Riot Goin' On*
Yes: *Fragile*

1971 in 100 Albums

The Move: *Message From The Country*
John Prine: *John Prine*
Santana: *III*
Michael Nesmith and The First National Band: *Nevada Fighter*
Nilsson: *Nilsson Schmilsson*
John Martyn: *Bless The Weather*
Elton John: *Madman Across The Water*
David Bowie: *Hunky Dory*
Wings: *Wildlife*
Emerson, Lake & Palmer: *Pictures At An Exhibition*
The Mahavishnu Orchestra: *The Inner Mounting Flame*
Freddie King: *Getting Ready*
Frank Zappa: *Fillmore East June 1971*
Alice Cooper: *Killer*
The Kinks: *Muswell Hillbillies*
Status Quo: *Dog Of Two Head*
Loudon Wainwright III: *Album II*
Shuggie Otis: *Freedom Flight*
Judy Collins: *Living*
Carly Simon: *Anticipation*
Laura Nyro and Labelle: *Gonna Take A Miracle*
Gil Scott-Heron: *Pieces Of A Man*
Judee Sill: *Judee Sill*
Colin Blunstone: *One Year*
Badfinger: *Straight Up*
The Staples Singers: *Staples Swingers*
Led Zeppelin: *IV*
The Electric Light Orchestra: *ELO*
America: *America*
George Harrison: *The Concert For Bangladesh*

SELECTED BIBLIOGRAPHY

Aubrey, Crispin and Shearlaw, John, *Glastonbury: Festival Tales* (Ebury, 2005)

Beckett, Andy, *When the Lights Went Out: Britain in the Seventies* (Faber and Faber, 2009)

Biskind, Peter, *Easy Riders, Raging Bulls* (Bloomsbury, 1998)

—— *Star: The Life & Wild Times of Warren Beatty* (Simon & Schuster, 2010)

Blake, Mark, *Pigs Might Fly: The Inside Story of Pink Floyd* (Aurum, 2008)

Boyd, Pattie, *Wonderful Tonight: The Autobiography* (Headline Review, 2007)

Bracewell, Michael, *Roxy: The Band that Invented an Era* (Faber and Faber, 2007)

Bruck, Connie, *Master of the Game: Steve Ross and the Creation of Time Warner* (Simon & Schuster, 1994)

Cann, Kevin, *Any Day Now: David Bowie, the London Years 1947–74* (Adelita, 2010)

Carlin, Peter Ames, *Bruce* (Simon & Schuster, 2012)

—— *Catch a Wave: The Rise, Fall and Redemption of the Beach Boys' Brian Wilson* (Rodale, 2007)

Clapton, Eric, *The Autobiography* (Century, 2007)

Cohn, Nik, *Ball the Wall* (Picador, 1989)

Davies, Hunter, *The Glory Game* (Mainstream, 1972)

Davies, Ray, *Americana: The Kinks, the Road and the Perfect Riff* (Ebury, 2013)

Davis, Clive, *Inside the Record Business* (Morrow, 1975)

Davis, Erik, *Led Zeppelin IV* (Continuum, 2005)

Doggett, Peter, *You Never Give Me Your Money* (The Bodley Head, 2009)

Edmonds, Ben, *Marvin Gaye: What's Going On and the Last Days of the Motown Sound* (Canongate, 2002)

Faithfull, Marianne, *Faithfull* (Michael Joseph, 1994)

Farren, Mick, *Give the Anarchist a Cigarette* (Pimlico, 2001)

Fisher, Marc, *Something in the Air: Radio, Rock and the Revolution that Shaped a Generation* (Random House, 2007)

Fong-Torres, Ben, *Willin': The Story of Little Feat* (Da Capo Press, 2013)

George, Nelson, *Where Did Our Love Go?: The Rise & Fall of the Motown Sound* (Omnibus, 2003)

George-Warren, Holly, *A Man Called Destruction: The Life and Music of Alex Chilton* (Viking, 2014)

Gladwell, Malcolm, *The Tipping Point: How Little Things Can Make a Big Difference* (Little, Brown, 2002)

Goodman, Fred, *Allen Klein* (Houghton Mifflin Harcourt, 2015)

—— *The Mansion on the Hill* (Jonathan Cape, 2003)

Gordon, Robert, *Respect Yourself: Stax Records and the Soul Explosion* (Bloomsbury, 2013)

Graham, Bill, *Bill Graham Presents* (Doubleday, 1992)

Green, Jonathon, *Days in the Life: Voices from the English Underground 1961–71* (Heinemann, 1988)

Greenfield, Robert, *Exile on Main Street: A Season in Hell with the Rolling Stones* (Da Capo Press, 2006)

Holder, Noddy, *Who's Crazee Now?* (Ebury, 1999)

Hoskyns, Barney, *Trampled Underfoot* (Faber and Faber, 2012)

―― *Waiting for the Sun: The Story of the Los Angeles Music Scene* (Viking, 1996)

Houghton, Mick, *I've Always Kept a Unicorn: The Biography of Sandy Denny* (Faber and Faber, 2015)

Iommi, Tony, *Iron Man* (Simon & Schuster, 2012)

Johns, Glyn, *Sound Man: A Life Recording Hits with the Rolling Stones, The Who, Led Zeppelin, The Eagles, Eric Clapton, The Faces …* (Blue Rider, 2014)

King, Carole, *A Natural Woman* (Little, Brown, 2012)

Lewis, Miles Marshall, *There's a Riot Goin' On* (Continuum, 2006)

Lowenstein, Prince Rupert, *A Prince Among Stones* (Bloomsbury, 2014)

McDonough, Jimmy, *Shakey: Neil Young's Biography* (Random House, 2003)

McNeill, Legs and McCain, Gillian, *Please Kill Me: The Uncensored Oral History of Punk* (Little, Brown, 1996)

Mason, Nick, *Inside Out: A Personal History of Pink Floyd* (Weidenfeld & Nicholson, 2004)

Milner, Greg, *Perfecting Sound Forever: The Story of Recorded Music* (Granta, 2009)

Nash, Graham, *Wild Tales* (Viking, 2014)

Neill, Andy and Kent, Matt, *The Complete Chronicle of the Who 1958–78* (Virgin, 2005)

Neville, Richard, *Hippie Hippie Shake* (Bloomsbury, 1995)

Norman, Philip, *Elton* (Hutchinson, 1991)

―― *The Stones* (Harper, 1993)

Palin, Michael, *Diaries 1969–1979* (Weidenfeld & Nicolson, 2006)

Paytress, Mark, *Bolan: The Rise and Fall of a 20th Century Superstar* (Omnibus, 2002)

Selected Bibliography

Richards, Keith, *Life* (Weidenfeld & Nicolson, 2010)

Ritz, David, *Divided Soul: The Life of Marvin Gaye* (Grafton, 1986)

Ronstadt, Linda, *Simple Dreams: A Musical Memoir* (Simon & Schuster, 2013)

Sampson, Anthony, *The New Anatomy of Britain* (Hodder & Stoughton, 1971)

Sanchez, Tony, *Up and Down With the Rolling Stones* (John Blake, 2010)

Sandbrook, Dominic, *State of Emergency: The Way We Were – Britain 1970–74* (Penguin, 2010)

Schmidt, Randy L., *Little Girl Blue: The Life of Karen Carpenter* (Omnibus, 2010)

Scott, Ken, *Abbey Road to Ziggy Stardust* (Alfred, 2012)

Shipton, Alyn, *Nilsson: The Life of a Singer-Songwriter* (Oxford University Press, 2013)

Sounes, Howard, *Down the Highway: The Life of Bob Dylan* (Doubleday, 2001)

Stewart, Rod, *The Autobiography* (Century, 2012)

Thomson, Graeme, *George Harrison: Behind the Locked Door* (Omnibus, 2013)

Townshend, Pete, *Who I Am* (HarperCollins, 2012)

Turner, Alwyn W., *Crisis? What Crisis? – Britain in the 1970s* (Aurum Press, 2013)

Turner, Steve, *Trouble Man: The Life and Death of Marvin Gaye* (Michael Joseph, 1998)

Wall, Mick, *When Giants Walked the Earth: A Biography of Led Zeppelin* (Orion, 2008)

Weller, Sheila, *Girls Like Us: Carole King, Joni Mitchell, Carly Simon and the Journey of a Generation* (Ebury, 2008)

White, Timothy, *Long Ago and Far Away: James Taylor – His Life and Music* (Omnibus, 2001)

Selected Bibliography

Willetts, Paul, *The Look of Love: The Life and Times of Paul Raymond* (Serpent's Tail, 2013)

Young, Robert, *Electric Eden: Unearthing Britain's Visionary Music* (Faber and Faber, 2010)

ACKNOWLEDGEMENTS

This book started life as a column in *The Word* magazine. Some of its ideas emerged from conversations with Mark Ellen, Kate Mossman, Fraser Lewry, Alex Gold and Mike 'Seventies' Johnson. What larks.

Whether they realized it or not, talking to Rob Dickins, Andy Murray, Terry Reid, Chris Johnson, Paul Henderson, Jonathan Morrish and Danny Baker helped.

Thanks to Bill Scott-Kerr, Darcy Nicholson, Richard Shailer and Sally Wray at Transworld, Gillian Blake at Holt and my agent Charlie Viney.

PICTURE ACKNOWLEDGEMENTS

Although every effort has been made to trace copyright holders and clear permission for the photographs in this book, the provenance of a number of them is uncertain. The author and publisher would welcome the opportunity to correct any mistakes.

First section

Page 1: Paul and Linda McCartney: © Getty Images; *Rolling Stone* cover – John Lennon: © *Rolling Stone* LLC; Alfred Hitchcock: © Getty Images.

Pages 2–3: Angie and David Bowie: © Mirrorpix; David Bowie in Hollywood; Joni Mitchell recording *Blue*; Nick Drake; Mick Jagger and Bianca Pérez-Mora Macias: all © Getty Images; Stones fans: © Mirrorpix.

Pages 4–5: Stevie Wonder and Syreeta; Robert Margouleff and Malcolm Cecil; dancers from *Soul Train*; Francis Ford Coppola shooting *The Godfather*; Berry Gordy: all © Getty Images; Tony Sanchez and Madeleine D'Arcy: © Rex Features; Ahmet Ertegun at Mick Jagger's wedding; Jagger makes his wedding vows; Julie Christie: all © Getty Images.

Pages 6–7: *Rolling Stone* cover – Keith Richard: © Rolling Stone LLC; Glenn Cowan; 1 May Washington protests; Glastonbury Festival; Celebration of Life festival: all © Getty Images.

Page 8: defendants in the Oz magazine trial: © Mirrorpix; Jane Fonda in *Klute*: © Getty Images.

Second section

Page 1: *Rolling Stone* cover – Jim Morrison: © *Rolling Stone* LLC; Marc Bolan and Elton John: © Getty Images; Cat Stevens and Carly Simon: © Peter Simon Photography.

Pages 2–3: Rod Stewart and the Faces; Rod Stewart's house: both © Photoshot; George Harrison with Ravi Shankar and Allen Klein; Bob Dylan at the Concert for Bangladesh; Big Star: all © Getty Images; David Geffen and America: © Cache Agency.

Pages 4–5: Van Morrison; Jackson Browne; Neil Young: all © Corbis; Sly and the Family Stone; riot at Attica prison: both © Getty Images; the Loud family: © WNET; *Rolling Stone* cover – Beach Boys: © Rolling Stone LLC.

Pages 6–7: Elton John with mother and stepfather; Frank Zappa with parents: both © Getty Images/Life; Richard Perry and Harry Nilsson: © Lorber Films; The Who: © Getty Images.

Page 8: Elvis Presley: © Getty Images; Alice Cooper: © Rex Features; David Bowie: © Getty Images.

INDEX

Bombay Bicycle Club 297
Bonham, John 80, 81, 357–8; *see also* Led Zeppelin
Bonnie *see* Bramlett, Bonnie; Delaney and Bonnie
Boomer's Story (Cooder) 332
'Born To Be Wild' 17
Boston Rock Storybook website 275
'Both Sides Now' 319
Bottoms, Timothy 207
Bowie, Angie 59, 63, 188
Bowie, David 1, 58–63, 65, 188–9, 230, 285–6, 287, 290, 299, 341–5, 372, 373, 390, 392
Box Tops, the 281
Boyd, Joe 69, 75
Boyle, Susan 157
Boz Scaggs And Band 268
Brady Bunch, The (TV) 324
Bramlett, Bonnie 51; *see also* Delaney and Bonnie
Bramlett, Delaney 251; *see also* Delaney and Bonnie
Brando, Marlon 122
Branson, Richard 377
Breaking Bad (TV series) 256
Breteuil, Jean de 142, 200–1
Brewer, Don 85; *see also* Grand Funk Railroad
'Brides Of Jesus' 260
'Bridge Over The River Ash' 197
Bridge Over Troubled Water (Simon & Garfunkel) 38
'Bridget The Midget' 214
Bright Tunes Music 252, 253
Brooks, Ernie 274; *see also* Modern Lovers
Broughton, Edgar 220
Brown, Arthur 220
Brown, James 158, 258, 387
Brown, Richard 'Rabbit' 82
Browne, Jackson 263, 264–5, 360
'Brown Sugar' 134, 138, 139, 150, 154, 155, 156–7, 167, 169, 395
Brubeck, Dave 193
Bryter Layter (Drake) 68, 69, 71, 73–4, 390
Buckmaster, Paul 158
Budd, Roy 65
Burretti, Freddie 63, 285, 341, 344
Bush 157
Byrne, David 279
'By The Time I Get To Phoenix' 124

Cahoots (the Band) 379
Caine, Michael 74, 143
Cale, John J. 274, 276, 372, 387; *see also* Velvet Underground

California, Randy 355
'Call Me The Breeze' 387
Can 280, 299, 391
Canby, Vincent 321, 365, 366
'Candy Man' 268
Canned Heat 48, 141
'Can't Get Next To You' 127
'Can't You Hear Me Knocking' 154
Capitol Records 377
Captain Beefheart 260, 312
Caravan 151
Carey, Mariah 256
Carlin, Peter Ames: *Bruce* 208
Carlos, Wendy 111
Carnal Knowledge (film) 323, 365
Carpenter, Karen and Richard 31, 33, 37, 51–4, 309–10, 329
Carr, Ian 338
Carr, Vicki 51
Carroll, Jim 281
Cars, the 297
Carson, Johnny 11, 50, 51, 151, 291
Carter, Jimmy, US President 11
Carter, Mother Maybelle 319
Cash, Johnny 307
Castro, Fidel 11
Cat Stevens Sings Cat Stevens 209
Cavett, Dick 291–3, 294, 295
Cecil, Malcolm 110–11, 112, 114–15
Celebration of Life Festival, Louisiana 191–3
Chandler, Chas 18
'Change Partners' 169
'Changes' 189, 285, 345
Charisma Records 332
Charles, Prince 185
Charles, Ray 138, 216
Charlesworth, Chris 349
Chelsea Drugstore (shop) 175, 188
Chelsea Girl (shop) 175
'Chelsea Hotel #2' 208
Cher 51
Chicago (band) 378
Chiffons, the 251, 252
Child, June (Bolan) 217
Chilton, Alex 281–3; *see also* Big Star
Christie, Julie 148, 190, 203
Christie, Tony 363
Christopher Milk 61
Christy, June 36
Chrome and Hot Leather (film) 109
Churchill, Arabella 185, 186, 189
Churchill, Randolph 184, 185
Cicalo, Hank 35
'City Crazy' 363
'City Of New Orleans' 266, 269
Ciu Jian 167
Clapp, Rose 302

416

417

Coming soon

from David Hepworth

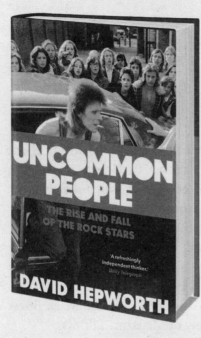

The age of the rock star, like the age of the cowboy, has passed. Like the cowboy, the idea of the rock star lives on in our imaginations.

What did we see in them? Swagger. Recklessness. Sexual charisma. Damn-the-torpedoes self-belief. A certain way of carrying themselves. Good hair. Interesting shoes. Talent we wished we had.

What did we want of them? To be larger than life but also like us. To live out their songs. To stay young for ever. No wonder many didn't stay the course.

In *Uncommon People*, David Hepworth zeroes in on defining moments and turning points in the lives of forty rock stars from 1955 to 1995, taking us on a journey to burst a hundred myths and create a hundred more.

As this tribe of uniquely motivated nobodies went about turning themselves into the ultimate somebodies, they also shaped us, our real lives and our fantasies. *Uncommon People* isn't just their story. It's ours as well.

'A refreshingly independent thinker.' *Daily Telegraph*

ABOUT THE AUTHOR

David Hepworth has been writing about, broadcasting about and speaking about music since the 70s. He was involved in the launch and/or editing of magazines like *Smash Hits*, *Q*, *Mojo* and *The Word* among many others.

He was one of the presenters of the BBC rock music programme *Whistle Test* and one of the anchors of the Corporation's coverage of Live Aid in 1985. He has won the Editor of the Year and Writer of the Year awards from the Professional Publishers Association and the Mark Boxer Award from the British Society of Magazine Editors.

He is a director of the independent company Development Hell and divides his time between writing for a variety of magazines and newspapers, speaking at events, broadcasting work and blogging. He lives in London.

'I was born in 1950,' he says, 'which means that in terms of music I have the winning ticket in the lottery of life.'

For more information on David Hepworth and his books, see his website at www.davidhepworth.com